The TEXAS CHAIN SAW MASSACRE

Companion

THE TEXAS CHAIN SAW MASSACRE COMPANION
1 84023 660 4

Published by
Titan Books
A division of
Titan Publishing Group Ltd
144 Southwark St
London
SE1 0UP

First edition October 2003
10 9 8 7 6 5 4 3 2

Picture credits

Did you enjoy this book? We love to hear from our readers. Please e-mail us at:
readerfeedback@titanemail.com or write to Reader Feedback at the above address. Visit our website: **www.titanbooks.com**. To subscribe to our regular newsletter for up-to-the-minute news, great
offers and competitions, email: **titan-news@titanemail.com**. Titan books are available from all good
bookshops or direct from our mail order service. For a free catalogue or to order, phone 01536 76 46
46 with your credit card details or contact Titan Books Mail Order, Unit 6, Pipewell Industrial Estate,
Desborough, Kettering, Northants NN14 2SW, quoting reference TC/MC.

The TEXAS CHAIN SAW MASSACRE Companion

STEFAN JAWORZYN

FOREWORD BY GUNNAR HANSEN

TITAN BOOKS

Acknowledgements

Firstly, to all the cast and crew members from the films who contributed to this book. Many went out of their way to help with resources, contacts and follow-up interviews. Without them this project really would have been impossible and this book is dedicated to them:

Wayne Bell, Joe Bob Briggs, Marilyn Burns, Robert A. Burns, Allen Danziger, Duane Graves, Ed Guinn, Gunnar Hansen, Kim Henkel, Brian Huberman, Levie Isaacks, Bill Johnson, Richard Kidd, Richard Kooris, Robert Kuhn, Eric Lasher, Jim Moran, Bill Moseley, Paul Partain, Lou Perryman, Sallye Richardson, David J. Schow, Brad Shellady, Jim Siedow, Mike Sullivan/Michael O'Sullivan.

Steve Pittis, without whose encouragement and resources I probably wouldn't have started on this project.

People who provided help, research materials and/or encouragement:

Chuck Grigson, Jay Grossman/MTI Video, David Hyman, Alan Jones (additional credit: sneering and contempt — I couldn't live without it), Stephen Jones, Craig Lapper, Edwin Pouncey, John Scoleri.

Others who provided research material or help in other ways:

Ryan Adams, *The Austin Chronicle*/Marc Savlov, Steve Beeho, Blue Dolphin Films, British Board of Film Classification, *Cinefantastique* magazine, CineSchlock-o-rama/G. Noel Gross, *Fangoria* magazine, *Film Comment*, Royce Freeman, Tim Harden, *Harper's Magazine*, International Cinematographer's Guild/Bob Fisher, David Kerekes, Living-Dead.com/Ryan Rotten, New Line Cinema, Kim Newman, Phil Nutman, The Onion a.v. club, Spencer Perskin, *Variety*, *Video Watchdog*/Tim Lucas.

And thanks of course to the staff at Titan Books (David Barraclough, Adam Newell, Katy Wild) for reminding me of the true nature of horror.

(In absentia: Tobe Hooper.)

CONTENTS

Publisher's Note
All quotes in the text are taken from interviews conducted by the author, unless otherwise attributed. For detailed 'who's who' information, please refer to the 'Cast of Characters' section, beginning on page 249.

UNEXPECTED

One recent spring day, Marilyn Burns and I took a walk on Regent Street, in London. We found a small pub and went inside for lunch. As we sat at the table contemplating our bangers and mash, Marilyn started to laugh. 'I never thought,' she said, 'that thirty years later you and I would be having a beer in a pub in London. All because of the movie.' The movie was *The Texas Chain Saw Massacre*, and Marilyn had played Sally, the one victim in that misadventure to escape alive. I had played Leatherface, the brutish killer who, at the end, had danced and swung his chainsaw in frustration at her escape. We were in London for a few days to promote the UK release of a new DVD celebrating the movie's thirtieth anniversary.

Marilyn was right: given what we had known back then, neither of us would ever have imagined such a thing. In fact, most of what has happened in these thirty years since the movie was released has been entirely unforeseen. When we were making *Chain Saw*, we were not expecting very much. Of course we wanted it to be a good movie. Of course we hoped people would like it.

But at best, I thought, it was just a low-budget horror movie. If we were lucky, it would earn enough money to make the investors happy, and a few hard-core horror movie fans would remember it for a while. After that it would fade into obscurity. We had even joked on the set that this, at least, was one movie that would never be on television.

Opposite:
Gunnar Hansen
in the role of
Leatherface, an
icon of modern
horror cinema.

I thought the highlight of the movie for me would be our ersatz première at a small theatre in Austin, Texas, just before Halloween 1974. The manager let me in for free after I convinced him I had been in the movie. Afterwards a few friends gathered in the parking lot, where they gave me a defunct chainsaw, and we signed the charter for the Gunnar Hansen Fan Club in red ink. We had a lot of fun that night. And that, I figured, was that.

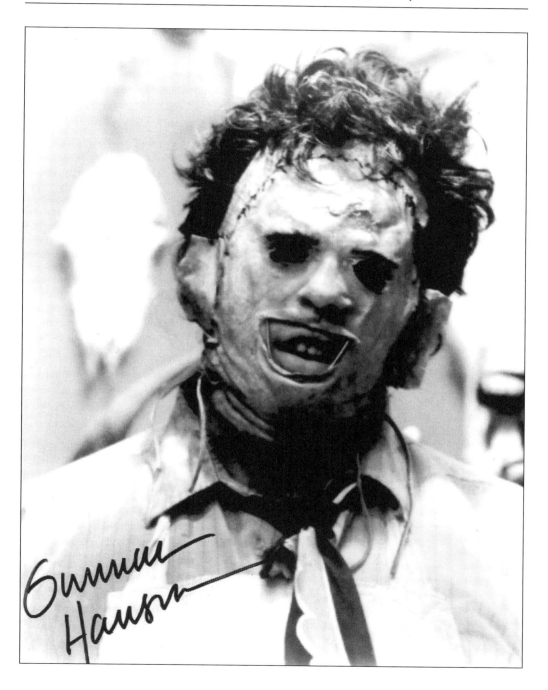

Well, wrong.

Almost immediately the reviews started coming in, and we knew that we had something hot. One Philadelphia newspaper published articles about how angered and revolted theatre-goers had been at the movie's explicit violence. They were, the writer claimed, leaving the theatre physically ill and demanding their money back. Of course, none of what they were complaining about is in the movie. For all its supposed violence, it is very tame compared to mainstream action movies such as *Raiders of the Lost Ark*. Almost all its violence is implied, even if some reviewers call it the original splatter movie.

These complaints were echoed by a talk show host who griped to his audience one night on national TV that movies like *Chain Saw* should get an X rating, not the tame R that it had received. My favourite angry review came in *Harper's Magazine*, which called *Chain Saw* a 'vile little piece of sick crap with literally nothing to recommend it.' Of course this condemnation only increased interest in the movie.

Then New York film reviewer Rex Reed stepped into the middle of this. He praised *Chain Saw*. Said it was the scariest movie he'd ever seen. Or something like that.

Suddenly the movie was very big. People were jamming the theatres to see it. People *talked* about it. Everybody, not just hardcore horror fans, had heard of *The Texas Chain Saw Massacre*. (And in spite of our earlier joking, I even saw it on TV one night in my hotel room in Paris. In French.) And, as we listened to all the hubbub, we realized that this movie was going to be more than we expected. This movie was going to be known. And it was going to make us a lot of money.

Well, wrong again. Eventually a few small royalty checks dribbled in, but we never got a big pay-off. No one knows how much money it made. Some estimate that it grossed $50 million. Others say $100 million. But we'll never know. Lawsuits popped up over a period of years — some involved with the film sued others to get at the money. It did no good, though — no one ever got much out of it. After all this time, the one thing I do know about the finances is that I didn't see any of those imagined millions.

Not that it mattered much. It would have been nice to get the money, but that wasn't why I worked on the movie. As I said, I just wanted to do something interesting during the summer. And I got that. I got to make a movie. I got to work with people who were very good at what they did and who gave their best effort. That is something I've carried with me — since then I, too, have tried to be good at what I do, and to do my best. I also learned how a movie is made, something few people get to see.

In these thirty years since *Chain Saw's* release I continue to be amazed by how it has turned out to be so much more than what we expected. Movie-makers want to copy the movie. Fans still want to see it. And everybody — not just fans — has an opinion about it.

Some people are still angry after all these years. How dare I, they demand, make such a thing? It represents everything that's wrong with the movies. I was the reason, one woman claimed, that a dozen people had recently been murdered in New York City.

But mostly the talk is positive.

I go to horror conventions a few times a year to meet fans (who would have expected that?). And here, not only do people remember and love *Chain Saw*, but each generation rediscovers it. I meet young boys and girls — thirteen or fourteen years old — who have just seen it for the first time, and are fascinated. I meet people in their fifties and sixties who saw it back in '74, and still have something to say about it. I meet people who are convinced it's true: 'I remember when it happened,' one says. 'It was in all the papers. It was very scary.' 'I knew the original Leatherface,' another claims. 'I was a guard at the Texas State Prison, and Leatherface was a prisoner there. He worked in the kitchen.'

All because of this little horror movie we made one summer thirty years ago.

And so, despite our expectations, *The Texas Chain Saw Massacre* is still around. And it's thriving. It has entered the culture — it's hard to pick up a chainsaw now without having it mean something menacing. People still tell me chainsaw jokes. (They're not funny.) Even people who don't know horror movies know who Leatherface is. A copy of *Chain Saw* sits in the collection of the Museum of Modern Art, in New York. Recently I bought a *Texas Chain Saw Massacre* lunch box. There are even Leatherface action figures, some eight or nine different ones, including a Bobblehead Leatherface. Who knew?

The movie has proved to be so much more than we could imagine at the time. And the proof was in Marilyn's laugh in that London pub so many years later. ∎

Gunnar Hansen

Gunnar Hansen
Northeast Harbor
April 2003

Prelude: Eggshells

"PSYCHEDELIC CRAP!"

Sallye Richardson: First of all, you think this thing revolves around Tobe Hooper and then you think, well no, maybe not — in part he is the central focus — but whose story is this? Is it a story about Tobe and his movies or is it a story about a lot of people at a particular time?

Gunnar Hansen: What you'll probably find about this is, we each have our own take on *Chain Saw* — this is like *Rashomon*, where we each tell the story… So between five of us we'd have five different stories…

Sallye Richardson: The thing about it is, I've heard a lot of different stories — it's interesting for me because I happen to know the truth — whatever anybody says, that's fine, but I happen to *know* the truth… And it's interesting that people have their own perspective on what happened — everybody sees things differently — some people stretch the truth, and would like it to look like something that it's not. So it's an interesting phenomenon — just like what you write will be a compilation of what you have experienced, filtering it through yourself…

After spending the greater part of the 1960s producing a large body of short films, documentaries and commercials, Tobe Hooper's first feature film was *Eggshells*, shot between 1969-1970. Its late hippie-period sensibilities — psychedelic visuals, fragmented, semi-improvised narrative — coupled with incomprehensible artiness left it something short of a commercial venture, destined to play at festivals (it won a gold award at the Atlanta International Film Festival) and a handful of university campuses before being sold as a tax write-off and never seen again.

Left:
Eggshells *poster*
artwork by
Jim Franklin.

Lou Perryman: My brother Ron and Tobe were buddies, they were partners, they were the two hot film-makers in town — they had aspirations, they talked about directors and scriptwriters, knew all the stuff. When I moved to Austin, I remember seeing Tobe editing a film for my brother on this 'hot splicer' — where you actually clip and scrape and then glue the pieces of film together, whereas a guillotine splicer is one where you tape it and it's your work print — and I knew he had this visual sense about him. So they would put these films together and talk about them — mostly I would go for cigars and Cokes...

Richard Kidd: I had gone to work for KTVC, a local television station owned by Lyndon Johnson here in Austin, while I was finishing my last years at The University of Texas (UT). I met a fellow camera person also working in the news department, Gary Pickle. So Gary and I decided to leave the television station and start a film company, it was that simple — we didn't have too many ideas about it, we just thought we could do it on our own. That must have been about 1966. There was another fellow recruited from the TV station, Mike Bosler, who has since died. I guess we did that for about a year, and that's when we hooked up with Tobe and Ron, both of whom would come into the category of being real creative types. They were trying to make films, do commercials, get started in the business, but they didn't really have an office, they were just kind of doing it out of their homes. We had rented a small office building near the state capitol, we were an honest-to-goodness legitimate business!

Sallye Richardson: I graduated from UT film school with a degree in film — the department was still very new. After I graduated I went out and did a documentary for a children's mental health facility, then I met Lou Perryman and we did a second film for the same people. I took the film into Richard Kidd's company Motion Picture Productions (MPP), where I could use their equipment in exchange for bringing the film in. So I used their post-production facilities, and that's how I got started with the company. I met Tobe there. I learned so many things about photography from both Tobe and Ron Perryman — Ron was so good at lighting, he had a speciality of doing the long slow shot — he would set up and wait for the sunset, or he would set up with a long lens with someone running in the distance and there'd be a real slow pan that would be so delicate, and it would be lit incredibly. Ron and Tobe complement-ed each other so well because Tobe was quick and upside down and sideways and Ron had the meticulously slow, beautiful shots — he did so much beautiful work. Ron shot commercials too, and they always had a beautiful quality — softer, slow, beautifully lit, meticulously crafted. They liked working together because they added something to each other, a lot of things they did together were really neat... I was always sad that Ron was not able to put it together to go forward with his career...

Lou Perryman: Tobe had made another movie, a short film, way back, *The Heisters* — I think it was shot in 35mm. I remember being on that set, must have been about '62...

Sallye Richardson: I believe it was his first film, I think he just made that by himself — he's probably the only person with a copy of it — it was a comedy, a slapstick thing. He brought out this giant pie, and this guy gets hit in the face with a pie that's about as big as a door...

Lou Perryman: Tobe and Ron were invited to join MPP by Richard Kidd. In some ways he's the one who had the dream of a film company — Ron and Tobe were the artists and they wanted to do 'art', and Richard's grabbing a camera and running down to a bank and clicking off a bunch of shots and making a commercial out of it. They were just horrified — that's not art! But he kept it alive, he paid the bills...

Sallye Richardson: Richard Kidd was a phenomenal film-maker, though he's a commercial film-maker, not an artist. He was able to keep that group of artists together in some manner and still support a company, and it was through his wiles that it managed to stay afloat. I don't know how he did it sometimes! He knows how to get something out — and forget the art! MPP became Film House because Ron and Tobe along with this other guy, Gary Pickle, tried to make it 'less Richard' — they felt like they needed a new name, but it was still basically 'Richard Kidd Productions'. Everybody left him but he survived — moved to Dallas and became even more successful!

Richard Kidd: MPP changed its name to Film House, maybe '69 or '70. When Gary and I started up, we couldn't think of what to call it so it ended up Motion Picture Productions. Talk about a stupid name! So when we got Ron and Tobe, they said,

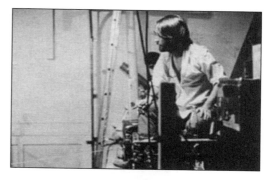

Top:
Tobe Hooper at work.

Above:
David Ford (left) and Tobe Hooper (right) receive the gold award at the Atlanta International Film Festival.

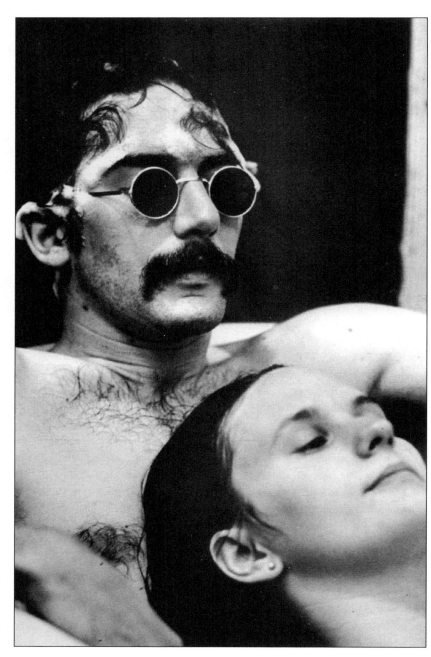

Right:
The mysterious
'Boris Schnurr'
(aka Kim Henkel)
and Mahlon
Forman relax.

'We need to come up with a better name than MPP,' so that's where Film House came from, and that was the operational name till the mid-'70s when everybody split and RKP was born.

Sallye Richardson: If there was a commercial to shoot for the bank in Austin, Richard would say, 'Tobe, you got to go do this one.' He would give him the sheet the agency had provided — Tobe would look at it, and we'd go down and there'd be, say, ten people we were supposed to interview. But Tobe would be walking around doing hand-held stuff — that was who he was. If he needed a set-up shot he'd maybe take Ron. He'd bring it back, drop it off with us, then go away until it was ready. Then he'd sit down at the Steenbeck and he would perform this miracle. He'd have film hanging round his neck, taped to his coat — and in almost no time he'd have this imaginative thing that was just great. Perhaps not exactly as the Austin National Bank or the agency would necessarily have liked, but it was so magical that, gosh, who couldn't like it! He was a great cameraman and has always been an excellent editor.

Richard Kooris: I knew the guys at MPP — I freelanced for them on occasion, but in the early '70s I started a production company called Shootout with some students, one of whom was Danny Pearl, and we became competitors with MPP. We had a little office above a chiropractor's. Initially we didn't own any equipment, then we got a six-plate Steenbeck — a 16mm editing table — and we'd rent cameras, do whatever work we could get. The other guys were Larry Carroll, Ted Nicolaou and Courtney Goodin…

I had known Richard Kidd for years, and of course Tobe — he started making films when he was really young, and down at MPP was where he got his education — and a guy named Ron Perryman, who was a sort of mad genius. He's Lou's older brother — I haven't seen him for years, he's sort of a recluse, I don't think his health is too good either. He was a wonderful photographer, just a brilliant photographer, but he was a very strange individual… He had a great eye, and was technically really inventive — he built cameras and cranes and all sorts of devices.

Richard Kidd: Ron was pretty much a recluse even by the early '70s. He was a true talent but he wanted to do it his own way, and he didn't want anybody messing with him — you could never send Ron on a corporate job without handlers and managers and producers around, someone to run interference!

Robert A. Burns: I grew up in Austin, as did Tobe — Tobe and I met in 1965 at a small impromptu party after some small stage production in Austin. We decided to have it at my tiny house trailer but it got broken up before it started when the weird park owner thought I was opening up a whorehouse (I wish!). He then threw me out of the park.

I worked with Tobe on a couple of his projects. He did a fine little short picture called *Down Friday Street*, not a documentary *per se*, just a short thing about 'too bad they're tearing down all the old houses and building parking lots.' That must have been about '65, right after I met him, and it was basically him and I. Most of it was in Austin, some was in Dallas, mostly him shooting it and me helping him. He edited it together and it won some awards.

Richard Kidd: In the '60s Ron was kind of a guru to Tobe. Tobe was a great cinematographer, had a really good eye, but he loved collaboration, which Ron really provided him with — they'd talk over shots for hours, figure out some crazy way to rig the camera, hang the lights, whatever. They just went out and shot *Down Friday Street*, I don't think they even had a sponsor. When I saw it, that's when I wanted to get hooked up with Ron and Tobe. I thought it was great — these were the kind of guys we needed to be working with.

Sallye Richardson: First there was *Peter, Paul and Mary* [a documentary about the folk singers], which was almost a movie, then there was *Eggshells*, which was almost a movie...

Fred Miller: [*Peter, Paul and Mary*] was directed by Tobe Hooper and mainly shot by Tobe and Ron Perryman. Their heroes were D. A. Pennebaker and the Maysles brothers. We set out on a venture budgeted at $500... There was only one company doing film in Austin at the time, Motion Picture Productions of Texas, owned by Richard Kidd. Tobe, Ron, and Gary Pickle were part-owners of that company and they became the crew. We started that night in San Antonio... For six months we toured together and shot about 100 hours of 16mm film. Tobe and Ron edited and sculpted the show. I only had a feeling of what it should be like. They knew how to make *cinéma-vérité* movies. They taught me. [*The Austin Chronicle*, Dec 1999]

Richard Kidd: I was very much involved in that one. We used three cameras on that, I shot one, Tobe one and Ron shot one. That's actually a wonderful documentary, it was an hour long, a classic 'follow them around the country' kind of deal, paid for by a crazy guy on his credit card: he was an assistant minister of the Baptist Church in Austin. Fred and I knew each other somehow, he came down to the office — he didn't have any money but he had credit cards, so I went along with that deal and said, 'OK, as long as you can cover all the expenses we'll participate,' and that's how it got done... We must have shot half a dozen concerts round the country, interviews, the whole bit... There was concert footage and interviews with the three principals, either backstage or at home. It probably still exists in the vaults of PBS [Public Broadcasting System]. It was great.

Eric Lasher: Tobe's actually in the movie a bit because there are two cameras and he's on stage and there's some feedback going on during rehearsal and they're asking him if he's responsible — 'Oh no, not me!'

Robert A. Burns: And then Tobe had this strange film called *Eggshells*. It started off as a documentary-type thing about some folks living in 'hippiedom' — and of course this is after hippiedom really ended and the people weren't particularly hippiesque, just living together in a house... After they'd shot a ton of stuff, they decided to inject a story and it was made up as it went along. It was neither fish nor fowl, but they decided to try releasing it as a feature.

I was doing a lot of advertising things and he came to me and I ended up putting together a press book. *Eggshells* showed in like two places... It was just this kind of odd little oddity, there would be some kinda time capsule-esque aspect to it now maybe. Some of this stuff has become campish, but this was just odd. It has some moments of creativity but basically it's this pointless thing. It would have more nostalgia value in Austin than elsewhere, 'cause it shows things that aren't there any more.

Left:
Mahlon Forman in
Eggshells.

Lou Perryman: So Tobe brought *Eggshells* in. I was a hired hand — they provided me with a Volkswagen van full of beer, and every day I went to the movie, 'What are we doing now?' I'd load the magazine, carry the camera, set the camera up, charge the batteries — it was basically just him and me, they added other people as the film went on. I think Ron shot a few things, maybe helped out with some stuff.

Tobe Hooper: It's a real movie about 1969. It's kind of *vérité* but with a little push. Like a script on a napkin, improvisation mixed with magic. It was about the beginning of the end of the subculture. Most of it takes place in a commune house. But what they didn't know is that in the basement is a cryptoembryonic hyperelectric presence that managed to influence the house and the people in it. The influences in my life were all kind of politically, socially implanted. [Interview with Marjorie Baumgarten, *The Austin Chronicle*, 27 Oct 2000]

Tobe Hooper: … some sort of strange presence enters the house and embeds itself in the walls of the basement and grows into this big bulb, half electronic, half organic. Almost like an eye but it's like a big light. It comes out of the wall. It manipulates the house. Animates the walls. Anyway, that's sort of what it is. I think that the film is a mixture really. It has sort of a Paul Morrissey look at times, like *Trash*, and other times it has a *Fantasia* look. [Interview by Donald G. Jackson, *The Late Show* fanzine, 1975]

Below:
Ben Skabarsak
(Ron Barnhart)
acts coy.

Richard Kidd: I was trying to keep the business functioning, actually bring money in the door, pay salaries. So I would go out and find advertising agencies that would pay for commercials, sponsors who'd pay for documentary work. Of course what Tobe wanted to do was produce theatrical things, so there was this constant conflict — you know, 'Of course, Tobe, but who's paying the bills?' He never got anybody with any money! The concept of raising money was totally lost on him! He wanted all the cameras, editing and lights that a business offered, but he didn't want to go out and shoot that nasty commercial stuff! So for a few years we'd alternate between people trying to come up with an idea they could sell theatrically or to television and in the meantime do the local bank commercials that were paying the bills.

So Tobe found someone in Houston with a bit of money, God knows, probably an oil and gas guy, and he agreed to fund just the cost of film and processing. We supplied the equipment and editing and some of the crew. I went on some of the shooting, but I never could get too excited about it, it was pretty weird: the story of a couple of young kids Tobe had recruited from the university who have this 'out of mind' weirdo experience and go through all this psychedelic crap! So it was the classic late '60s/early '70s head trip [laughs]. That was shot in 16mm, but I don't think it ever got picked up and shown.

Allen Danziger: I think about twenty people saw *Eggshells*! You're not missing much… My involvement came about via the couple the movie was originally centred on, David and Amy. Then Kim Henkel got involved and another couple. I had met David and Amy when I was doing social work here in Austin. They got involved with programmes I was doing to get rights for poor people, welfare recipients. Sallye Richardson and her boyfriend Jim Schulman lived downstairs for a while, and Sallye knew Tobe, so I met Tobe through her and Jim. We started talking and when they found out that David and Amy were involved with my programmes they asked if they could do a scene of them coming in and talking with me — I guess you could say *cinéma-vérité*, no lines, they just said, 'Here's the scene, they're coming in to talk to you' and let the cameras roll. And that was the start. After that, they asked if I would do another thing — there was a big anti-Vietnam war demonstration going on and they shot some stuff with me there. And also at the wedding, where they got married in the park, I think I'm in that. My son, who was about eight months old, was in it, and my wife Sharon made him an Uncle Sam hat. I have a picture somewhere of him in that car with the bubble on top… It was a bizarre movie.

Sallye Richardson: Allen and his wife Sharon lived underneath us — we had a duplex, my husband and I lived upstairs. That's how Allen got involved in *Eggshells* — he met Tobe through us. Tobe liked his looks and he did it for very little [laughs]…

Tobe Hooper: It was a very low-budget film, maybe $40,000 or $60,000. I shot it in 16, and blew it up to 35mm. I remember loading it into the trunk of my old MG, and thinking that it was quite an accomplishment… It's a film about the disintegration of the peace movement, toward the end of the Vietnamese war. [*Fangoria* 12, 1981]

Sallye Richardson: I think it cost about $40,000. But I don't think it ever got distributed — it got a distributor, but didn't get shown… I believe it was *Eggshells* we shot some morgue footage for. We went to Houston and we rented this place where they take you when you're dead to take the blood out and stuff, 'cause we couldn't find one in Austin. And we got this guy, like a guy off the street, who agreed to be the dead person and lie on the slab 'cause nobody wanted to do that. I think Tobe paid him $100... I remember shooting in that place — it wasn't very much fun at all... But I don't think he ever cut it in. It was supposed to be part of the beginning.

Lou Perryman: In a morgue? Yeah, I was there... It was a sidetrack that was not useful, it didn't make it into the picture. Tobe was fishing for a film in all this material that he had in front of him... There was some guy who had showed up, I've forgotten his name or how he showed up, he was kind of a hippie character. And Tobe decided he'd been killed in a motorbike accident or something, and the next thing we were down in a funeral home outside Houston. So we shot a fake embalming process, where you see them open the carotid artery and the blood drains out and then the embalming fluid goes in — it was fairly ghastly...

There *was* an interesting scene where we shot two of the actors literally fucking — but it was not shot explicitly. It was a closed set, just me and Tobe and the two actors. I was holding this frame with some mirrored mylar on it and Tobe was shooting into the mylar and I was giving him a distorted reflection of their coupling...

Spencer Perskin: I can't remember when I first started hanging out with Tobe at his office where he did editing — at the corner of 8th and Nueces, I think. He mostly did short films in those days, but had plans for feature length films, too. When he finally was ready to make *Eggshells* he gave me the opportunity to do music for it. I wound up doing about half the soundtrack, some on sitar with Jim Franklin tapping tablas, some with Shawn Siegel... We appear in the movie as Shiva's, playing for a wedding which is actually taking place there at the gazebo in Wooldrige Park by the courthouse. However, you don't hear the band in that scene. We went up to Robinhood Brian's studio in Tyler to do the music. Tobe told me we were doing sitar so I brought Jim with me because he had some tablas and could play a little. We did some sitar stuff, and I think some other solo stuff. Then, all of a sudden, Tobe says, 'Where's the band?' and I say, you never said bring the band. But Tobe wanted some rock'n'roll so I called Shawn in Austin and said, 'How soon can you come?' and he said 'Pretty quick,' because Tobe had dough. So when Shawn showed up, it being a good six hour drive to Tyler from Austin, we did our usual pre-game warm-up and then went right to work. Tobe needed some rough raucous rock and we just had the two of us, so Shawn did piano and organ and I threw on drums, bass, guitars, and, if I remember correctly, some fiddle. We did my instrumental piece, 'Thing in D', to which a Volkswagen is blown up in the movie, too cool. [From 'Stars We Are', on Spencer Perskin's Shiva's Head Band website]

Wayne Bell: Tobe and I were friends. I was a college student and I worked on *Eggshells*. I had known Tobe before that, when I went to work, right out of High School, for the film production company MPP, later called Film House, here in Austin, of which Tobe was a co-owner. Two of the guys there — Tobe Hooper and Ron Perryman — were very talented and I naturally gravitated towards them. And that's how Lou got into the film business — through his brother recruiting him. Lou came up and began to get to know cameras. This would be the summer of 1969 — although shooting began on *Eggshells* in the fall of '69, my first involvement was in summer 1970.

Levie Isaacks: When I was at UT we turned out 25,000 students against the war in Vietnam — it was pretty much unheard of that that would happen in what had always been considered a pretty conservative city.

Wayne Bell: The protests against the Vietnam War really went onto another level around that time. There was a massive peace march in Austin and this TV station I was associated with at college sent me down to do some coverage and I ran into Tobe. They were filming these — hippies basically [*laughs*] — so I got in with them and helped out, and we filmed the rest of the day. Then I ended up spending my summer working on

Below:
The wedding
in the park.

Eggshells. My guess is that a lot of the more pedestrian stuff was shot during the preceding spring — people hanging out, you know. A lot of that stuff was basically improvised — I've listened to a lot of the audio, the synched sound that was done — there was no script, it was, 'Here's the set-up here, see if you can get it to there.' And there were definitely some non-actors. Kim had a girlfriend named Mahlon and they were both in it. They had this great old painted car with a bubble on top. One of the first shots I did was a scene out in the country where they blow up the car. The car 'evaporates' — it was on a platform over a pit and when the puff of smoke goes off, the platform blows and the car disappears. That was the idea.

Boy, was it a character doing the explosives — Henry Holly [*laughs*] — oh man. Being the kid of the group I got stuck driving with Henry and his shrieking wife, dragging a trailer full of explosives. They were haranguing each other and the car was swerving back and forth — at one point we did a 'gas and pee stop' — and I got out of the car and went over to the van with Tobe and the others, got in and said, 'I'm riding with you.' And nobody questioned it. Henry had a reputation... The ride back was great, and we really got to know each other.

Shortly after that we would get into these jam sessions. I come from a musical background, whereas Tobe and Ron were non-musicians but very creative guys. So we would play together, just experimenting with all kinds of instruments: dulcimers, percussion instruments, children's toys, some electric stuff — there weren't really synthesizers then. Some of that music is in *Eggshells*. There's a lot of other music written by songwriters, and other players as well, so the score is quite eclectic. There are a few places where the score gets kind of strange... I don't know that any session I played on is in *Eggshells* — Tobe and Ron would also have these jam sessions when I wasn't there. And that was the precursor to the *Chain Saw* music.

Eggshells in a way was dated the moment it came out — so tied to a particular time, not only in the things happening on screen but the whole mindset, and it's going to look laughable and quaint at different times because it's so 'of its time'…

Lou Perryman: I think Tobe gave me an assistant director credit on *Eggshells*. It was supposed to be a movie about two sweet sort of hip kids in college that the producer Dave Ford knew, and Tobe took it crazy from there — 'Hmm, they're going to watch it for about five minutes if it's people sitting around eating wheat germ, hell' and so he began to add these fantasy characters. That's where he met Kim… It was a hippie movie about people that were hip and smoked dope and lived this alternative lifestyle and had various crises… I think it was sold as some sort of tax write-off, so it's basically never played again.

In the culmination of the picture, Kim goes off in this old car with a bubble on the top, it's all painted up like the American flag, takes it out in the middle of this field, sets it on fire, throws his clothes in and runs away nekkid, then the car blows up.

I remember on that shot, at the last minute somebody handed me a Nagra [tape recorder] and said, 'Go get some sound,' and I went over and got behind these bushes and got ready to turn it on then thought, 'That guy said something about not starting any electric motors, aren't these electric motors in the recorder? But my God, I got to get some sound but I can't turn on the motor…' Finally I decided I had to get the sound and turned it on, and the instant I turned it

on, the explosion went off, I thought I set it off! The car was over a pit which it was going to drop into, then the explosion and gas would go up in line with the camera so it looked like the car blew up — the platform they'd built was not the right width for the tyres, so it looked really cheesy getting the thing on. And the dynamite, like twenty-five sticks of it, was already in the pit and I think there was another seventy-five with the gas. And to get the car onto this

TIME AND SPACED FILM FANTASY

a film by tobe hooper

EGGSHELLS

thing, we had to pull it with a rope, and so somebody had to steer it. So I ended up getting in the car or leaning over into it and steering it while it went up on the ramp, leaning over this dynamite pit...

Sallye Richardson was involved in some way — it was hard to tell what anybody's particular job was — you know, it was just put together that way... I do remember Sallye being out there when we blew up the car, that was excellent...

Sallye Richardson: I took all the photos — including the one on the poster, the boy and girl in the bubble — seems to me I took that when we were out blowing up the car. That was the first time I'd ever blown up anything, it was real exciting. I think Ron was doing that too — we had three cameras there, maybe four, it was a lot of fun.

Richard Kidd: I remember seeing some of it in editing — we'd all collectively hold our noses at how bad the two kid actors were — it was pretty terrible from that standpoint. But it did have a gigantic big car explosion. The two hippie kids drive their painted-up old car into the country, to the woods, then they walk away from it, and as they walk away it magically explodes and disappears. Tobe had this great idea, and Ron helped him rig it, where they dug a hole about twelve feet deep then put two by fours together and rolled the car out over the hole, with fifty gallon drums of gasoline and explosives under it. For the big scene I was shooting one of the cameras, we'd gotten three or four together to do it — as Tobe pointed out, 'Hell, we only get to shoot it once!' Then they trigger the explosion and the car disappears in a puff of mushroom-shaped cloud, drops down into the hole — it was a great-looking special effect, but, you know, we're probably lucky nobody got blown up! [*Laughs*]

In 1971, Tobe Hooper and Jim Siedow both acted in *The Windsplitter*, a low-budget exploitation number also produced by David Ford. Bobby Joe Smith, a small town boy-turned movie star, returns to his home town with long hair and motorbike to encounter *Easy Rider*-style prejudice and violence. Hooper played one of the Wilson Brothers, local thugs who take a dislike to Bobby Joe. Mahlon Forman, Kim Henkel's partner at the time and another *Eggshells* veteran, also appeared.

Kim Henkel: I was a grip on *The Windsplitter*, that's where I met Ron Bozman, who became the production manager on *Chain Saw*. He was my fellow grip in some cases, most of the time he was the assistant cameraman. If it got a release beyond David Ford going around booking it into a couple of theatres himself, I don't know. I think David Ford just never had a great deal of judgement when it came to material [*laughs*]… You know, you have to remember that I took the screenplay of *Chain Saw* to him and offered him the opportunity to be part of it and he declined…

Sallye Richardson: I was assistant director on *The Windsplitter*, I shot the one-sheet as well — it was funded by Dave Ford, the director was J. D. Feigelson, and it had an LA cinematographer and lighting crew. We shot it in a little town outside Houston, but I don't think it ever got much distribution. Jim Siedow played the father of the girl, and Tobe was in it: there are these three goofy guys who get everyone in trouble — he was one of them. I think Tobe always wanted to be an actor too; he was very enthusiastic. He and J. D. were kind of friends at the time, partly because of Dave Ford being the money man behind both their movies. It had local backdrops — there's a scene in a local bar, but it's more like a little place where old guys go to play dominoes — with real locals. It was a very historic little town.

Jim Siedow: I didn't know Tobe back then. *The Windsplitter* was shot in Columbus, about thirty miles from Houston. When it came to making *Chain Saw* — the unions had some kind of deal where you can make a movie if there's a SAG member in the cast and a SAG technician. So I was the SAG actor that Tobe got to be in it — I was the only professional actor.

Tobe Hooper: Kim was one of the actors in *Eggshells*. That was how we met, and as we worked together, Kim helped to develop it. Eventually we came to be collaborators on the script. Following *Eggshells*, we worked a year or so together, and worked out the specifications on several projects; finally we came up with *Texas Chain Saw*. [*Fangoria* 23, 1982]

Kim Henkel: I acted in *Eggshells* — well, after a fashion — and that's where I ran into Tobe. I wrote some short little pieces for it. It was mainly centred on two friends of mine — and it was because I knew them that I ran into the whole situation. After that, Tobe and I talked about something off and on for several years and then we finally settled on the *Chain Saw* project. Then we spent most of six to eight weeks one spring beating it out. ■

"WE JUST WANT TO MAKE SOMETHING FOR A BUCK"

Tobe Hooper: The true monster itself is death. All the classic horror flicks — *Dracula, Frankenstein, Psycho* — have this in common. They have a unique way of getting inside you by setting up symbols that represent death: a graveyard, bones, flowers. If you put them in the proper order then you create the most important aura known as the creeps. [*The Texas Monthly Reporter*, March 1974]

Tobe Hooper: It's a film about meat, about people who have gone beyond dealing with animal meat and rats and dogs and cats. Crazy retarded people going beyond the line between animal and human. [Bryanston press notes]

According to Tobe Hooper, the genesis of the *Chain Saw* legend runs as follows: one Christmas he found himself in the hardware department of a large branch of Montgomery Ward's, brooding about a film project and cursing the holiday period crowds, when his attention was drawn to the chainsaws as a useful aid to a hasty exit... After escaping the crowds and store, the whole concept for *Chain Saw* then apparently manifested itself to Hooper in thirty seconds!

Tobe Hooper: The structural puzzle pieces, the way it folds continuously back in on itself, and no matter where you're going it's the wrong place. That was influenced by my thinking about solar flares' and sunspots' reflecting behaviours. That's the reason the movie starts on the sun. It's amazing how it all kind of zeitgeisted into my head so quickly. [*The Austin Chronicle*, 27 Oct 2000]

Lou Perryman: I think Tobe starting getting the idea about chainsaws when I was living like a hermit with another fella out in the woods — we had a chainsaw and a lot

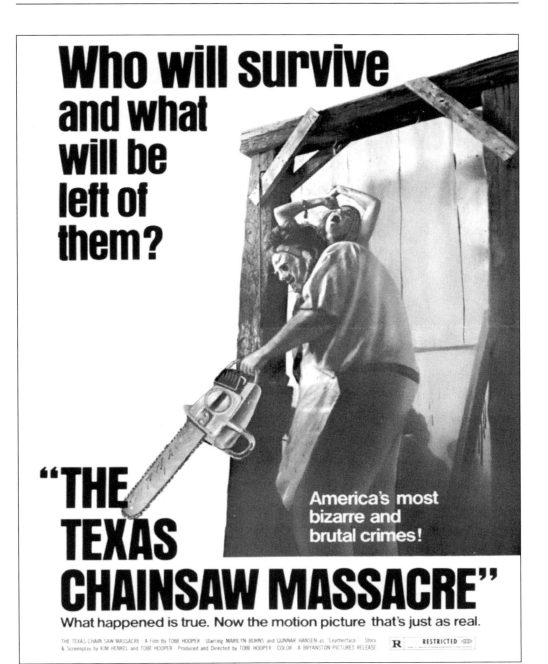

of stumps, and a wood-burning stove, that was the only way we could heat ourselves. So I had this chainsaw and he was terribly scared of it: 'Oh God, be careful with that chainsaw, be *careful* with that chainsaw!' The next thing I know, I'd moved to Colorado and he and Kim had written this script, *Headcheese* as it was called...

Tobe Hooper: The old EC comics were collections of short horror stories... They were absolutely frightening, unbelievably gruesome. And they were packed with the most unspeakably horrible monsters and fiends, most of which specialised in mutilation... I started reading these comics when I was about seven. I loved them. They were not in any way based on logic. To enjoy them you had to accept that there is a Bogey Man out there... Since I started reading these comics when I was young and impressionable, their overall feeling stayed with me. I'd say they were the single most important influence on *The Texas Chain Saw Massacre*. A lot of their mood went into the film, along with some of Hitchcock's methods of manipulating an audience. [1977 interview with Glenn Lovell and Bill Kelley, *Cinefantastique*, Oct 1986]

The brush with Christmas crowds, chainsaws, horror comics, the hippie hangover of *Eggshells*, and the legend of Wisconsin ghoul Ed Gein (see page 238) combined and ignited with whatever else was happening in Tobe Hooper's head to provide a springboard. In what would prove to be one of the great collaborations of horror cinema, Hooper teamed up with Kim Henkel, and the twosome began to hatch a plot...

Kim Henkel: The initial idea was both of ours, though maybe I would say more Tobe's than mine if I had to split hairs about it... But what we did was sit down and talked through the script, worked through it scene by scene in terms of action, what was going to happen from one scene to the next, then I would go off and write the scene.

Bob Burns knew Gunnar Hansen. I knew Ron Bozman from *The Windsplitter* and had a lot of confidence in him — I knew we needed someone who could really organise things, because we were dealing with a lot of people who were not particularly good in that realm. So I talked him into coming down and doing that. He did his best given that harem scarem crew of people...

Robert A. Burns: The people involved in *Chain Saw* were local except for a couple of friends of Tobe's (Jim Siedow and a couple of crew). Ed Neal was the only one I knew previously — we had crossed in the drama department at the University of Texas years before — I didn't know him real well but he was the only person I had met before, cast-wise... The crew was all out of UT's film department — everybody wanted to get the credit and experience, like you do when you're just starting out, and it's amazing how many members of the crew have gone on to very successful careers in film-making.

When it came time to do *Chain Saw*, I had known Tobe for eight years; I was the person to do art direction 'cause Tobe knew what I did, and I had a well-established reputation for being able to make something out of nothing. I'd put things together and taken them apart all my life. I had a large old office where I did graphic arts and advertising — and there was no production office, so we did the casting out of my office 'cause I had a lot of space there.

Tobe and Kim came here and brought this script and said, 'Let's do it' and I was familiar enough with Tobe to know that he'd fling himself into something and it'd become the be-all and end-all. So I was a little cautious but they said, 'Don't worry, we just want to make something for a buck.' But ultimately he did end up flinging himself into it and it became nightmarish...

Richard Kidd: Tobe and Ron were such a creative, energetic team you didn't want to lose them. They were working at Film House up until Tobe got the *Chain Saw* money together. I made a deal to supply equipment to them on a rental basis, I think it was a half money, half credit kind of deal. At that point Tobe was soliciting the help of anyone he could, everybody he knew. We owned three Eclairs, and they were always Tobe's favourite camera so he couldn't stray too far from our cache of goodies! We didn't have a colour lab though, the film had to be sent to Dallas. We could do sound mixes and editing and of course we had lighting and film gear, but we didn't have any processing. As I remember he wound up putting together two or three different deals — he wanted some things we didn't own, like dollies. And we couldn't let our gear go all the time 'cause we were trying to do the other stuff, so there was another rental company up in Dallas that was supplying him as well. But Tobe was really a very lousy business person — he was a great, creative ideas guy, but as far as business was concerned...

Below:
Kim Henkel on
location.

Warren Skaaren was a twenty-five year-old whiz-kid graduate who had majored in art and sculpture at Rice, and was working for Governor Preston Smith following graduation. Impressed by the millions New Mexico had generated from its newly founded Film Commission, Smith's press secretary Jerry Hall and one Bill Parsley, who worked for the Texas Legislature, persuaded Skaaren to draft a memo for Smith proposing the formation of a Texas Film Commission. Smith went for it, and the Commission was created in May 1971.

Bottom:
Left to right:
Tobe Hooper,
Marilyn Burns,
Daniel Pearl,
Jim Siedow.

Jerry Hall: Warren was eager to apply for the position of executive director. I asked him if he knew anything about the movies, and he said, 'Not much.' So I gave him the job.

Warren intuitively knew what to do. When I was growing up, my parents owned a silent movie house in Stanton. I'd been going to movies all my life — I loved movies — but that was about all I knew about them. Warren understood immediately, and then taught all of us, that this in fact was a business — a rough, tough business. And the whole idea was not to take sides or get involved in the politics of the production of a movie. He found their locations for them and he stayed out of their business. Warren made us understand that these people were dead serious about what they were doing. [Interview by Marc Savlov, *The Austin Chronicle*, 15 Jun 2001]

Kim Henkel: It was through me that we got to our principal financing. Warren Skaaren and Ron

Bozman had been classmates at Rice University, so through my friendship with Ron I came to know Skaaren. When I completed the script I took it to him and asked him if he had any suggestions or thoughts. He made some introductions for us and introduced us to Bill Parsley. (His name is Bill J. Parsley, hence the aka of Jay Parsley.) He worked for Texas Tech University — he was officially the Vice President of Student Affairs. In reality what that meant was that he was the lobbyist for Texas Tech University — he hung out in Austin and did his best to induce the legislature to send money to the university.

Robert Kuhn: I was involved in the financing of *Chain Saw* — what happened was the Texas Film Commission had just been created and the guy who had lobbied it through was a guy called Warren Skaaren, who became the first Executive Director of the newly formed Commission. I knew Warren before that. Parsley, Hooper and Henkel went to him and he brought them over to me because they wanted a couple of corporations [Vortex and MAB] made up. Then I got to know Ron Bozman during the shoot. I had an old motor home they used for wardrobe, make-up, actors' lounge — all in one place. I'd go out and start it up — it'd sit in one place and the battery would run down... So that was my major contribution — but I was also an investor. There was a $60,000 budget originally and I invested $9,000. The reason it was nine instead of ten was there were some other little pieces there — Parsley gave Marilyn Burns a part, Kim Henkel's sister bought a little part of it. I knew I was throwing away that $9,000 — but it was certainly far and away the best investment I ever made. There was a lot of misery went with it but the return for the investment was better than anything else I've ever done!

Marilyn Burns: I worked with Warren Skaaren on the Texas Film Commission. He came up with the title *Texas Chain Saw Massacre*... Originally I was working in this children's home and there were things going on — I was going to write about them, and these politicians I knew basically said, 'Don't write anything, here's a job on the Texas Film Commission'...

Gunnar Hansen: It was the Austin State School, for the profoundly retarded and mentally disturbed. I worked there for a while too, but I could never get a permanent job...

Marilyn Burns: So I talked to the politicians about doing a movie as a tax shelter and they liked the idea — and Tobe and Kim were around, Tobe had a name for his commercials, and he'd done *Eggshells*. So this little group got together, and I think it was Ron Bozman told Tobe he knew a girl...

Sallye Richardson: Most of the money to shoot came from Bill Parsley wanting to buy a vehicle for Marilyn — you know, I've often wondered about her character being called Sally, if Tobe did that with a purpose...

Marilyn Burns: Warren Skaaren knew the producers — but I didn't know what a brilliant artistic, creative guy he was. He also did the sculpture at the beginning of the movie. He had a mind to do the politics and play the game and get ahead and become the head of the Film Commission... So I remember telling the politicians when it first started that it would be a wonderful idea if they invested some of their money in a tax shelter. Back then you could put up a lot of money for a film, and if it totally flopped and never went anywhere, by golly you got your tax shelter back. So I suggested it would be a great idea to put their money in a movie — it would never get produced, they'd have nothing to worry about, none of their friends would know they invested in a bad low-budget movie! Well, guess what... And they said, 'Marilyn, you said it would never go anywhere!' I said, 'Well, you never know... ' And they were so furious that they were going to be associated with it — I believe the title was *Scum of the Earth* back then, at first — and that their politician friends would know they'd invested in *Scum of the Earth*! But Jay Parsley became so proud as the years went on...

Kim Henkel: *Scum of the Earth* was not a title either Tobe or I ever considered. It could have come from others connected to the film, but I'm unaware of it.

Robert A. Burns: As to titles, the first (as far as I know) was *Saturn in Retrograde* (old hippiedom at work). The shooting script contained the title *Headcheese*. During the long editing time a number of titles were considered. *Leatherface* was rejected as possibly being confused with the Marines term 'leatherneck'. As I understand it, the final title came about as a joke during a poker game — I don't know who all was involved. As you probably know, *Scum of the Earth* was a rather well-known title of the famous Herschell Gordon Lewis film not that many years before, so would not have been considered for *Chain Saw*.

Scum of the Earth was also a film by S. F. Brownrigg, produced in 1973 and retitled *Poor White Trash II* for release. It was one of the earliest productions developed by the Texas Film Commission...

Kim Henkel: Skaaren did the sculpture that's up on the grave at the beginning, and thought up the title. But what he did in our case was rather unusual — he provided an introduction, but for the most part (to the best of my knowledge) his job was to try to induce production companies from out of state to come to Texas to film there.

Robert A. Burns: Warren Skaaren was the first head of the Texas Film Commission — other states had them, New Mexico had one, and a whole load of low-budget stuff was shot there, and they said, 'Hey, Texas needs to get in on this.' He was running it, then he quit the Film Commission about the time we did *Chain Saw*, and he was in business with the main investor, a guy named Bill Parsley, and they had a company in Dallas. Originally he put Tobe together with Bill Parsley, so he was the money guy — and he ended up owning a big part of the picture... Skaaren was a very typical Hollywood-type of guy — gets involved in things then really soaks you, finds something and latches onto it and takes lots of credit for it... Then once *Chain Saw* was finished he was additionally contracted to shop the film around.

Marilyn Burns: Tobe and Kim had just written this incredibly strange script — and the idea comes from Ed Gein up in Wisconsin. He's the man that *Psycho*, *Silence of the Lambs* and *Chain*

Saw came from — this one man inspired those three great horror movies... When they found him and his furniture, his food and everything — well, the Leatherface family was all based on that, so he inspired three different movies — we just added a chainsaw and the word Texas.

Gunnar Hansen: I just heard there were these guys in town who were making this movie — I was a graduate student — and it was too bad, they had hired a guy to play Leatherface, but he was holed up drunk in a motel and wouldn't come out, and did I want to try out because they were desperate. I was thinking, 'Well, it's just a summer job, I'll be able to tell my grandchildren about it' — that's all I thought it would be.

Paul Partain: How did I get involved? It was a dark and stormy night... wait, that's my novel. I auditioned for it. Kim Henkel's wife was a student teacher at Martin Jr. High School where Ms. Nan Elkins was the drama teacher. Nan and her family had a dinner theatre where I hung out acting in anything and everything that came

Top:
On-set meeting (left to right):
Kim Henkel,
Allen Danziger,
Marilyn Burns,
Tobe Hooper,
Teri McMinn,
Paul Partain.

Above:
Publicity shot of Paul Partain.

along. One day Nan comes to the theatre with news of a weird movie that her friend's husband is involved in and guess what? They need actors. They were looking for everything except the roles of Franklin, Sally and Jerry. Those roles were pretty much off the table by the time I arrived. They really wanted somebody freaky for Hitchhiker. I can be freaky, so I showed up. I read for the freaky guy and wound up reading Franklin's lines to feed the guys auditioning for Hitchhiker. I thought I was auditioning too and it really did not sink in that I was just holding the place for somebody else who Kim and Tobe had in mind. In retrospect, I believe the more I read Franklin, the more I liked the part and the more the role became mine.

Two things I believe were deciding factors: first, on what turned out to be the last audition, as a parting shot, I told Kim and Tobe that I truly believed I could bring a depth to Franklin that they did not know was there, and that I wanted the part. Secondly, and probably most importantly, there was a conversation (I am told) between Kim and Tobe where they were trying to decide between their first choice for Franklin and me. I had, just a couple of months earlier, completed shooting a nice-sized supporting role on my first feature film, *Lovin' Molly*, which was directed by Sidney Lumet (aka Big Time Director). The quote that came back to me was '... if he's good enough for Sidney Lumet, he's good enough for us... ' Marilyn worked on *Lovin' Molly* as Blythe Danner's stand-in, and I knew Ed Neal, who had worked at Ms. Elkins' dinner theatre as the romantic lead in *Bell, Book and Candle*.

Right:
Leatherface gets
to grips with Pam.

Allen Danziger: Because of my role in *Eggshells*, my understanding is that when *Chain Saw* came about, Tobe and Kim came directly to me and said, 'We have a part we'd like you to do.' I didn't even have to read for it...

Gunnar Hansen: They asked me three questions before they hired me. 'Are you a violent person? Are you crazy?' When I replied, 'No, not more so than normal,' they finally asked, 'Can you do it?' 'Sure, it's easy,' I said. They loved the fact that I filled the doorway. [*Fangoria* 70, 1988]

Richard Kooris: Tobe asked me if I was available to shoot a movie, he didn't tell me what it was, and when I told him I was already booked to do a B (Z) grade movie he talked to a bunch of other people and wound up doing it with Daniel.

Daniel Pearl: I had bumped into Tobe once at the lab in Austin... He called me five or six months later and said, 'Daniel, I'm doing this film. It's really important that I have a Texan shoot this film. I've seen some of your stuff on television. I want you to shoot this film.' There was a delay in getting started... I asked Tobe when we were going to begin and he said, 'Daniel, we're making this film for $80,000 and we've got $70,000. As soon as we find the other $10,000 we start production.' So I called a friend who had a wealthy family and told him about an opportunity to invest in a film. I brought him the screenplay and five hours later he called and wanted in. I was given four percent of the film for finding an investor and I gave small percentages of that to my crew. The rest of the crew were my classmates and associates from film school. Ted Nicolaou was the soundman and Larry Carroll was one of the editors. [International Cinematographer's Guild interview by Bob Fisher]

The friend with the 'wealthy family' was the mysterious Richard Saenz, *Chain Saw*'s associate producer, alleged marijuana smuggler and one-time fugitive from justice, whose exact whereabouts are still unknown.

Lou Perryman: I had ended up in Boulder working on a newspaper with Sallye Richardson, she was a photographer or photographer's assistant, I was a typesetter. I remember she came back from Texas and told me about this movie... I don't remember if I called Tobe or he called me. But he ended up sticking me between Daniel Pearl, the shooter, and his normal assistant, a guy named Mike McClary — I think because he didn't trust them — he was worried, if not paranoid, about getting some film rolling. I had worked with him for years, we had travelled all over... Tobe and I had worked together enough that he could say, 'Put the camera here' and I would figure out how to get it there. He wanted someone to get the camera there, pull focus, make sure you didn't flash the film, carry the heavy gear. And I came down and they were still in casting, though you could say that Marilyn Burns came attached... I found a place to stay, with a friend of mine, Tyson McLeod, who was the third actor in Eagle Pennell's first short film *Hell of a Note* — the one film he ever acted in...

Debate on the subject of the Ed Gein story's influence on Hooper and Henkel's script has continued over the years. Some say *Chain Saw's* story is directly based on Gein...

Kim Henkel: We were aware of the Ed Gein story, of course. Obviously Ed Gein was the character who made things out of human bones and skin and that was the inspiration for that aspect of the story. But there was actually another murder case in Houston right about that time, I believe they were called the Candyman Murders. The focus of all the media attention was Elmer Wayne Henley, who'd been involved with an older man, Dean Corll. And his responsibility was to lure victims into the lair of the older man, then the older man would sexually abuse them, and Elmer Wayne and another kid would participate. At some point in this process the third young man became a victim and Elmer Wayne became frightened and killed the older man, which is how it all came to light. What there was about it that struck me was a scene I saw on TV, where Elmer Wayne Henley was being taken to show where some of the bodies had been dumped. And he was a skinny little pigeon-chested white trash kid, like someone out of an Erskine Caldwell story, and he drew himself up to his full height and said how he was going to take his punishment like a man. What struck me about that was operating in accord with a certain set of values and taking his punishment, and at the same time that lived happily in conjunction with this bizarre and sexually twisted set of murders. So we referred to this as 'moral schizophrenia' when we were writing the script. And we played with that with our characters. Most notably where you see it occur is scenes like where the Cook brings Marilyn Burns back to the house and stops when he sees that the door's been sawed down and gets very upset because that exhibits a lack of pride in one's home. And this kind of sensibility, this kind of sense of 'values', co-exists with the murderous rampage that's going on.

Gunnar Hansen: I didn't know about Ed Gein at the time, but I know it's connected to Ed Gein because I was very curious to learn everything I could — I'd never been on a movie set, so whenever I had a chance I would talk with Kim and Tobe. One evening we were sitting in the van, waiting for a shot to be set up — for a few days we had an RV — and I asked them where the idea had come from. They told me there was this guy in Wisconsin, Ed Gein — and this was the first time I knew that *Psycho* was based on him — they said, 'He was the inspiration, we decided to have a *family* of Ed Geins' — and the family together shared all the characteristics of Gein. So I don't think the intention ever was to make a movie about Ed Gein, but he was the seed of the idea. The Grandma, the furniture, the skin lamps — that's all Ed Gein. I don't think it was such a strong thing that Kim and Tobe thought they needed to tell everyone else about it.

Robert A. Burns: I had not heard of Ed Gein, and Tobe didn't really refer to him much. I certainly didn't do any research on him for the film. I think a tiny little grain of the story was suggested by Ed Gein...

Above:

Pam struggles on the meathook.

Allen Danziger: It did come up — I can't remember if it was during the movie or after it — he was the fellow *Psycho* was based on...

Jim Siedow: There was a guy up in the state of, I forgot, but he did the same kind of thing, but just to two people. Ed Gein or somebody like that. That's where they got the idea from.

Paul Partain: The only mention was because of the opening statement in the film about this being a 'true story'. When I asked, Kim told me that there was a germ of truth about a guy Tobe had read about when he was a kid. The rest all came from the fertile minds of folks raised with their feet firmly planted on the enriching earth known as Texas.

The most commonly repeated story is that Tobe Hooper had relations in Wisconsin who terrified him as a child with tales of Ed Gein, skin suits and cannibalism...

Robert A. Burns: [*Laughs*] Tobe creates his own believable reality, and thereby he can tell it to other people and they'll believe it because he's not lying to them! Tobe tells people these stories about being terrified by tales when he was a small child — but this happened when Tobe was fourteen years old! But Tobe has *himself* convinced of that! Like he told people he was going to make *Chain Saw* for $60,000 — he had *himself* convinced of it...

Gunnar Hansen: You know, on the last day of shooting I heard Tobe talking to Bill Parsley and he said, 'We got this in the can for $60,000, but if I'd known at the beginning what I know now we could have done it for half that'!

Amazingly enough, there seems to have been a notion that *Chain Saw* might somehow qualify for a PG rating...

Robert A. Burns: That was the original plan, but once shooting began it took on a life of its own without any thought of rating.

Kim Henkel: I don't know where that comes from. The thing of it is, teenagers don't want to go to see PG movies, they want to see R-rated movies! So what we wanted was an R-rated movie — what we feared was that we might have problems getting an R rating at all...

Tobe Hooper: I put in a lot of telephone calls to the MPAA asking their advice — how do I get an R rating — no, actually I said, 'How do I get a PG rating and hang some-one on a meathook?' [*Texas Chainsaw Massacre: The Shocking Truth*]

Below:
The Family pose
for publicity.

John Dugan: I do remember them one night sitting around and trying to write a scene to try and get Marilyn's blouse ripped off... but believe it or not Tobe was worried about the rating — being able to get it on television! [*The Texas Chain Saw Massacre: A Family Portrait*]

The structure of the 'Bad Family' is somewhat confusing — who are those guys and what is their relationship?

Kim Henkel: Well, I think I'd prefer just to leave that a mystery!

Robert A. Burns: The first thing I thought was, 'Where are the women in this family?' You have three generations of men in this house, where are the women? They said, 'Oh, ah, that's kind of the mystery of the thing.' I said, 'You got to put something in that implies there were once women around, graves outside — you've got Grandpa sitting in the attic, have Grandma sitting there, you know' — and Grandma was my contribution to the script. I said, 'At least put a *dead* Grandma up there to indicate that at some point there were women in this family, that they didn't just spontaneously rejuvenate.'

Gunnar Hansen: It never occurred to me that there were no female members of the family — if you think about it, it makes sense, because in effect Leatherface is saying, 'Well, we need a woman around the house now,' because he's obviously taken on the role of the housekeeper. He's been in the kitchen making dinner, so he's taking the mother role...

After he's killed Jerry, Leatherface gets very flustered and ends up sitting there with his head in his hands — he's having a bad day, like the washing machine has broken down or some other domestic disaster has occurred...

Gunnar Hansen: Dinner won't stay dead... It's never stated explicitly, but there's a misconception — we always thought of the family as three brothers: the Cook is the older brother — most people think of the Cook as the father, but our intention was that he was the eldest of the three brothers.

Above:

A flustered

Leatherface.

Jim Siedow: Well, in the script — they never made it plain in the movie — but in the script we were three brothers. Nobody ever mentioned the father or the mother, just the grandfather and grandmother upstairs. I was more or less the boss of the brothers, but we were definitely three brothers.

Another hot *Chain Saw* topic of debate is the nature of the script. Was it just rough notes or guidelines? Was it made up on a daily basis as shooting progressed?

Sallye Richardson: I don't even remember the script! I know that they worked on a script and there were little pieces of paper with dialogue on them... There were some ideas that were guidelines, and those guidelines were like any great film — they were just changed on the spot: if it didn't work for the actor, if it sounded stupid, it was fixed — it wasn't like you had to say it like it is. Then in editing you fixed it again — if it didn't sound good but you got it on film, then you tried to fix it. And that's when it was made, in the editing — a lot of the time you're trying to save something — it's not like you're working with a Robert Towne script where it's finished and you just cut it and go home...

Allen Danziger: Most of my lines are ad-libbed. I said, 'I can't say these lines!' and they said, 'Allen, just make them up, do your thing.' So some of the lines like, 'Hey, he's going to get you — he even has your zip code' — those are my lines. I think, for me, they were looking for more of a comedy relief — I think they cut some of that down when they realised, 'Hey, we've got something here.' I think some of it was going to be a spoof, there were references to cannibalism with the sausage — they cut some of the humour out and played it somewhat straighter. Although there's laughs galore when you look at some of the things going on: 'Look what your brother did to that door,' the scene where they've taken her out of the barbecue place and he's talking about utility rates going up — that's way out there...

Below:
The three
Leatherface
masks.
Left to right: the
Pretty Woman,
the Old Lady, the
Killing Mask.

Robert A. Burns: The script was shortened considerably. The original had many pages of the kids driving around, with much late-hippie banter. Much of it was rewritten day-by-day during shooting. The abandoned house sequence was added in, as the found location was across the street from the main house.

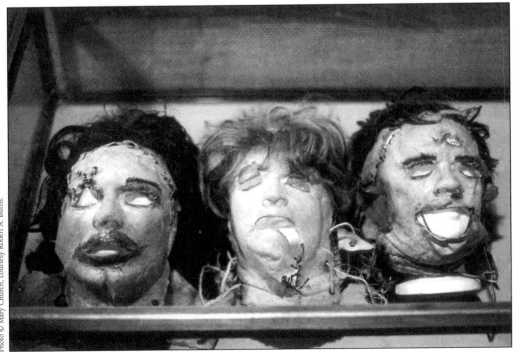

Photo © Mary Church, courtesy Robert A. Burns.

Kim Henkel: We made a lot of changes, but no real structural changes — a lot of internal changes. I'd be writing dialogue on the back of napkins...

Gunnar Hansen: There were a lot of changes — but I don't think it's anything unusual — we were getting quite a bit of new material, but I'm surprised to hear people say the script was being created as it went along. My feeling was — it's dynamic, things are always changing as you go along. For instance, Leatherface originally had lines, and the lines in the script had meaning. I wrote down what those lines are supposed to mean. And we sat down and we ran those lines, we shot the scene, and Tobe said, 'It doesn't work, there's too much intelligence in the character.' So we redid it. Leatherface knows what he wants to say, but he can't get his mouth to make the right sounds. He has the idea of speech, but he can't express it — he just makes sounds randomly thinking that it means something.

Some examples of Leatherface's 'speech' from the script, with Gunnar's translations:
A ab e y ob er ewe ober (How are you, welcome home, supper's almost ready)
Iba goba igee em a (I've been a good boy and I got 'em all)
Aba de ah du o dey (How do you do today)
Aga does uh er (You get beside her)
Li o ba fu gapa gil (You can do it Granpa, kill her)
Aba do hil li ito giba giba (That'll do it, let her have it, get her)

Kim Henkel: Leatherface is one of those characters who is what he wears — his character changes according to the face he puts on...

Gunnar Hansen: What I took to be the great disadvantage for me — that I had neither voice nor face for the character and all I had was my body to play the character with — was actually a great advantage in fact: it forced me to spend the time trying to figure out the character physically. So I had a very strong idea of his personality... I had really worked on figuring out how I was going to represent that character physically. I don't know much about acting — and I knew even less then — but if I had had my voice and face to use, it would never have occurred to me how important it was to create a physical posture, to create a presence that I could step into to be him. So what appeared to be the terrible burden of the character became what made it possible to make the character real.

The whole idea [of Leatherface] was that the mask reflected who he was now — my feeling was that under the mask there was nothing — if you take the mask away there's no face there — that's how I tried to play him, and I think that's why he's such a horrifying character. So the mask defines who he was — he was androgynous any-

way — in *Return of* he's played very effeminately, but he's not effeminate, just androgynous. So the three masks were the killer mask, the old lady mask and the pretty woman — and the pretty woman was because we had company and he was getting all dressed up for dinner, so he put on the pretty face. But that was the idea: the masks express what's going on in his mind, in his little pea brain...

A popular favourite with 'critical thinkers' is highlighting the 'worlds in collision' aspect of the script, the 'good family' of wholesome youngsters decimated by the 'bad family' of slobbering, dispossessed white trash...

Kim Henkel: I think it's more ambivalent than that, but I'm uncomfortable with such questions. *Chain Saw* is not unlike most urban myths — what they all involve is a certain kind of transgression and then there's a response to that transgression, and these characters who are purportedly the good ones, they transgress: they trespass and then they endure the consequences. And all those urban myths involve a stereotype, generally of American teenagers, and indeed when Tobe and I were working on it, we referred to the teenagers in almost generic terms: before we came up with names we referred to them as Ken and Barbie because they were clearly cardboard cut-outs of kids and they weren't designed to be characters so much as archetypes. The more interesting people in the film of course are the bad guys, which is generally the case.

We did have a little bit of fun, particularly with Marilyn Burns and Paul Partain. You stick a guy in a wheelchair and instantly you're going to have a bit of sympathy, but then you play against it by making him an obnoxious and unattractive whiner, and his sister has to contend with him and all his unpleasantness: I think that strikes a chord with a lot of people [*laughs*] who have brothers or sisters who are a bit difficult — sibling relations are sometimes challenging...

While the script was being completed, pre-production was underway in the hands of Robert Burns. From building bone sculptures to preparing Leatherface masks to outfitting rooms with corpse art, Burns delivered an entire film's set decoration and effects on a shoestring budget.

Robert A. Burns: Being the writer/director, Tobe had his original ideas about how things were supposed to be, but he knew what I could do with the script. I had free rein to take it where we knew it should go. The original budget was supposed to be $60,000, and it could have been done for that. It ended up being about $125,000. Including my salary the art budget was only about $3,000. I had to beg, borrow and steal (all of which I was known for) for materials.

Opposite top:
Robert Burns
relaxes with some
of his 'bone art'.

Opposite bottom:
Burns at work
in his studio.

Sallye Richardson: Tobe was always good at getting people to do something for nothing — trying to get a bunch of people who really love what they do and having them do it for free — and that's about how *Chain Saw* got to be put together. A lot of people who really wanted to work and in the end got a little bit for a lot.

Wayne Bell: By the end of the film I felt I'd learned a lot — that's what a film like that should be doing: you don't have enough money to pay people properly, so if you have people who show potential you help them grow into it.

Robert A. Burns: I spent many a long day tracking that prop stuff down. Dottie Pearl [make-up and wife of Daniel Pearl, director of photography] worked for a veterinarian who had land outside town where he left dead animals to be recycled by nature. This proved to be quite a trove. Mary Church [assistant art director and stunt woman], with whom I lived at the time, had family in farm country where we harvested many cow skeletons. Once the collection began many friends brought disgusting things by to add to it. I had a friend out in LA whose girlfriend worked in some sort of dentistry school and he said, 'Hey, want some teeth?' I said, 'Sure,' so he sent this little plastic bucket full of teeth...

People always looked on me as slightly eccentric — they would give me things they found in the woods! The armadillo — Mary and I were out collecting things and were driving along and found a freshly hit armadillo. I said, 'Hell, I'll learn to do taxidermy,' so I went out and got a book on it and taxidermied the armadillo! About a week later I came to the office and found this dead squirrel tied with a piece of string to my doorknob!

The people from the insurance company next door to my store front office would come in and there'd be these little old ladies saying, 'Oh, isn't that cute,' about all this stuff that was supposed to be disgusting!

I also did the effects and co-ordinated the stunts, minor as both were. I even poured my own sugar glass windows because we couldn't afford store bought. All that stuff took quite a long time — I started working on it in April, and the idea was my involvement was supposed to be three months, but it ended up being about four.

For the masks, I experimented a lot to find just the right materials to create the parchment-like look of thin translucent leather. I finally settled on a combination of an extremely thin layer of fibreglass insulation enclosed in latex, which aged naturally to the right colour. On exposure to light the fibreglass starts to darken, so it didn't take long, and liquid latex is rubber band colour. Human skin is thin, so I was trying to find something that would 'turn', and that had the necessary translucency — I didn't want to have to paint it because paint is opaque.

Opposite top and bottom: The Killing Mask in progress.

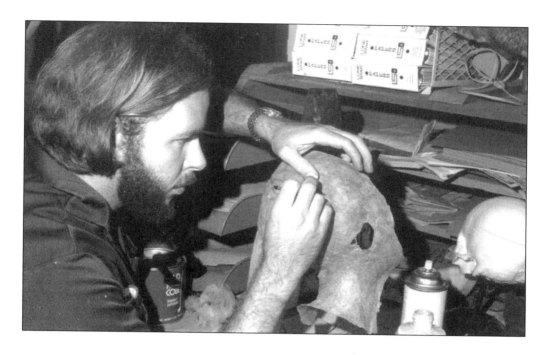

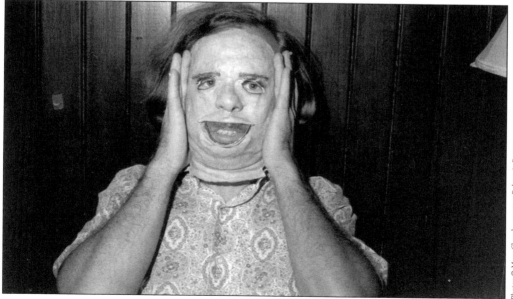

Sallye Richardson: I was living at Tobe's — I had introduced him to my best friend Paulette from High School, and they were living together — I had a little room at the back, it was like living with family... Kim would come in the evenings and he and Tobe would work on it. I'd be there and I would talk to them about what we were doing the next morning, then we'd drive out to the set. Tobe would fuss around thinking about camera angles and I would get people going because I knew what we were doing and how to do it, making sure everybody had their stuff for the day, plus taking stills as I went around all the time. So I was basically working behind him, getting stuff ready that he didn't have time to do — he'd be over setting the lights 'cause there wasn't really anyone who knew. Danny Pearl was good at lights but he was still very young — he learned a lot on that shoot, a lot... A lot of us had been working in commercial film for some time — whatever we could get to support the company — and Danny had just come out of school, he didn't have any commercial experience.

Daniel Pearl: Tobe definitely knew the shooting style he wanted. He wanted to shoot handheld. He had been a documentary, *cinéma-vérité* shooter before he started directing. He knew that I had shot a lot of handheld film and wanted that sort of fluid movement and tension. There were no handheld 35 blimp cameras available for us, so we had to shoot in 16mm for a 35mm blow-up. [International Cinematographer's Guild interview by Bob Fisher]

Photo © Mary Church, courtesy Robert A. Burns.

Right:
Burns in the 'Bone
Room' (before...)

Left:

Pam in the 'Bone

Room' (after...)

Sallye Richardson: We were very influenced by *vérité*. When I was a senior in college it was already something I was studying... They had a core of people to work with, it was different from Hollywood. American independent film-making was really influenced by the French, maybe not intentionally, but it just happened like that — you got a bunch of people who knew each other and could work together and could count on each other. Maybe it had something to do with the fact that these were people who wanted to do it so badly that they would do a lot for a little...

The house where the Leatherface 'family' live was located in Quick Hill, Austin, built in the 1890s.

Robert A. Burns: Some friends of mine were renting the place and were very proud of the fact that it was so well kept up. So there were people living in the house — it was a nice old Victorian place, they were hippiesque people, at one with nature and at one with the house, and they were very concerned we not mess it up. And we said, 'We're not to going to mess up your house!' — and of course we just came in and stomped all over it. We tried to be very careful in making it look run-down so as not to damage it too much — a fanciful pipe dream in the world of film-making. We were there longer than we were supposed to be... It didn't add to the camaraderie of film-making. It was a very tough shoot...

When we made the contract we were going to pay their month's rent for the house and told them they didn't have to move out, we'd only use three rooms — which is true — and we'd only shoot for five days. Of course once we started filming there was no way they could live there, they *had* to move out, and we ended up shooting there for about three weeks. And one of them came to me and said, 'You said you'd only be here for a week, we can't live here — don't you think you should give a little more compensation?' So I went to Tobe and Kim and they said, 'What? Can't we get any cooperation from anyone? Are they trying to wreck our film? What are they saying?' That sort of attitude pervaded the whole thing...

Allen Danziger: A few years ago, the house where the movie was shot was falling into disrepair. Somebody bought it and moved it to a place called Kingsland where it's now a steak restaurant, The Kingsland Old Town Grill — they restored it and it's beautiful. Cut it up and moved it, which is cool. They don't really play up the chainsaw thing...

Robert A. Burns: The house that they stop off at, where Sally's grandfather supposedly lived, the ruin, that was written in because it was opposite the house we were shooting at. This abandoned house was surrounded by mesquite trees, it was all owned by a big lime and limestone company — it was a great place to shoot all the chase scenes. They were all done within a short time span — we lit it and ran one way, then ran back the other way, like you do when you're making low-budget pictures...

The gas station/barbecue place was about thirty-five to forty miles away... I don't know how they found it, maybe it was something somebody had driven by and seen, or if it was the Texas Film Commission — one of the things they have traditionally done best is helping find locations. It was just a gas station, I built the barbecue thing beside it, that was totally constructed. It was just made out of textured masonite — there was no fire in it or anything, it was all lighting effects. I was not there when they did it but the first time they shot Marilyn coming in and flinging herself into this building it bounced around — 'Hey don't do that!' — she didn't realise it was all fake...

By the time casting, pre-production and location scouting were completed, spring was turning to summer and the weather was warming up...

Robert A. Burns: We started shooting — or tried to — in June but had to stop because they were just not prepared to shoot yet. When Bill Parsley put up the money he did so with the proviso that we start shooting by 'x' day — which is not the way to do it — because I think he was afraid of them taking the money and blowing it even before they started shooting. But pre-production doesn't really cost anything, it starts costing when you start shooting. So Tobe agreed to start shooting the film when we were totally unprepared, and I think we shot for about a week then had to stop, shut things down for a week to actually get organised.

Lou Perryman: They had to reshoot. They shot a week's worth of footage and it all came back bad, they couldn't use it. The cameras were bad, or we didn't know enough — whatever, it was all out of focus. But Tobe was really good at getting what he wanted on *Chain Saw* — he had a very good visual way. He'd picked up so much by doing film, by looking at story and understanding that a hippie movie was not going to be the breakthrough — and he did something that would shock the system. He was generally fairly demanding. It was much more, 'Let's get in line, let's get this shot' than *Eggshells*. And Ron Bozman also brought a lot of that professionalism to it, particularly after the first week of filming didn't turn out. He had to crack the whip and say, 'Let's be professional about this and stop screwing around.'

Sallye Richardson: I remember a lot of bitching about Danny Pearl at the time — whether or not it was Danny's problem... I think he shot it out of focus — it might have been the lighting was screwed too. It was a big thing at the time because it cost us a lot of money.

Kim Henkel: You know, I think we did have a focus problem at some point. I don't remember that Daniel Pearl was particularly at fault. The more likely scenario is there was a lens that wasn't properly calibrated — maybe it was his responsibility to do that, but the largest problem was lack of organisation, and that was a direct product of lack of prep time, rushing to get things done with too little money.

I didn't really know much about the film business. Tobe was the most knowledgeable person, the most experienced in terms of film. So I took him at face value, but the truth is Tobe wants the position and the power, but he doesn't really want the day-to-day responsibility that should come with that kind of position. So either somebody recognises that and picks up the slack or things are less than what they should be. And I think there was some adjusting to that situation. Ron Bozman really was responsible for organising things and making them work.

Daniel Pearl: We were about a week into shooting and were sort of flying by the seat of our pants. The executive producer heard from someone else that we needed a shot list. He thought that would make us more productive. So they shut us down for four or five days and Tobe was forced to write a shot list. When we started shooting again, Tobe told me he just wrote the shot list to get the guy off his back. So anyhow, we were outside shooting the sequence where Leatherface has just taken his first victim inside the house. We cut to Pam, who was sitting outside on this quite bizarre swing made out of railroad ties. She got up and walked towards the house. We had forty-eight feet of dolly track with a flat platform. I realised that if I laid down on the dolly holding the camera over the edge, I could fit under this swing, get behind the girl, and use the swing as a frame with the house almost a dot in the bottom of the frame, keeping the track just out of the shot and follow her as she walked to the house. That way, the house would grow and grow, and go from seeming very small until it dominated the picture. It's terrifying for the audience because they know what she's walking towards. I told Tobe my idea and he said, 'Daniel that's incredible.' Around this time, the producer figured out we weren't following the shot list. He told Tobe we had to move on to the next scene. Tobe tried to explain my idea but the producer insisted he live by the list. Tobe really stuck his neck out but history has proven him correct. It's the shot that has gone down in history. [International Cinematographer's Guild interview by Bob Fisher]

The film finally began shooting on 15 July 1973, and took anywhere from thirty-two days to eight weeks — it's a measure of how traumatic the shoot was that most err towards a longer period. Certainly few cast or crew members found the time flying past as they relaxed and enjoyed themselves on what was for most of them a first feature...

Lou Perryman: It was a hard shoot, and it was shot pretty much in sequence — there was no coming back to a location more than once that I recall. Certainly as costumes degraded it was cheaper and easier to have your continuity going so that if you got a splatter on something it was on there for the rest of the picture.

Gunnar Hansen: A lot of people ask if it was fun — fun was the one word that never came to mind. We shot twelve to sixteen hours a day... We didn't have a trailer, we didn't have any place to sit that was out of the heat — everything was very limited — because of that the conditions were very difficult. We couldn't do a lot of takes...

Ed Neal: The thing that helped us a great deal was the 115 degrees Texas weather. By the time your clothes hadn't been washed in six weeks it got easier and easier and

easier, as we took on the environmental aspects of the family, to *become* the family...
[*The Texas Chain Saw Massacre: A Family Portrait*]

Paul Partain: Getting around in the chair was tough. I worked really hard and then felt guilty at how poorly I could get around in it. You see, my Grandfather, a very strong fellow, had a stroke which put him in a wheelchair and he could not use his right arm or right leg and he got around quite well. There I was with two good arms, was working like a dog and not doing very well at all. Any time I would get to feeling like I couldn't do it, I just thought of my Grandad and all he was able to do. Many times I would try to get around using just one arm and I will tell you it is a damned difficult deal. Pray you keep your health and that you are never bound to such a device.

Below:
Daniel Pearl
sets up.

Wayne Bell: The way sound is recorded is there's the sound mixer back at the recorder and there's the boom man who is actually dancing the microphone. In more involved movies there's more than one microphone and therefore wires coming into the recorder, so he truly does mix. In the scene inside the van, Ted is mixing — we planted mics either on people or inside the van, and Ted is down behind the luggage at the very back of the van, not seeing any of the action at all. That's one of the few times where there was any actual mixing. The rest of the time it was just one boom mic — 'Where is that boom mic, what's it doing?' That's where the dance is — I thought, 'That's where the real creativity is.' Booming is more akin to dancing because your dancing partner is the actor — the actors and the scene they're creating in front of you: it moves here, moves there, gets loud here, quiet there, and changes from performance to performance. You have the feeling of being the most immediate person to the movie that's happening in front of you — it's going right into your ears first. You're having to respond to nuances of performance — and of course the camera operator, who's having to pull focus if the actor gets closer to the lens, is also having to respond — you're right there in the moment.

We had a little baby buggy which Ted improvised as the sound cart — and most of the time he was recording straight into the Nagra with no mixer involved, so the critical decision was 'Where's the microphone?' I far preferred it to being where Ted was. So I loved it — for a guy just getting into film-making, yeah — I was right on it!

Lou Perryman: My contribution to the chainsaw was, I was familiar with them. You get on a take, get Leatherface to run over to the chainsaw and start it up and it doesn't work! Well that's really screwed up. I became the uncredited chainsaw professional: start it up, choke it and turn it off so that the carburettor flooded with gas, then turn it back on, set it there and it's ready to go. Give it one crank and it's off. So I was the one who figured that out, I was a contributor in that way... One of the good effects is mine: Tobe and Bob were in a big argument, they were fighting all the time, and Tobe's like, 'I want it big, I want it *big*, I want it *extravagant*,' and Bob just didn't... Tobe says, 'Get a big nail, a really big nail, and nail this watch to a tree, nail this fucking watch to a tree.' So Bob gets like a sixteenth of an inch nail, it's just not a big nail and Tobe was throwing a fit about it. I went over to my box and got out a big old railroad spike and went over and nailed that goddamn watch to the tree... And the other one was, we were out on the highway after picking up the Hitchhiker, he's getting ready to cut his arm and bleed. Bob had got this little bulb thing that makes a plastic frog hop, held a couple of thimblefuls of blood, and Tobe was throwing a fit — 'Goddamnit, that's not enough blood!' — and Bob got pissed off and went back to town! There we were sitting on the highway with no effects. I said, 'What the fuck is the problem?' They told me what the deal was and I said, 'Give me that!' and got out a big ear syringe that I used for dusting off the gate and the lenses. I filled it full of blood and I fixed it up to the tube rigged to the back of the knife and said, 'How about this?' and ran the knife from my ribs to my armpits and there was blood galore and Tobe goes, 'Yeah, that's it!'

Sallye Richardson: Bob Burns, oh God — he and Tobe argued a lot... Tobe would say, 'I want this' and he would say, 'Nah, nah... ' and Tobe would say, 'Yeah, that's what I want, go out and get it!' and Bob would say, 'Nah, you can't do that,' and he would come up with something Tobe didn't want... Tobe would say, 'Go get me an armadillo, I want an armadillo, just go out in the road and get me an armadillo — there's plenty out there!' 'I ain't gonna get no armadillos, I can't find any armadillo', and then later he'd show up with one...

Allen Danziger: I think for the most part Tobe didn't lend too much to me. He maybe pulled me aside a couple of times and tried to direct me to something. The opening part in the van — I didn't know anything about astrology, it was like speaking Greek — and I do remember him giving me some direction with those lines.

Sallye Richardson: Tobe knows what the scene is, he knows what he's going to do — but at the same time Kim stimulates him with ideas. Tobe might think, 'I need some dialogue to get me from here to here' so he'd ask Kim to write something. And then hopefully when he got back to the editing room, he'd be able to piece together all the little bits to make a cohesive story out of the sequences...

The scene most like that was the one in the van — Danny didn't shoot it, he might have shot some of the exteriors, but Tobe shot inside. He just sat in the van and picked up stuff they were saying. He had the idea of what he wanted them to be talking about — which was astrology — he knew he needed particular thoughts to be in their heads to get them from here to there... So Tobe would probably say to Kim, 'What do you want them to say here?' and Kim would write some dialogue. I think Tobe sees the screenplay more as a guideline — though I doubt scriptwriters think that! He's not an actor's director, he's a film-maker...

Allen Danziger: Tobe was like a dark presence, he had this cigar like some Erich von Stroheim, lurking in the background... But he was always very nice to me and because I had the least invested in it — I didn't want to be an actor, I was a social worker — it was more like fun for me, I just took it for what it was. But some of these guys, like Eagle Pennell and Tobe — they're really bright but they have their own demons...

Left:
Tobe Hooper
shoots the van
scene, with Paul
Partain and
Marilyn Burns.

There was a scene when we were at the gas station, just about out of gas, and this little troll comes over and spits soapy water on the windscreen — well that scene took all day, it should have taken an hour. It took all day because in one of the takes, as I'm talking to Jim Siedow and this troll was putting on the soapy water, I somehow hit the windscreen wipers and they threw the water all over Jim, so he's talking to me with all this soapy water dripping down his face. Well, that was it for me, it was over: I could *not* say the lines, we were on the floor, we just couldn't do it. Tobe got so flustered that he walked off the set and Kim finished it... Tobe just lost it...

Daniel Pearl: We would purposely lead the eye away from the side of the frame where Leatherface was going to make his entrance. By the time you realised he was in the frame, he was already doing something scary. You know the scene where Leatherface jumps out and gets Franklin? Just prior to that, Franklin was moving and he was holding a flashlight. It was very sketchily lit on a very dark night... He's moving his flashlight around, so your eye is going to the thing you can see most

Below:
The Family
prepare Sally
for butchery.

clearly. You put a bright thing in the frame and the eye will go to it. So, you're creating a little distraction because you know the way people will respond. We had this flashlight moving around and the audience is following it. Leatherface enters the frame and the scary song comes on at the same time. Franklin swings the beam of the flashlight onto Leatherface. He was just sketchily lit before that. Now, you see him and the chainsaw smack dab in the middle of the frame. You also heard the rrrrrrr. People jump out of their seats. It was scary and surprising. [International Cinematographer's Guild interview by Bob Fisher]

Paul Partain: ... out of the darkness comes the sound of that big saw cranking up and then there is the most God-awful sight you ever want to see, eleven foot twenty-seven inches tall, leather apron, somebody else's face for a mask and that damned smokin' chainsaw coming right at you. I am an actor, and so is Ms Burns, but we did not have to do a lot of acting at that point. Marilyn hooked 'em to parts unknown and I screamed my ass off. The shot, the first time we saw Leatherface, was as close to real as we all could make it. Now when the close up came for old Franklin's demise, that was a bunch of fun. The camera was looking over my left shoulder. Most of the lighting was coming from a 'sun gun' flashlight in my hand. The deal was that Leatherface was to come into the light with the saw and take a swipe at Franklin again and again. Dottie Pearl, our make-up lady, was squatted off camera on my left and Tobe was in the same position off camera on my right. We all three had a mouth full of red Karo Syrup and every time Leatherface came into the light, we would spit. The result is that with each pass, the apron and saw gets more and more bloody. If you look really close you can see drops of blood in the air. Very effective. At the end, Tobe had a cup full of blood and he threw the contents. Said it could have been when they hit the heart... As I recall that scene was a lot of fun and everyone was laughing when it was done. [Living-Dead.com interview by Ryan Adams]

Jim Siedow: When we first started that scene in the BarBQ shack where I'm beating Marilyn up — that was hard — we started out and I couldn't do it. They'd keep telling me to make it look real — 'Hit her!' — they couldn't use anything that looked fake, so I'd start and — 'No, you got to hit her harder, hit her some more!' Marilyn said, 'Hit me, don't worry about it.' And every time we'd try it she'd come up with a few more bruises. Finally I got with it and started having fun doing it and started really slugging her and we kept that up — we did eight shots — and when they finally said 'That's a take,' she just fainted dead away — the poor girl was beaten up pretty bad. [*The Texas Chain Saw Massacre: A Family Portrait*]

Marilyn Burns: They enjoyed dropping that hammer on my head! It was a sledge-hammer — they took off the metal part but the handle was made of oak, so every time it hit my head it was killing me. And it made a nice big clunk when it dropped into the bowl, but it gave me a bloody head and a couple of bumps — but everyone was so crazed by then they were saying, 'Let's kill the...' and enjoying it.

Gunnar Hansen: In fact, that was the one time when I forgot it was a movie... During the scene when Marilyn breaks free and heads towards the door, at that point the Hitchhiker says something like 'Kill the bitch'. I remember thinking, 'Kill... the... bitch,' and I turned to kill her — and the physical act of turning made me remember where I was.

Marilyn Burns: In the scene where Sally jumps through the window, she's jumping from the ground floor to the ground floor — it's just a big picture window. And Tobe says, 'Oh Marilyn, we want your stunt double [Mary Church] to do that scene,' and I said, 'Why Tobe? I'm just going to be jumping through a bunch of sugar glass onto the ground and I want it to look like me.' And he says, 'No, no, we can't take any chances.' So Mary jumps through the sugar glass onto the mattress with a blonde wig on. For me, the next morning, it's like 5.30am and nice and humid, and the sugar glass has crystallized into hard chunks and it's no longer crunchy but hard. And Tobe has this scaffolding there that's like six to eight feet. I asked, 'What's that for?' and Tobe says, 'Oh this is where you jump out the window. You're going to climb up there and you're going to jump and we're going to throw the sugar glass in your hair when you hit the ground.' That's why I limped for the rest of the picture.

Gunnar Hansen: The worst was the scene where Leatherface chases Sally up the stairs. Mary Church doubled her for the dive out of the window: it was from the second floor, but they put a mattress and an angle brace at the edge of the eaves, so when Mary dived out she goes about five feet forward and two feet down. Because they wanted to protect Marilyn. But then there's the shot where Marilyn lands in the dirt by the back porch — they took Marilyn up on the roof and dropped her from the roof! And it was an old Texas house and the porch was high up — they dropped her ten feet! That didn't seem to bother anybody at all.

Marilyn Burns: They got their realism. I think that was one way round having to save a lot of money — you just went for it. A little reality never hurts a picture — could have hurt *me* quite a lot though. There was a week they spent on my eyes, where we came in and they took pictures of my eyes, and they'd say, 'Just be still Marilyn, tear up' — well, it's real hard to get your eyes to do just exactly what the director wants them to do...

People used to say, 'Wow, it looks so real, it's got such a quality.' We'd say, 'We shot it in 16mm to give it that grainy, documentary look,' and people would say, 'Wow, that's such a good idea!' — well, we couldn't afford anything else, we shot it like that because it was cheap.

Ed Neal: The scene where Siedow's chasing me around in front of the truck with artsy-fartsy lights behind and all of the smoke — it's not even smoke — it's dirt! This really works because it's all natural elements — I'm grovelling in the dirt! The reason I'm grovelling and trying to get down into the dirt is because the stick that Siedow's punching me with is made out of hardwood! And he's beating me! I can hear my skull cracking! I'm going 'Aaarrgh!' and Hooper's going, 'Great, great, that's great stuff, give me some more of that!' [*The Texas Chain Saw Massacre: A Family Portrait*]

Allen Danziger: ... when I got my brains bashed out? To this day, I'm still getting headaches! I guess it was a rubber mallet. I felt that during that particular scene I was acting — I got myself away from everybody else, I closed my eyes, I had them block the whole scene out for me. This part was my Stanislavsky method — you know, I went into myself (didn't like what I saw) and got ready for the scene. In fact, when we shot it the first time they said, 'Allen, your scream was incredible, but there was nobody in the scene with you' — Leatherface hadn't even entered the room!

Paul Partain: It was hot — Texas in the summertime is hot — the world was not air-conditioned in 1973, but we got by. Some of us still do to this day. There is a good line from a Johnny Rodriguez song: 'It's hot down in Texas, yeah, I call it my home. If I ain't happy here, I ain't happy nowhere...' There is also the bumper sticker that says, 'If you can't stand the heat... get the hell out of Texas.'

Allen Danziger: I couldn't compare the scenes in the van with what it must have been like in the house, with the smell of the rotting bones and feathers, people throwing up... It was hot in the van, but that's Texas, it's ninety-five degrees, and you've got the cameras in there. The scenes would finish and everyone would scurry in to the trailer to get fixed up, except when it came my turn they'd say, 'Allen, there's nothing we can do with you, we can't help you.' There wasn't a lot of time spent 'foofing' me up — I had that Afro in the movie, the bellbottoms... And I want you to know I'm still upset about my shirt! I loaned it to Ron Bozman because they were doing a long shot they didn't need me in, they borrowed my shirt and I never got it back! I'm still upset about that! My favourite shirt!

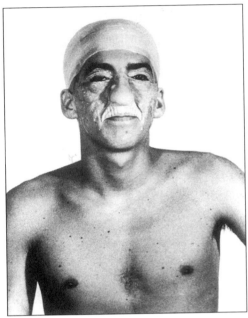
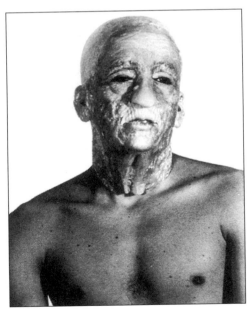
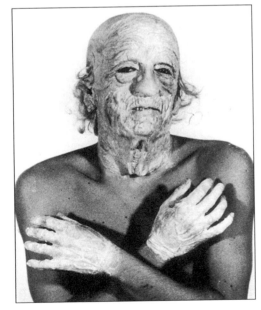

Kim Henkel: John Dugan, who played Grandpa, was my brother-in-law. He was an actor in his own right. He went to a well known drama school in Chicago, he now lives in Indiana.

Gunnar Hansen: We had to shoot that day because of Grandpa — we had only three faces for him — we had to shoot everything with him in it in three sessions and that was it, so we had to do the dinner scene that day. [*The Texas Chain Saw Massacre: A Family Portrait*]

Marilyn Burns: There was this relation of Kim's who wanted to be in the movie, and the only part left was Grandpa, so it took twenty-three hours of make-up. Like, we had such a big budget that we didn't think, 'Hey, we should get an old guy to play Grandpa' — no, let's get a plastic surgeon and an eighteen year-old kid and make the cast wait while the plastic surgeon layers latex all over him so it can melt in the light...

Gunnar Hansen: They had three faces but it took so long to put the first face on he said, 'No, that's it, no more.'

Jim Siedow: They had this young guy playing the grandfather — and they had someone come out to do the make-up, and it took hours. Marilyn and I said that round Austin there were plenty of old men who would be glad to do that job and they wouldn't even require too many more lines!

John Dugan: The guy who did the make-up, Dr Barnes, a plastic surgeon, had made two masks with liquid latex. The first time they put it on it took seven hours, then we shot for twelve maybe. The second time they only had one more mask for me, which they cut up into sections and put on with spirit gum. So the second time they wanted to shoot myself and Jim Siedow out because they couldn't afford to pay him any more and they didn't have a third mask to use for me. So I was in make-up for I think twenty-six hours, and this was Texas in July — it was really uncomfortable. [*The Texas Chain Saw Massacre: A Family Portrait*]

Sallye Richardson: God, we were ready to just burn the house down after that twenty-six hour shoot — I don't know what they did with the house, but I'm sure it had to be fumigated. It was a terrible mess, just awful... All the things on the table — it was real, it wasn't stuffed...

We had to shoot it out — partly because everything was rotting, partly because of the time constraint. I think we only had John Dugan for a certain number of days — he was more of a professional actor then, and we had to pay him by

Opposite:

Four stages of

John Dugan's

Grandpa make-up.

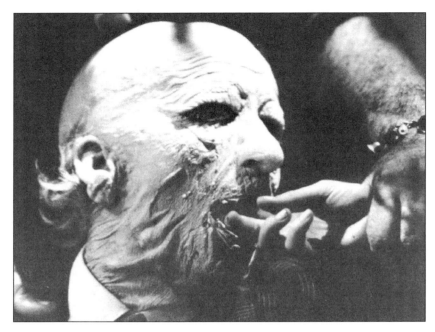

Right:
Grandpa gets to
grips with Sally.

the day. It went on all night and into the next morning, it was very hot — and Marilyn's screams, she was really screamed out...

Marilyn Burns: It was gruelling. It was intensely low budget. What you saw was real — that was real torture, 110 in the shade. It was a very hard picture to make. You can't be locked up for twenty-six hours for the dinner sequence with chickens melting and headcheese that's been out for days in the heat without us all getting sick.

Jim Siedow: It's hard to forget! The main reason it ran that long is — they were on a very low budget — I had to leave the next day, I was on contract only for that week, after which I was supposed to show up for a play. So they had to finish that scene, and they just kept going... That was my fault [*laughs*]. That was the hottest weather in Texas too. They had food on the table and it was getting rotten and the smell would make you sick. They had a skeleton they made a lamp out of... Well, you turned the light on those bones and they started burning and the smell of burning bones along with the rotten food was very bad. And there was no air conditioning — and of course Gunnar and I wore the same clothing all along, it was never washed. So we smelled just as bad! It was alright though — it was an experience!

Wayne Bell: Not only was I stuck in it, but I was up high with the boom, and heat rises as do a lot of the smells, so I was getting it worst. It was really hot... I recall having to put things down and go outside — got to breathe some air... But I was digging it — for a young guy, what a great lot of fun to be in the middle of...

Lou Perryman: Oh yeah I was there. They got Sally tied up at the end of the table and Leatherface is coming up 'goo goo'-ing and coming up toward the camera — I mean, he smelled *so bad* that I had to pull focus and as soon as I hit my mark I leaned back and stuck my head out the window so I could breathe some fresh air. They wouldn't let him wash his costume, they wouldn't let him in the chow trailer — they had some sort of a mobile home where they fed us — and they were bringing food out to him because he smelled so bad. So we would sit out there talking about art and literature and paintings — you know, with a beautiful sunset, all this stuff and there he was in this costume, sometimes with his mask on! But he did smell bad... But that's a low-budget picture for you — nowadays you got six distressed shirts that are all just about the same — but no matter how much *he* washed the *clothing* stayed the same. Course you had all the bones and headcheese and there was a rotten smell all over that house...

Gunnar Hansen: I was the smelliest element of the set... The problem was they had one costume for me — they daren't have it cleaned — they were afraid it would get lost or the colour would change... So I wore the same clothes twelve or sixteen hours a day for a month. [*Texas Chainsaw Massacre: The Shocking Truth*]

Robert A. Burns: The dinner sequence was the main stinky thing — shooting for about thirty hours in the middle of Texas summer time made it very sweaty, and the unpleasant-ness of the shoot added stress that made its way on-screen. And it was supposed to be the middle of the night, so they had to black out all the windows. So it was a totally airless room with all these bright lights and great amounts of sweat — every-thing in there started to stink — and poor Gunnar, they were afraid to wash his suit in case it fell apart or it wasn't the same. That's the way the whole thing was — there was no laundering — so it brought out the worst possible odours of everyone and everything in this place. It was pretty rank. The main stink — well, I made this little thing with a chicken head and chick-en feet in the middle of the table that was starting to stink — but not as bad as everybody claimed.

Below:

Left to right:

Robert A. Burns,

a chicken,

Ted Nicolaou,

Tobe Hooper.

But there was no reason for it... Everything ran longer, there was no preparation — Tobe didn't believe in it, it was 'spontaneity' that made it: 'We are artists, we are not scientists', all that kind of stuff, it kind of went overboard. Then they ran out of money and they were going round asking people if they could take deferments — people were working for very little to begin with! — and I thought, great, this really helps...

Ed Neal: Here was this table, and all of the action going round and round this table — which took like thirty something hours to shoot with the same group of people. Here was this table with the sausage that had been on the plate for two and a half weeks for continuity purposes — it couldn't be moved off — and these lights at about 8,000 degrees shining down... and this stuff was decomposing in front of your eyes and four inches from your nose. And Burns had this idea and nails this chicken head and feet to a board and that sucker was rotting right in front of you. And they had things over the window to keep the light out... and there's no air... no ventilation whatsoever. Everybody's puking and pissing and moaning... A lot of people couldn't see the end of the tunnel — they couldn't even remember how they got on the god-damn train! [*The Texas Chain Saw Massacre: A Family Portrait*]

Below:
Ed Neal (left) gets
a whiff of Bob
Burns' infamous
'chicken art'.

Kim Henkel: Oh yeah, I was there for every fucking minute of it... It was unpleasant...

Lou Perryman: There was this goat on the lot — there was a barn out behind that house with a goat in it. It was a small barn, but still a barn, and one day the goddamn thing collapsed and a beam from up top just nailed that goat behind the head and killed the sonofabitch. We go out and there's this dead goat and we're thinking, 'Damn — but better him than us'! It seemed like part of the karma for this whole outfit that something like that would happen.

Gunnar Hansen: The caterer was also the craft services, usually it's two separate things. Anyway, they made a big plate of marijuana brownies and neglected to tell us... So there was a point where we were all very stoned — and we'd get really hungry, forget that the reason we were really hungry was from the brownies, and we'd go and get another snack! I'm convinced that's the reason we had the infamous twenty-six hour filming sequence... There's a shot where Marilyn comes up the steps before she dives out the window with me behind her, it's like a three or four second shot — and Tobe and the cinematographer discussed the lighting in that shot for hours...

Marilyn Burns: I wasn't eating the brownies, but Gunnar was, and then I found out he'd had three and what's in them. And he's got to chase me up the stairs with a chainsaw and he's going, 'Wow, I feel so woozy. Man, something's wrong.' When I hear about the brownies, I think, 'Oh, we're in trouble' — I mean, I trust Gunnar 100 per cent, but not Gunnar on brownies, with a chainsaw, running up the wooden steps, take forty-four, oh no...

Gunnar Hansen: If you watch that shot where Leatherface kicks the door in — I knew I was very stoned at that point and I was really worried because we had only one door and I didn't want to ruin the shot, so it had to work. I kept thinking, 'I've got to remember to kick the door in and not stop.' And if you look at that shot, I kick the door in then do this thing [*twitches his head around*] — the reason was, the cameraman was so stoned that when I kicked the door in (the camera was on the floor) he jumped up and ran out of the room! So I turned and watched him run out of the room, then remembered, 'Oh, the stairs' and turned back...

Chain Saw is virtually devoid of on-screen violence, yet its reputation as one of the most violent films of all time endures. Was there a decision to avoid blood-letting, was it a budgetary constraint or was there a conscious attempt to give the illusion of graphic horror while not actually showing much?

Robert A. Burns: I always insist that graphic effects, no matter how 'realistic', distance the audience from the event because they subliminally know that they are manufactured. This cushions the impact for the audience — 'It's only a movie.'

Tobe originally wanted me to make an appliance of the meathook coming through Teri's chest and squirting blood. I talked him out of it. That scene is still one of the most memorably gut-wrenching in filmdom without a single drop of blood.

Levie Isaacks: Wasn't it banned in Europe for being the bloodiest film of all time or something? When you look at it, all the violence is implied and there's really not much blood. But that steel door slamming shut — what a great image — it makes your mind shoot into all kinds of possibilities that you could never create in a person's mind by showing it to them. Those images were just great... Right now I work on a TV show, *Malcolm in the Middle*, and I've learned so much about comedy — so much of it's out of implication rather than being literal. And that's the funny part about watching other people being miserable, it's much more in thinking 'This could happen to me' than what's happening to *them*... That's what scares you, because you imagine yourself in the scene, your mind takes over — it becomes truly horrifying from the standpoint of what your own mind can tell you.

Sallye Richardson: I never thought it was horrible, I thought it was funny — I always thought it was funny.

Kim Henkel: Tobe and I always thought *Chain Saw* was a comedy anyway, to a large extent...

Above:
Bob Burns' balsa
wood wrench.

Sallye Richardson: The only time I got scared was when I was editing in LA. Tobe was back in the hotel sleeping — in the morning we were going to do the final, *absolutely* final mix — and that was the night the movie was really born. I got scared, I got really scared, because it became something other than what it was, it went to another dimension, it was like a spirit went into it, it became that entity that people now look at. A spirit went into that *thing* — it wasn't always there, but after that it was *always* there... It was that magical thing, it wasn't just a piece of film any more — then that's when I got scared. Then when they put the final mix on it, it really began to live. But still it doesn't look horrible to me because I see it in terms of shots, pieces of celluloid.

Various props and 'special effects' (including a balsa wood wrench thrown at Leatherface by Ed Guinn's truck driver in the last sequence) were used to achieve the surprisingly realistic on-screen violence. Pam's meathook impalement proved to be the most difficult because she was wearing only a halter top and shorts.

Gunnar Hansen: They rigged up a little harness to fit around her waist and legs, made of nylon pantyhose. The crew wired it up with a little loop in the back that I just threaded over the meathook, which was then facing away from her back. [*Fangoria 70*, 1988]

The pain caused by dangling from a meathook, her weight supported by only a pair of tights, caused actress Teri McMinn to feel like she was being cut in half. As with so many shots in *Chain Saw*, realism was achieved by genuine pain inflicted on the cast and crew.

Robert A. Burns: The most graphic violence effect in the film is the chainsaw dropping on Leatherface's leg. This was done by taking a metal plate and wrapping it across his leg for protection (the chain itself was filed smooth), placing a steak over the plate, and duct taping a baggie filled with blood over the whole mess. Even with the metal plate, Gunnar was burned slightly by the friction of the blade heating up the metal. I should have realised this and put a piece of leather under the metal.

Below:

Pam gets hung up.

For running over the Hitchhiker I made an articulated dummy from PVC and stuffing which I strung up across the road with wire I was actually holding in my hand (standing on top of a ladder) while it was struck. Wonder I didn't kill myself. [From www.robert-a-burns.com]

Marilyn Burns: When I first heard it was banned in England, I thought — how, why, with all the stuff that's out there, on the screen — how did this get picked out...?

I've heard the accusations about gratuitous violence towards women — those people just don't get it — I survived! I made it through! I was not a victim — Sally got away — she kept running back to the wrong places all the time, which wasn't too bright of her, but you know, in the heat of pursuit... But the girl got away — and she's so ecstatic at the end of the picture because she did get through. Gratuitous violence! There'd been very few females in horror movies before that who had survived at all!

Gunnar Hansen: And there are three men killed and only one woman...

Marilyn Burns: No one complains about the gratuitous violence against men!

Gunnar Hansen: Violence in a movie that serves the point of the movie is not gratuitous, and this movie — where you see virtually nothing — the violence in *Chain Saw* serves a purpose, which is to scare the bejesus out of you. So it's very hard to call it gratuitous. People just want to say that because it's a horror movie...

Allen Danziger: Because I worked for the Austin-Travis County Mental Health I kiddingly say it's my way of atoning for that movie — trying to do something good

Right:
Blood-soaked and
hysterical, Sally
finally escapes.

in the community. My parents couldn't believe it — they were trying to figure out what was good about it because their son was in it! It's hard to say there was anything morally good about it.

Chain Saw's detractors have been known to fixate on what they perceive as a sexual element in Sally's endless torment...

Kim Henkel: Well, it just wasn't about that. The odd thing is that the *victim* poses it as a possibility — but that's the only suggestion of it — and they laugh at her! [*Laughs*] That wasn't part of their game...

Gunnar Hansen: My feeling was that the only hint at sex in the movie is where Sally says, 'I'll do anything.' I don't know what Leatherface is thinking except he's kind of banging on the table going 'moo', but the Cook has got that gleam in his eye, he keeps doing this [*twitches*] and looking toward her — I always think that was his reaction to her saying 'I'll do anything.'

Marilyn Burns: Oh, she didn't really mean it, God, ugh! ■

FIXING IT: THE JOYS OF POST-PRODUCTION

Robert A. Burns: It's so hard to make money on a film — and when you make one for $125,000 that makes millions, you're golden. The point is you make money for your investors so you can go back to them again. These investors would never invest in another film as long as they lived and wanted to lynch Tobe! That to me is a cardinal sin — to make money for your backers and have them want to kill you!

Lou Perryman: It was such a low-budget project that every night after work I literally had to go jump in dumpsters looking for cardboard boxes to ship the film off to the lab. It was just bizarre — I can't believe anything like that occurs.

Allen Danziger: It was a lot of fun — but the thing is, there's still residual feelings that people didn't get a fair shake from the movie, especially as it did real well. It was a massacre after the movie was made and released.

Gunnar Hansen: We got nothing from this movie — I got to keep the boots because they were mine. I mean, these people were so cheap they told us that because they paid us so little they'd have a big cast party, a wrap party, and they'd have stills there and what have you. So at least we could get some stills...

Marilyn Burns: Yeah, well, I didn't go to that cast party.

Gunnar Hansen: There wasn't one.

Opposite:
The Hitchhiker
amuses himself
with Sally.

Sallye Richardson: Everybody was so tired, everybody was under such pressure, there

was no money... Sometimes a time constraint helps the artist, because if you didn't have it you might never be done: you can fix it and fix it and fix it, but to what end...?

Robert A. Burns: The editing just took forever — Tobe continued editing and shooting inserts for months. Most of the cost overrun came from the time involved in post-production. That's the reason it ended up costing $125,000. He had some people that were helping him edit, but he ended up basically taking over.

Wayne Bell: Let's see, Larry Carroll was the editor...

Sallye Richardson: Larry still gets a credit and he didn't do anything! Everything that Larry did was torn up, but a deal was struck whereby if Larry would leave he would get a point and he would get that credit, and I was so happy to have an opportunity to do it, at the time I just didn't care — just get him out of here and let's do it!

And I don't have a still photographer credit — every still that was ever shot, I shot it. I was ADing and taking the shots at the same time — but I didn't know enough to ask for it, I was young and dumb, it was really exciting, so I blew it. I shot vast amounts of film — I imagine Tobe still has it all tucked away.

They started the editing, I wasn't hired — maybe because they wanted someone they thought had experience, maybe it was a chauvinistic thing, I don't know... I had gone back to Colorado, I was doing lithography on a newspaper, working the nightshift. I guess Lou worked for that newspaper too, 'cause he wasn't around for the editing.

When Tobe called me they had edited some of the van sequence — he had wanted someone to edit so he could say, 'Here's the film, go edit it, let me come in and I'll see if I like it' and he thought Larry could do that. Larry was already on board when we were shooting, he was handling getting the film processed, I believe he was doing some synching up. But he just destroyed it from Tobe's point of view. Larry was not from the kind of thinking process that we had all been in, he wasn't able to work with Tobe the way a lot of us were. That's when he called me in, and we tore it all up and started anew.

Wayne Bell: There's a lot of places where I think the music is mixed low because it only marginally worked and was merely a presence, whereas if we could have taken a little more time editing the music, it could ride a little higher in the mix and maybe cast its spell a little better. The way we made the music, the *technique*, was right, it's just that in marrying sound to picture, Tobe was in such a hurry that it wasn't crafted quite as well as it could have been. The effect of the music would have been the same, it would just have been tailored a little better so that the music could step up at certain moments and could have more *accurately* cast its spell. The power of music and editing is something that film-makers who are just starting should bear in mind — you shoot the movie on location, but you make the movie in the editing. You can somewhat apply that same philosophy to music: you record the music but then you actually make the score in the editing.

Sallye Richardson: *Chain Saw* was made in editing. It wasn't a case of a scene in the screenplay being 'x' pages long — the scenes were as long as they were *supposed* to be, it was instinctive. Tobe knew what he wanted from, say, the van scene, and it didn't have anything to do with how much footage he was going to shoot... And that's why Larry Carroll didn't work out, because he didn't understand that. Tobe came in, and he decided the ebb and flow, the building of the scene — he had ,that overview that he was able to project onto it, and that was never in the screenplay.

Below:

An original

newspaper ad.

Bottom:

Sally screams

at dinner...

Richard Kooris: They actually ended up doing the last of the cutting on the Steenbeck in our little production office — they ran out of money and needed a place to go to make some last minute changes, so they wound up bringing it up, they spent a week or two. They were in there at night and we were doing our stuff during the day.

Sallye Richardson: We had rented this place, an editing facility of somebody's, but we couldn't leave the film there, we had to clear it out every morning. We worked at night and slept in the day: I'd go to work about 5pm and I'd have to carry everything I was working on that day up the back stairs, maybe five, six cans or more. I'd start work and Tobe would show up later, maybe after a meeting with Kim — and he was always going to the movies, he'd catch the last show, just about every night — and he'd edit for a while, or mark up, or suggest things to me, then he'd go and I'd work till about 7am and have to pack everything up again.

Right:
Sally continues to
scream at dinner.
Note the
'arm chair'.

Wayne Bell: There was a Steenbeck in Tobe's living room... It seems like we did a lot of music sessions early on, more playing around — you got to understand, we were having fun, which is why we got into it — but once that Steenbeck got in his living room, it got into serious editing time.

Sallye Richardson: We had to move the Steenbeck to Tobe's living room because we ran out of money. I had to manipulate the film on a table! You opened the front door of the house and the Steenbeck was right there, then the kitchen's behind it, then a little room that was probably a study, where Tobe would sit on the floor — he had a sound system in there — and if you had an audience, you would go in and sit in front of him on the floor, because we were just kind of old hippies, right? People would come and go, though by that point it was pretty much just Wayne doing sound.

Wayne Bell: Sometimes Tobe would have been cutting on a scene and was thinking about it, but in terms of conception, as far as real musical direction went — sometimes we'd do 'ice', or sometimes we'd do 'bones' or 'chase', 'hot', 'cold' or 'suspense'. The music of *Chain Saw* was just the two of us together playing — I would invent a few things that I would bring in, but it was mostly just playing around and jamming and seeing where things would go. There was a little bit of overdubbing, but not much.

The stuff where we have the sunspot, the sun corona footage, that's one we envisioned in our minds — we weren't looking at a picture, but at least considered in our minds that footage. I think the principal instruments there are cymbals. I'd do some stuff at my studio, at home, then we'd do more with the cymbals — I got into music as a percussionist, I'd played piano as a child, but once I hit puberty drums were my rock 'n' roll instrument. A lot of sounds were slowed down or treated — the most electronic thing in the *Chain Saw* music is a lap steel guitar. The synthesizer seen in my studio in the *Shocking Truth* documentary — an ARP 2600 — isn't used in the *Chain Saw* music, but I still find uses for it in sound design. Under that ARP is a picture of my mom and dad — all the pig sounds and cow sounds in *Chain Saw*, that's my dad! You'll hear them at different speeds — that's all my father.

In the opening, those little sting noises, that's mine, but the track of the guy in the dark cutting up stuff, that's Tobe. We arrayed Tobe with knives, some vegetables, some chicken bones, uncooked chicken parts — we set up Tobe with that stuff, I got the recorder in the other room, set up a mic and basically did a little foley studio, a little performance space, and Tobe performed that whole sequence. We recorded a few takes, and from that comes the sequence of the grisly cadaver art. The shot of the reveal at the end, Ron Perryman helped do that. It was actually done at sunset — I think we were out at Bagdad Cemetery in Leander, which has now been subsumed by the growing city of Austin, but it was out in the country then.

Sallye Richardson: We could see it wasn't working, and Tobe felt he needed something at the beginning — it wasn't quite there... We'd be editing and it'd be like four in the morning and Warren would come and say, 'You got to finish! You got to finish this! Are we done yet?' We'd say, 'No, we're not done yet! We're not done!' Warren would say, 'You've got to finish, we don't have any more money!' and Tobe would say, 'The beginning doesn't work, we've got to fix the beginning!' So we shot the opening scene with the corpse statue of Warren's, bought the sunspot footage from NASA in Houston and added the crawl. I believe Ron Perryman shot the corpse

Below:

Leatherface as

'Pretty Woman':

eat your heart out,

Julia Roberts.

scene. Ron had this big crane he was building in his garage — it was a new invention for the film industry — and Tobe knew it was good, so he used it for that shot

Lou Perryman: Ron had built a big wood-framed dolly, a boom sort of thing. He was onto the idea of having a crane/dolly that was operable by one person, which is just not tenable. He spent a long time working trying to get something going in that regard, a predecessor to the Louma Crane maybe...

Sallye Richardson: John Larroquette, who does the voice for the opening crawl, was my friend, I knew him from Colorado. I told Tobe, 'I've got the perfect voice', called John and asked him to do it. So Tobe flew out to LA and they recorded it at Todd/AO.

Levie Isaacks: The voice that opens the picture, in the graveyard scene, that's actually my voice. John Larroquette does the opening sequence, but once you get into the graveyard, there's a news reporter in the background talking about the macabre killings — that's me: that's how long I've known these guys. I was doing television news at the time, they asked me to come down and read the news reports, and we've remained friends over the years.

Kim Henkel: The film got edited, which was started in the upstairs office, then moved to Tobe's. Then what you do is you cut the negative — that was done upstairs at Bill Witliff's, then what happened in LA was the sound mix and the blow-up. Each of those are processes in that linear chain. It didn't move to Bill Witliff's until after it was edited. When the editing process is complete, then you have to match the work print to the negative and actually cut the negative.

There was a problem we ran into because 16mm is different from 35mm: when you're cutting 16mm negative you have to do A/B rolls and we screwed up something in that process, and that meant a major problem which cost us some money — but the film wasn't literally re-edited in the sense that its construction was changed. These were technical and physical problems. You have to get everything into sync.

Ron Bozman came back in when we were doing the negative cutting, which took place at Witliff's. Once that was done and there was an answer print, they took it out to LA and did the sound mix. There are some things you have to do when you blow up from 16mm to 35mm — you can't just lay the 16mm sound on a 35mm track and marry them — we're talking about different links, scales of material. When you do the blow-up from 16mm you have to mix the sound so it would sync up with the 35mm print, that's what they did at Todd/AO.

Who will survive and what will be left of them?

"THE TEXAS CHAINSAW MASSACRE"

COLOR · A BRYANSTON PICTURES RELEASE [R]

Sallye Richardson: I think in the end we had twenty-five tracks [of sound]. I'd been up for days without sleep, I don't think I'd even taken any uppers because I was just so tired... Tobe had done the sound mix for *Eggshells* at Todd/AO and it's the oldest, most wonderful place in the world to go — Tobe loved Hollywood history, and that's where he got the feel of it, mixing *Eggshells*. So he wanted to take *Chain Saw* there. He had a meeting with Warren so he told me, 'You've got to go, I want you to have the experience,' because he'd already booked the day. But I didn't particularly want to take the film out to LA on my own, to some place I hadn't been — look at all these tracks! So he put me on the plane with all the tracks and the work print, and sent me off to LA. I got to the hotel and I went into the bathroom and starting hitting my head against the wall, 'Wake up, wake up! This is a big deal!'

When I got there it was a magnificent, wonderful thing — they sat me down and took everything from me and said,

'It's OK now, you're here, let us do it for you. Everything's fine now, we can fix it...' So we loaded everything up, and some of the splices on the tracks had stretched so there were blips. If it didn't work someone would re-splice it — you can't cut it because you're in sync, you have to try to re-splice it. I had a medium-sized theatre to myself — at the front of it was a little putting green, I'd never seen anything like it! The first day we got down through the van sequence, then the next day Tobe arrived and started re-doing everything!

After we finished all the mixing we had to conform — when you take the negative and match it to the work print, that's what you put into the lab — and came back to Austin, and Warren got Ron Bozman to sit on Tobe, to keep him on target. Bill Witliff donated his place, so we moved into the second floor of his beautiful house, and he ended up putting up a lot of the money for the final finish, about $5,000, and he got points for that. Ron helped me pull the shots — it wasn't really his job, he was the production manager — in this upstairs room, for a feature film! That kind of scope of project should be done in a lab, because of the cleanliness — but we didn't have the money to do it in the lab. And we made a mistake, it was my fault we made it — we got about halfway through before we realised, and we had to raise more money...

So I had to remove, on every track and every scene, two frames at the head and two frames at the tail, the historic trims, which I still have... Then we had to remix, and Tobe was able to enhance the soundtrack through the remix. And that was when it took off, the magical thing that was above and beyond what anyone could have or would have anticipated. We finished the colouring, did some tweaking, had the screening to get the rating, then were able to print — we left it at the lab, and it was like giving your baby away...

But basically, once post-production started, nobody touched that film apart from Tobe and I. I carried it up and down those stairs, I'm the one who cut the tracks. And if you think Marilyn Burns screamed for one day — it took me maybe *two weeks* to cut that track... If I think about it now, I think, who would want to cut those awful, ugly sounds, and *live* it, because you really have to live it. I wouldn't want to do that kind of stuff any more, I'd want to do 'happy stuff'...

Lou Perryman: It was a screwy deal from day one — and there was confusion about the investor's shares...

Robert A. Burns: When they got it done — and of course they'd had to come up with other money along the way, so they'd sold off some of it, it's a long, sorry, story

— they make a deal with a known Mafia company! And they get screwed and it's like, 'Duh!?' — well, the guy running the company is called 'Butchie' Peraino!

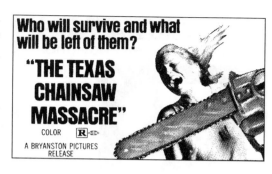

Who will survive and what will be left of them?

"THE TEXAS CHAINSAW MASSACRE"

COLOR [R]

A BRYANSTON PICTURES RELEASE

Kim Henkel: When we had a completed print we showed it around. The picture was finished and it had been blown up to 35mm before Bryanston saw it. Then Bryanston acquired it and got all the materials from Todd/AO and the lab in LA and re-[colour]timed it there — the prints they struck were from the timing they did there rather than the timing we did in LA. That's why the prints looked the way they did. Tobe had carefully timed it out in LA to give it a particular look and when Bryanston got hold of it they did their timing and it came out looking kind of green... In fact, at some point, I think it was when Bryanston still had it, they printed one of the reels backwards — I did actually see it in a theatre where one of the reels was printed backwards, so the steering wheel on the pick-up truck was flopped, it looked like you were in Britain! I don't know how many prints were out there like that...

Chain Saw's finances were indeed a screwy deal. The original $60,000 budget had been divided between Bill Parsley ($40,000), Robert Kuhn ($9,000), Kim Henkel's sister ($1,000) and the mysterious Richard Saenz ($10,000). Parsley, through his corporation MAB, owned fifty per cent of the picture. Kim Henkel and Tobe Hooper, through Vortex, owned the other fifty per cent. Parsley's deal appears to have been that if at any time Vortex was unable to raise extra finances or complete the picture, he would own the entire product. To complicate matters, cast and crew members working on deferred salaries had been given points in Vortex in lieu of payment. Assuming that Vortex owned 100 per cent of the picture, they were perfectly happy with the arrangement. But each point was initially only worth half a point, due to Parsley's interests. And in order to finish the film and keep it out of Parsley's grasp, Henkel and Hooper were forced to barter further percentages of Vortex's shares and potential profits. As Vortex's ownership percentage shrank while they struggled to complete it (a syndicate of backers including Bill Witliff put up another $23,500 during post-production for which they received nineteen per cent of the fifty per cent owned by Vortex), so the cast and crew points correspondingly shrank. If the final post-production budget totalled $125,000, the cast and crew points must have been worth less than a quarter of what they expected...

Chain Saw opened on 11 October 1974 in the USA, distributed by Bryanston Pictures. Bryanston was a new company formed by members of the Peraino family (with Louis 'Butchie' Peraino as President) and financed by profits ($100 million at a conservative estimate) from the ground-breaking *Deep Throat*, the film that brought pornography somewhere close to mainstream acceptance in the US. Bryanston set up offices in Los Angeles and New York and, by the end of 1974, trade papers (including *Variety*) were naming them as the hottest independent distribution company around. Bryanston did not boast of their ties to *Deep Throat* and organised crime, but they were certainly no secret.

Robert A. Burns: I don't know how the deal with Bryanston was done because later on a lot of people like Roger Corman said they never had a chance to look at the picture — Warren's side of it was he showed it to lots of people but the only ones interested were Bryanston.

Skaaren said he previewed the picture to Crown International, 20th Century Fox, Warner Bros, Columbia (who made an initial offer then withdrew it) and Universal. All had turned it down.

Kim Henkel: I seem to recall Tobe telling me someone who saw it making the remark that as a director he 'wasn't altogether without talent'.

Sallye Richardson: I know he went to all those places. When we were out in LA, Warren spent a lot of that time visiting people, talking to them — maybe Bryanston offered him a better deal than he could get elsewhere. It didn't work out that way in the end, and that was his error.

Marilyn Burns: But see, we didn't know about Bryanston's involvement in *Deep Throat*. Bryanston suddenly emerged and they had *Return of the Dragon* — a brand new, up and coming company, no connection to anybody. They had John Carpenter's *Dark Star* too, so we seemed to be in good company. It was only after we started following the money that we found out about *Deep Throat* — oh my God...

Kim Henkel: I don't know if other people knew of their involvement in *Deep Throat* — at least I didn't, and I doubt if Skaaren did. We were hooked up to Bryanston by a guy named David Foster, a well-known producer in LA. The original *Getaway* was made in Austin, and at the time Skaaren was Film Commissioner and Foster was one of the producers. This is all speculation, but I guess Foster told him, 'Go see these guys, they're spending money,' so we made the deal with Bryanston based on that tip from Foster, and Skaaren says, 'We have to take care of him if we want this deal.'

Below:
Bryanston's
original trade ad
announcing
Chain Saw's
incredible box
office takings.

It appears Warren Skaaren carried out his initial negotiations in Los Angeles, and the distribution contracts were signed by Skaaren and Ron Bozman in New York. Skaaren and Bozman had secured thirty-five per cent of Bryanston's worldwide profits on *Chain Saw*, with $225,000 up-front. But because Hooper and Henkel had been forced to barter Vortex shares (Warren Skaaren received a $5,000 fee, fifteen per cent of Vortex and a further three per cent of the film's gross profits, David Foster a $500 fee and one and a half per cent of Vortex's profits), and the majority of cast and crew salaries had been deferred, Bryanston's advance put virtually nothing into the pockets of those who'd actually made *Chain Saw*.

As a further blow, it soon became obvious the film was generating impressive profits, but its box office performance was not translating into returns for the investors or film-makers. Tobe Hooper told the *Los Angeles Times* in 1982 that within two months of *Chain Saw*'s release he heard rumours of Bryanston's true background. Suspicions gave way to the obvious fact: the film-makers were being defrauded of their profits. Bryanston's occasional accounting over the next eighteen months claimed their thirty-five

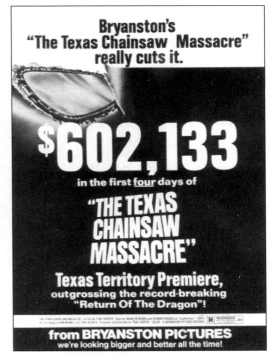

per cent had netted a mere $5,700 — and this after they'd announced (in a full page trade ad) takings of over $600,000 in the first four days! After six months of auditing Bryanston's books yielded nothing, Robert Kuhn was hired to sue Bryanston.

Allen Danziger: I talked to Warren Skaaren over the phone, trying to figure out what was going on. I would collect clippings that showed it [*Chain Saw*] 'with a bullet' — all of a sudden this movie is making a fortune and we're not seeing anything! And then it started to come out that Bryanston was Mafia-owned and the money was gone. I was thinking that here was my ticket out of possible poverty — because everybody had a percentage of the movie. I had one per cent — more than some people — so you're thinking one per cent of a million, that's a lot of money! And then they say you've got one per cent of a pie that's been cut up so many times... I think that we did get something — $200 or $300 — and it's like 'What???' To give him his credit, I think Bob Burns was the first one to say, 'What's going on here? We're getting killed.' Eventually things got sorted out, but we went from thinking we'd get thousands to getting a few hundred... At first I was very upset — but these were people who had very little experience, who then get taken in by the Mafia, people who make the Sopranos look like Boy Scouts! Go figure!

Right:
Sally and the
cattle truck driver
(Ed Guinn) beat a
hasty retreat.

Left:
Marylin Burns
crawls away in
genuine pain after
being dropped ten
feet from the
porch roof.

Robert A. Burns: When questions started being asked about money, these people were so anxious not to appear backwoods rubes that they ended up acting like it. The more they were pushed around [by Bryanston] the more they let themselves *be* pushed around... When we first heard about it we went in and said, 'Hey, go and tell them we want our money,' and they'd say, 'We don't want to end up ruining this good relationship.' They ended up filing suit at the same time as it appeared on the front page of *Variety* that Bryanston was bankrupt, and the Federal Government was already ahead of us!

Then there was some very entertaining legal stuff that went on till '82, when a court-appointed trustee was put in charge of things and the money situation was finally resolved — but the original money was long gone by then... And of course, for every dollar that came in thereafter, five should have come in before.

Robert Kuhn: Warren Skaaren and I went to New York to talk to Bryanston because they weren't accounting or filing any reports or paying any money. We went to see Lou Piranha as I called him, and met him in his office. We'd given him notice to audit the books and went down there, but he said his bookkeeper was sick and wouldn't be back for a week or two. So I said, 'You've got to let us see those books.' He had these two big goons on either side of him, and he looked at me and said, 'You ain't got the balls to sue me.' Anyway, we did, but it was the beginning of a long saga. And what he'd done was he'd sold off everything — people had never looked at his original contract — and Joseph Brenner Associates claimed to have rights. So of course we ended suing *them*. Eventually we got the movie back and then did a deal with New Line.

Years of suing and counter-suing followed, with writs relating to *Chain Saw* flying around like confetti. Bryanston had unpaid debts for movie prints, six-figure sums were passed on from company to company — and all of them seemed to end up at the door of the film-makers. By the time it ended, almost everyone except *Chain Saw's* original cast and crew had made untold thousands. In cases relating to *Deep Throat*, three members of the Peraino family were ultimately found guilty of interstate trafficking in pornography and given prison sentences. New Line finally re-released *Chain Saw*, and the video rights were sold to Charles Band's Wizard Video for $200,000, but the damage had been done. Box office receipts for the first seven years of *Chain Saw's* life may have totalled anywhere from $30 million to $100 million — no one knows just how much... Perhaps it's better that way.

Below:

Leatherface in hot

pursuit of Sally.

Kim Henkel: You know, this is just an incredible saga of being taken to the cleaners over and over again — people have tried to figure out more ways to fuck us over on this deal than I ever would have imagined — I mean, even Kafka would be hard pressed to deal with it.

But the *Chain Saw* saga never ends, and Kim Henkel and Robert Kuhn recently became embroiled in another distribution fiasco, this time over foreign territory rights.

Kim Henkel: We licensed certain foreign rights to a company called Raven and they went out and sold a bunch then disappeared from the planet — we couldn't even find a place of business for these people...

Robert Kuhn: The Raven thing: there was a guy who'd done some work with us — matter of fact he had presold Japan for *Return of* — who went to work for Raven, and he'd always been straight

Left:
Lobby card
signed by Ed Neal,
from one of
Chain Saw's
many reissues.

with us. So Raven licensed it for foreign markets — and they sold it and took all the money! We should have tried to get them indicted — we did get a judgement against them for about a million dollars. We had to get people to stop paying Raven — we got them to quit doing that, showed them we had a court order, so they began sending the money to us, but some of the foreign rights holders just stopped paying entirely when Raven were out of the picture! It's really difficult to get someone halfway round the world to pay you if you don't know much about them to start with. International lawsuits! We have enough difficulty here suing someone from out of state let alone in another country. It's just a nightmare.

Chain Saw certainly has quite a spectacular history.

Kim Henkel: [*Laughs*] Spectacular's maybe not quite the word...

But by and large the majority of copies out there are accounted for... in some way... now... aren't they...?

Kim Henkel: Who the hell knows? I certainly hope so, but God almighty... ∎

30 YEARS AFTER
AND IT JUST WON'T DIE!

Chain Saw played at the London Film Festival in 1975, the Director's Fortnight at Cannes in 1975, won the Jury's Special Prize at Avoriaz 1976, plus prizes at the Trieste Festival and the Antwerp Festival in 1976.

Kim Henkel: It had an unusual history: it came out and had some good initial response, but then faded a bit. Then it got invited to Cannes and began to draw attention from different quarters...

Most of the cast and crew were fairly young when they worked on *The Texas Chain Saw Massacre*, for many it was a first feature — given the way *Chain Saw* took off after release and its subsequent reputation, did the participants feel they might be doing something unique, that this film would be different from anything made previously?

Kim Henkel: We did in one sense and in another absolutely not. There was no way of course that we could imagine that, God almighty, thirty years after this thing and it just won't die! But at the same time, we had a sense that we were going out to do things that pushed the limits, and we didn't really know to what extent we were doing it because we were not subject to the process of homogenisation that goes on within the mainstream of the industry — and even its fringes if you're in LA. And we were outside of all that...

Opposite:
The Family take
it easy.

Tobe Hooper: I knew when I was shooting it that it was special because everything that was happening led me to that conclusion, both in the shooting and in the genesis of the project. Those feelings were based on what was in the marketplace and what I had seen (and I had seen practically everything). I had a good feeling about

it at the time, about it being a film that would get lots of play dates and basically get another job for me. In that respect, I knew it was special because I knew that there was nothing like it, but no, there was no way of anticipating that it would become a title as important as *Gone With the Wind.* [Interview by Marc Savlov, *The Austin Chronicle,* 2 Nov 98]

Jim Siedow: Heavens no! When Tobe asked me if I would do it, my wife and I read the script and we thought it would be a pretty good class B drive-in movie, and that's all we thought it would be. Hell, what happened to that thing is just amazing. I tell ya, you can't imagine the letters and telephone calls I get — after thirty years! Hundreds of people that want my picture and autograph — they say it's the best show they've ever seen — it's really amazing after that long. It really did create something.

Ed Neal: No idea at all. There was no doubt in all our minds that the thing would show at about three drive-ins in south Texas, and that'd be the end of it, and we'd all have a laugh over it when we got old. When it went crazy, we were totally astounded. You know, when I first saw all the publicity on how well it was doing everywhere, I just figured it was media hype, a publicity campaign they put out because they couldn't get it booked anywhere. I had no idea that the publicity reports, for the most part, were basically *true!* [*Fangoria* 23, 1982]

Below:
Japanese poster.

Paul Partain: We were young alright. The script was powerful from the get go. You knew that if this film was ever shot, edited and released, it would be unlike anything ever seen. What we didn't know was just how good it would look when it was done. I remember seeing the trailer, totally unexpected before watching a real movie at the Village Cinema IV in Austin and thinking, 'Wow! This looks just like a real movie!' Total shock...

Allen Danziger: No no, just the opposite — I would see some of the rushes and Tobe would say, 'Is there anything you think we could do to improve the movie?' and I think I said, 'Turn the seats away from the screen!' I thought it could be a major turkey. Then when the movie was finished and they went into the editing room and added some of the earlier scenes and then started the crawl — I think that changed it, as well as the change of title from *Stalking Leatherface* to *The Texas Chain Saw Massacre* — I think those two things were brilliant.

Daniel Pearl: I thought it was going to be a good film because of the screenplay. Did I think it was going to make the impact that it did? I couldn't possibly have imagined that. I went through serious soul searching after it was released and became a big hit at Cannes. I was twenty-three years old, and I was wondering if I would ever hit that plateau again. [International Cinematographer's Guild interview by Bob Fisher]

Sallye Richardson: No, no, no, never, no, never, nah [*laughs*]. I never expected that — even when the movie took off that night in LA, I never thought it would be *that* successful.

Gunnar Hansen: I didn't think it was going to be big — I thought it would be like *2000 Maniacs* — five years down the road, I thought, the investors will have made their money back, maybe a small profit and there'd be a few hardcore fans, that's all I expected. Some time after it came out, I'd taken a friend to show her the location and a car of young guys pulled up and came over — they didn't know who I was — and one of them said to me, 'You know, that's where they made that movie' — I think that was the first inkling that I had it was going to be big.

Robert A. Burns: Oh God no — there are those inklings in films, but usually they're wrong! You think, 'This is going to be something big,' and it fails... When we were doing it no one was looking at it as anything particularly ground-breaking at all. But there was an enormous amount of raw energy that helped carry it. But almost instantly — Bryanston did a brilliant job of marketing it — it became a cultural, folk-art phenomenon. It's like it somehow created the idea that such an event really occurred and became the event itself — it was like a documentary of the event itself rather than a movie.

Marilyn Burns: Well, I always thought it was going to come out, it just *had* to — heck, I was starring in it! It better! I just wanted it to happen so bad, so I believed in it. Then I started to dream I was left on the cutting room floor! When I saw it, I was so grateful I didn't get cut out of it. As an actor, there's so many things you tell your friends about and then if they blink or go to the bathroom they miss your part, so I was happy to see I was still there.

Lou Perryman: You couldn't tell at all that this was any sort of classic, at least I couldn't. I have to admit that I bought in with a naysayer on the set who was just talking about what a snake-bit outfit this was and I hung out with him. I told people honestly, I couldn't tell at all what was happening — it just looked like a horror film of some sort, killing people — and it was not going well, there were a lot of problems. But that's what you have on a film, problems to solve, and I think I brought some idea to it that you could foresee a problem and get it taken care of before it causes something to completely stop.

One of the most enduring legacies of the original *Chain Saw Massacre* is the notion suggested by Robert Burns: that 'it happened', that it really is a documentary. This notion was not solely the domain of gullible drive-in movie viewers: in early correspondence, Stephen Murphy, then Secretary of the British Board of Film Censors, refers to it as 'fictionalised documentary', while Stephen Koch's delirious raging in *Harper's Magazine* asserts 'this work is best discussed alongside the so-called snuff movies, a variety of largely South American sadomasochistic pornography which bills itself, at least, as showing the actual murders of women...' Was that notion created deliberately by the film-makers, or did it arise as an 'urban legend'?

Kim Henkel: Well, both of those things. We shot the film in 16mm and blew it up to 35mm, and we actually did a very good job of it, but when Bryanston got hold of it, in making prints they were very sloppy with their timing. When you blow up 16mm to 35mm you're going to have some grain, but when you do a sloppy job of the timing that's going to be exacerbated. So the film was actually grainier than it should have been — which lent it a quality of authenticity. There's a sense of something along the lines of *cinéma-vérité*, and Tobe had come out of that school of film-making, doing documentaries where there's a lot of hand-held camera work. It was also at the time when films like *Medium Cool* were coming out — a lot of sense of what the medium itself means, kind of structuralist concepts, even though we didn't call them that or refer to them as that at the time, that's indeed what we were playing with.

And Bryanston was a participant in that as well. I think the people there genuinely thought it was — not a documentary, but a fictional account of an actual occurrence. They misunderstood, for instance, the crawl, the roll that precedes the film. We had no intention that anyone would believe this was a real event. This was supposed to be in the tradition of those overblown radio dramas of the '30s, like Orson Welles' *War of the Worlds* — we had no intention of actually deceiving anybody, it was an atmospheric endeavour on our part. God almighty, it flabbergasts me to think that anybody would ever take something like that seriously, but evidently a lot of people did!

Wayne Bell: I must say that half the credit for its power in our memories goes to its title. The movie delivers, so only half the credit goes to its title — but the way it was named is an important component in its lasting effect on us. When it was written it was called *Headcheese*, and I read the *Headcheese* script... When it was shot it was called *Leatherface*, and it was only late in the post-production process that this name came out. And an important part of the legend is on the one-sheet — 'What happened is true!'

Below:

Spanish poster.

That is part of the title's power — that it implies a real event — and the one-sheet bold-facedly lies that what happened is true! I've always had a problem with that, and that is — it's Hollywood, it is Hollywood to lie... You know, at the grocery store checkout there's this trash — the *National Enquirer*, a couple of others — that say these outrageous things, and of course we've become jaded or knowledgeable enough to know it's not true, but isn't it weird that a thing which is essentially not true is given this prominent position there at the counter where you can't help but see it...? So this puts *Chain Saw* in a category with those things! I had a problem with it then — and Tobe would say (I don't know what Tobe would say now) 'Well, you know, there was this guy Ed Gein...' and talk about the connection to truth — but it's not true. It's a total fabrication — just a horrendous reality giving these guys a launching point to build something on which to spark the ghoulish side of their imagination...

Nothing
Could Ever
Prepare You For
The Horror Of...

THE TEXAS CHAINSAW MASSACRE

NOW ON VIDEOCASSETTE

Above:
Poster for Media's
video release.

Jim Siedow: That was one of the great things about the way Tobe wrote and directed the movie — he made people see things that weren't in it. He made them think things that weren't in the movie at all. And they came out with their own ideas about the whole thing.

There are so many people who actually believe that what you do in that movie is what you are! That you do it for a living! I had one woman get really mad at me when she saw it — 'You raped all those girls!' I said, 'I wasn't there that day I guess.' There are so many stories that people thought were true...

Allen Danziger: Exactly — people to this day think it's a true story. It's unbelievable how the cult of it is such that 'It happened'. I think a year or so later there was some jerk here in Texas who cut up some missionaries and stuffed them or something... So I think all of that played into the melding where it gets to be, 'Oh yeah, this is a true story.' When they ask me and I say, 'No' they're disappointed. Everybody thinks Texas is a crazy place — take Charles Whitman. Just as a sideline, I was working for the Peace Corps when I first moved here and I was driving down Guadalupe Street on my way to cash a cheque when he was killing everybody — I was on a motor scooter, and a cop yelled at me to get off the street! So there's the notion that Texas is like some place out of the Wild West — that was *my* notion when I first came down here in '64, I was disappointed when there weren't horses at the airport! I couldn't believe there were cars!

Brian Huberman: I did see the *Chain Saw* series as being part of the Texas 'folklore' thing — in my documentary, there's a digression where I go into a cemetery, and there are two graves that make reference to the Texas revolution, one of them of a woman who survived the Alamo, another of a man who survived the Massacre at Goliad — and the connection was clear to me, the use of the word 'massacre' suggests something much broader than, say, a Ripper-type piece. And also the word 'Texas' — I think mythically we associate it with westerns, open spaces, the frontier — 'massacre' fits in well with that. So the connection of the two genres is *kind* of surprising — it is for me at any rate — but it's part of the richness of the film.

Robert A. Burns: Everyone wants to believe it's based on something that happened in Texas — it's like an urban myth — you go to LA and someone will say, 'Oh, my brother-in-law, he can take you to that house where it happened, he's been there!' Originally some people were concerned by the script — 'What is this going to say about Texas?' — but it was, 'Oh no, we're only going to shoot it here,' but then it ends up being called *The Texas Chain Saw Massacre*. Texas already had a bad reputation because of the murder of JFK, and *Time* magazine did a piece where Texas was spelled using graphics — like the 'A' was a Ku Klux Klan hat... So we'd just come out of a terrible reputation when the picture started.

Many of *Chain Saw's* participants have gone on to impressive careers in the film business, careers launched by a $125,000 movie in 1974. For some it opened doors, for others it caused them to close in their faces — has it proved to be a stigma?

Paul Partain: No. In the world of an actor, it is nice to have something that is immediately recognizable. *Texas Chain Saw Massacre* is the most recognised film title in the world (so says E!). The odds against an actor, any actor, getting in such a film are astronomical. You are more likely to get hit by lightning — twice. The recognition is what you make of it. It can be a door opener or it can be a source of pain and anger at all the things that did not happen, or at all the things that did happen. Stigma. Interesting choice of word, and one that fits — but not for me.

Tobe Hooper: It took *Texas Chain Saw Massacre* nearly eight years to become respectable in the eyes of the film industry. When the film became respectable, so did I. [*Fangoria* 92, 1990]

Kim Henkel: It has been absolutely a mixed blessing — it's branded me in a way that it's almost like one of those rhetorical questions — 'When did you stop beating your wife?' — you're in the position instantly of having to labour against all sorts of misconceptions and preconceptions [*sighs wearily*].

Robert A. Burns: The first thrust of the publicity for the film was the look of the design, and it received much praise for it. But the experience was so upsetting I didn't care if I worked in film again (I had a magazine that I edited and published) and I didn't for a couple of years, until Peter Locke tracked me down for *The Hills Have Eyes*. That was a much more pleasant situation and the rest, as they say, is history.

But it's long been a double-edged sword. One time Michael Nesmith was making a picture — I lived in LA for a couple of years — called *Time Rider*. So the producer (Harry Gittes, Jack Nicholson's producer on *Drive, He Said* — Nicholson's character in *Chinatown* was named after him) called me up in Austin about going to LA to do *Time Rider*, sent me a script and I flew to LA. And on the way I was supposed to do some location scouting. Gittes really wanted me to be production designer on the picture. But Michael Nesmith and William Dear, the director, they were predisposed against me because my reputation was in 'blood and guts' — and they wanted to shoot it in trendy, cool Santa Fe rather than uncool El Paso. And these two just kept saying, 'All these pictures you've done, they've just got bones everywhere!' So I showed them pictures of a western I had done, but they just found fault with everything. And they kept talking about the bones — 'We don't want bones all over our set!' And I swear to God, when that film came to town I went to see it with a friend who didn't know anything about my history with it. And at one point this person said to me, 'Why are there bones all over this movie?' The bad guy had a necklace made out of finger bones... And in the desert, instead of getting cattle skeletons, they'd got butchered bones, so there were like chopped up bones all over! So sometimes it's like, 'Oh no, he's that *Chain Saw* guy,' others it's, 'Hell, yeah, I'm the *Chain Saw* guy!'

Ed Neal: It was only after it became a 'cult movie' that it began to affect me. It's like something that you'll live with for the rest of your life — it's not like you can stop being 'The Hitchhiker'... Now there are several producers, directors who think, 'Oh, that's all he does, these kind of roles.' [*The Texas Chain Saw Massacre: A Family Portrait*]

Allen Danziger: I'm still milking that fifteen minutes! The funny thing is, I went from a starring role to an extra, in Willie Nelson's first movie, *Honeysuckle Rose* — I'm in a 'cameo' shot, you can see my shirt! My career took a nosedive! After that I think I was in *The Tomato That Ate Cleveland*... The other thing, I was asked to do a couple of vignettes in *The Whole Shootin' Match* — Eagle Pennell, also an unusual guy, kind of a strange guy. When you hear about directors, how they explain about each scene, walk you through it — this was a different deal... I shot a couple of scenes, then left for Colorado. When I returned he'd decided to go for one of the vignettes and turned it into *The Whole Shootin' Match*. I think they gave me shares instead of payment — the movie got a lot of acclaim.

Through a large amount of hard work, a certain measure of luck (and a large measure of bad luck), *Chain Saw* quickly achieved a place in cinema history. Does it deserve that place?

Left:
One of the
two original
French posters.

Paul Partain: Absolutely! But, I am concerned that the audience has gotten so much younger, even reaching into elementary school. I think the film is much too intense for those so young. I could live with that kind of censorship.

Brad Shellady: I truly believe *Chain Saw* to be the *Citizen Kane* of the horror genre, and discussion about it and interest in it will be infinite...

Sallye Richardson: I think it deserves its place in the evolution of film — whether it was a horror movie or not, it doesn't really matter, it's really well done — maybe well done based on the limitations that we had, but...

Lou Perryman: In the way that it was effective, yeah — but I'm not a big horror buff — I do not need to be frightened by death, I've had enough of that shit in my own life, I don't need horror. Am I fond of it? Fondness, yes... You know, I'm driving a cab and every once in a while I'll mention to someone I worked on it and it's like, 'No shit!' It was a breakthrough film, a classic of horror certainly — and I don't overestimate my contribution to it at all. But yeah, I worked on the first one, acted in the second, was offered a role in the fourth — I feel pretty good about it.

Gunnar Hansen: I've done thirteen pictures, but they're all lacking the genius of *Chain Saw*. I'm pretty proud of the movie. People misunderstand it... Even now Tobe, after the fact, will say, 'This movie is about the disintegration of the American family' — and recently he said [on the *Masters of Horror* DVD] 'It's not for nothing that this movie came out right after Vietnam'... I think an honest answer to the question of 'What's it about?' is, the movie is about scaring the audience as much as possible, and I think that it does it very well — I think a lot of people can see other things in the movie. And if they want to and it's consistent with the movie and they're not just superimposing something that makes no sense, that's fine if they want to... But none of us was thinking 'this movie is about the disintegration of the American family' — Tobe and I were sitting around one night waiting for something to get set up and Tobe said, 'Kim and I sat down and said, "Let's take everything that ever scared us in a movie and put it into this"' — and I think that's what they were thinking, they weren't thinking some other deep, deep interpretation.

Kim Henkel: I have never been able to watch it — never been able to watch anything I've been involved with, so it's not just that. I'm usually involved in the editing process, looking at the thing for colour correction and all that — so by the time they're completed I've actually seen them — at least in bits and pieces — many times. But I avoid watching them — at all costs. I don't think that should be so surprising — like most people who've been involved in something creative, you see all the flaws. I mean, I've stepped into theatres or screenings just to watch a scene and see how the audience is responding but I've always found it a very unpleasant experience — and why should I subject myself to something that's unpleasant if I don't have to? I'm not such a big fan of horror movies anyway — I can't take the tension, I can't take the blood and guts — I go into these things and I have to hide my eyes!

But you know, it is what it is, there's nothing I can say about it that's going to change what it is or its place in cinema history. That's something I just have to accept and deal with...

Allen Danziger: Before the première I snuck into the theatre to see the trailer and I'd never seen myself on screen before — I ended up having a panic attack and running out of the theatre! I thought it was better than I'd anticipated, but because I was in it I didn't get the scariness. It was amazing when I would watch it with people and see the yelling and screaming and gasps — it took me by surprise. When you're so close and you're so entwined with something, you can't see it the same way as somebody coming in who has no idea of the tricks and so on that went into it. My friends all enjoyed it, they all had a good time. And even today — it's almost thirty years old and people still talk about it. People are finding me on the internet and sending me posters to sign — I had a guy come in from Amsterdam with a chainsaw for me to sign! They find me out — people call me and say it's the best thing they've ever seen, I'm saying, 'Get a life! You've got a problem here!'

There was something about the spontaneity of it, that there were people who weren't really actors and who were able to just let go and have a good time with it. For me it was fun — how many times do you get to say, 'Oh, I'm on a set' — I even had an answering service I put together: 'I'm sorry I can't talk to you but I'm filming!' That was a kick for me. I would have to say I enjoyed everything, even the hot times, long hours, having to do scenes over and over again — big deal, it was so unique.

Rex Reed thought it was terrific, I think it's in the Museum of Modern Art... I can't tell you, I'm not enough of a film buff to know, but it's touched a nerve somewhere that other things haven't. And if you look at it and compare it to movies that came after, there's a lot less blood and guts than in *A Nightmare on Elm Street* or *Friday the 13th*. But it worked because of the nature of 'The story you are about to see...' and how it played out, these weren't movie stars in it, these were people you could identify with — a guy in a wheelchair who was obnoxious — ordinary people.

Nothing has touched the first one — that last one even had Matthew McConaughey and Renee Zellweger, top actors, and it still didn't make it.

Below:

The Texas

Lunchtime

Massacre.

Bill Johnson: I thought the first film was awesome, it's a great movie, and deserves to be in the Museum of Modern Art. I wish the second one could have been as great — it's absurd, in the serious sense — but something disturbed me about that first movie.

Robert A. Burns: You know how it got into the Museum of Modern Art? Bryanston literally walked a copy over and said, 'Here's a movie' and they took it and put it in their vaults! And that started the whole debate about 'Is it art'! It was 'placed' in the museum — literally — by Bryanston! And that made the Museum of Modern Art say that from there on they wouldn't take films unless they'd requested them!

Bill Moseley: I saw it in 1974 in Boston. I'd always been a horror movie fan, but with a name like that — a title made up of the most horrifying things you could imagine — I was excited to see what was being foisted on America... The Bruce Lee film played and the audience was really into it, shouting at the screen, 'Come on Bruce!' you know — then *Chain Saw* started and it sucked the air right out of the auditorium. I think we all realised, just with the opening shots and the weird music — we all realised we were in for something very serious... And all that goofy spirit was gone and stayed gone throughout the movie.

When I came out of it I was deeply disturbed. I'd always thought of rural America as quaint, not threatening — when I saw *Chain Saw*, this was Norman Rockwell gone terribly wrong, so it affected me. I was a college graduate, into spirituality, I always thought I would be able to communicate with just about anybody spiritually, but the *Chain Saw* family — I realised these were people I could not communicate with, there was something missing... They were still human beings but there was something missing. There was no humanity, not a shred of compassion, empathy — there was nothing — I think that scared me more than anything.

I thought I'd try to see it a dozen times, then finally I'd see the zipper in the costume, I'd be able to say, 'It's only a movie' — but it never happened! Its power doesn't diminish — there's a timeless quality to it. There's really nothing that dates it. It could happen tomorrow. ■

"THE PORNOGRAPHY OF TERROR"

Despite its later artistic success at Cannes and the London Film Festival, *Chain Saw* was hardly greeted with open arms by the British Board of Film Censors when submitted for classification. On 28 February 1975 Stephen Murphy, then Secretary of the Board, sent an Internal Communication to his examiners.

'I saw last night *The Texas Chain-Saw Massacre*. This appears to be a fictionalised documentary which bears every sign of being shot on 16mm and blown up to 35mm. It is a very good film, which we must take seriously. To my mind, although this is quite frankly fictionalised, we are basically back on the kind of considerations we faced with *Manson*…

'I have informed the Company that I can see no hope of certificating the film in its present form. The Company are proposing to make some reduction in the terrorisation of the one who finally escapes. I have given it informally as my opinion that, despite this, we are unlikely to offer certification.

'The film differs from *Manson*, not only in technique, but also in the fact that, with the exception of one tiny incident where a perversion is hinted at, it has no sexual content. I think that there is relatively little blood around in this film. Its documentary air makes it even more severe and even more distressing to watch than *The Last House on the Left*.'

This communication predates the official viewing, so Murphy must have been invited to a private screening. *Chain Saw* was viewed for certification on 12 March 1975 and immediately rejected. Examiner comments: '(I) found the film sick making and very offensive and would certainly reject' '… to pass this sort of episode (the attempt to kill the girl as she struggles while being held over the bucket) as entertainment is to enter the Roman Circus stakes.' One BBFC document reveals: 'Mr Shadrick [of Hemdale International, its distributor] has made the 3 cuts suggested by Sec towards the end of the pic', so the rejected version had already been cut by Hemdale before submission…

On 14 March, Stephen Murphy wrote to Gordon Shadrick: '... I have to tell you that we do not feel we can offer certification to this film. I should make it plain we do not regard this as an exploitation piece: it is a film of considerable merit. The problem is, I think, our continuing worry whether studies in abnormal psychology are suitable for the public cinema. Both the Board and the Television Authorities, for example, have fought shy of basing material on the Moors murders. We ourselves, two years ago, turned down a very sincere and unsensational documentary study of the Manson family... I really feel we must reject this piece.'

John Daly, co-director of Hemdale, replied at length on 20 March, with a defence which, if slightly oddly reasoned, raises the still relevant point that an audience is free to choose whether it watches or not.

'... I must confess that I find the Board's attitude unreasonable and inconsistent. I do agree that the film has certain scenes which lift it above the level of a normal thriller, but I do not think you can compare it with a documentary study of Manson or the Moors Murders.

'What makes the *Texas Chain Saw Massacre* special is the marvellous acting and, if the Board is now not to give certificates to films that are well-acted, then the film industry may as well give up all hope.

'... so please accept the film for what it is — a well-made, well-acted thriller which, if there is not an audience who will want to see this film, then the film will not be seen. However, if the film is popular then it will be successful, which means the audience like

Left:
The original
English GLC 'X'
poster.

the film. We do not invite the audience in and lock the doors — they can walk out — that is their choice — but we do feel that this is a film which is effective because of its good acting and should not be penalized because of this.'

Murphy's response of 25 March contained some even more peculiar logic.

'… The comparison to *Manson* is consistent. Our reason for turning down *Manson* was that we questioned whether the public cinema was the right place for studies in abnormal psychology. The same reason holds with the Moors Murders. Both we ourselves (who were approached on this subject some years ago) and the Broadcasting Authorities (who have many feet of film available on this subject) have refused to contemplate a film on this subject on the same grounds. In both *Manson* and the Moors Murders there were sexual overtones, which do not exist, save for one fleeting reference, in *Texas Chain Saw Massacre*. But this was not an important element in the decision which was taken not to pursue these projects. In the case of *Manson* the film was unsensational, again inviting direct comparison with *Texas Chain Saw Massacre*. In other words, this decision is wholly consistent with Board policy as it has existed since before my time.

'Further, we have recently turned down another fictionalised documentary… which, by coincidence, also ends with the use of chain saws. [Presumably *Last House on the Left*, another perennial pain for the British censors.]

'I can see little hope that the Board will change its mind on this film. I can only suggest submission to the Greater London Council.'

The correspondence continued until May 1975, Murphy adding on 4 April, 'In terms of actual content of the film, we are chiefly disturbed by the appalling terrorisation of the girl and the violence, both physical and mental, to which she is subjected.' And on 5 May, 'In our view many people would find the film so repellent that even backed by research it would still be held up as an example of violent material which the Board ought not to certificate.' Murphy resigned from the BBFC in May 1975, replaced by James Ferman, who held the position until 1999.

Hemdale gave up its attempt to gain a national release and followed Murphy's advice, seeking a GLC (Greater London Council) X certificate, which was finally awarded in August 1976. The film's release around the country was sporadic, with some local councils banning it outright, others passing it.

In January 1977 Gordon Shadrick wrote to James Ferman, informing him there had been an accidental cut of twenty-eight seconds to the print showing in London. (The scene accidentally cut was Leatherface butchering Kirk. When videos began to appear, some bootleg versions were struck from this print, leading to the incorrect assumption that the film had been censored.)

In October 1982, *Chain Saw* having passed on to yet another distributor (ITC), a letter was written to the BBFC requesting they consider granting the film a newly introduced

R18 certificate. (The R18 category was introduced to deal primarily with sex videos, and would mean any videotape certified thus could only be sold in the few sex shops legally licensed by local councils.) Ferman's hand-written note on ITC's letter states 'Told Terry we would look at *Texas Chainsaw* again — no promises.' In May 1983 *Chain Saw*, with Tigon now listed as distributor, again went before the examiners, in this case two women and one man (Ken Penry, one of the examiners responsible for its initial rejection). In this case Penry elected for passing the film R18 uncut, commenting:

'... this is still to me the most effective of all the horror films. I can admire the expertise with which it is made, but I still find watching it a rather degrading experience with its persistent terrorising of the girl... now we have the Restricted 18 category this is the right classification for the film. Politically it would be appropriate as the Licensing Authorities that saw it and rejected it would not feel that they were going back on their earlier decision not to allow it to be seen in a public cinema. More importantly perhaps, it would mean that the sale of the video cassette would be restricted to licensed outlets only.'

Above:

Ticket order form for Chain Saw's *first English cinema run.*

The women examiners both felt the film could finally be released but needed cuts 'to reduce the terrorisation and humiliation of poor old Sally', in the words of one. Their opinions of the film's merits differed considerably, one of them stating, 'I'm not an aficionado of horror movies... I thought this the most indulgent of films, and indulgent in a particularly sadistic way towards female terror... the gleeful indulgence in Sally's extended terror during the last two reels is way over the top and for my money is not acceptable in either the 18 or R18 categories in the present quantity. There is a sadism in the three loonies' treatment of her, a kind of verbal and physical prodding, which left me feeling brutalised — and not because the victim was female, either. Ultimately one is left feeling that a good clean chainsaw death would have been almost preferable to the interminable torture to which she is subjected. And what an awful statement that is.'

The second female examiner's opinions were far more enlightened, though she still felt cuts were necessary. 'Maybe I'll be branded as the office ghoul, but I have to admit to enjoying this by now notorious movie. It is a classic piece of *grand guignol*, definitely not for the squeamish: but the squeamish, almost by definition, avoid this

Right:
Original English
video jacket.

kind of experience so that the audience is self-selecting.' (Which begs the question: why censor it?) She continued, 'Young people (like it or not) have a taste for this kind of film, and are we really to say that they have no right to see it in their local cinema (or hire it in their local video shop…)?'

James Ferman, who coined the phrase 'the pornography of terror' to describe *Chain Saw*, felt he *was* really to say that young people (and everyone else) had no right to see it — the examiners' opinions were ignored and the film remained uncertificated until his retirement, although it was revived for a limited release (only in the few cinemas under the jurisdiction of Camden Council in London) when a new print was struck in 1998. Ferman, contrary to his public persona, was not a reasonable, well-meaning, sincere and responsible director of the BBFC. His views on cinema were often bizarre, extreme and irrational, his judgements frequently motivated by personal opinions of a director's work, his desire to protect the British public from images of horror misplaced and inappropriate. It is significant that in the years following his retirement, the majority of films refused certificates under his regime have been released in Britain, mostly in their original uncut forms.

Finally, in 1999, *The Texas Chain Saw Massacre* was passed uncut on film (in March) and on video (in August) for the whole of Britain — almost twenty-five years since its initial US release. The BBFC issued a press release to alert the nation, signed by Andreas Whittam Smith, its ineffectual erstwhile President, and Robin Duval, its current Director.

'The notoriety of the film may owe a lot to its original rejection by the BBFC in 1975. It was passed for viewing in Europe, the USA, Australia and other countries. It received a GLC licence in the 1970s and was most recently shown in central London in 1998 under a licence from Camden Council. There is, so far as the Board is aware, no evidence that harm has ever arisen as a consequence of viewing the film. For modern young adults, accustomed to the macabre shocks of horror films through the 1980s and 1990s, *The Texas Chain Saw Massacre* is unlikely to be particularly challenging. Unlike more recent examples of the genre, violence in *The Texas Chain Saw Massacre* is throughout implied rather than explicit. By today's standards, its visual effects may seem relatively unconvincing.

'Possibly the most notorious feature is the relentless pursuit of the 'Final Girl' throughout the last half hour or so of the film. The heroine in peril is a staple of the cinema since the earliest days. It is nonetheless legitimate to question the unusual emphasis *The Texas Chain Saw Massacre* places on the pursuit of a defenceless and screaming female over such an extended period. The Board's conclusion, after careful consideration, was that any possible harm that might arise in terms of the effect upon a modern audience would be more than sufficiently countered by the unrealistic, even absurd, nature of the action itself. It is worth emphasising that there is no explicit sexual element in the film, and relatively little visible violence.' ■

Below:
Badge given
out at the
first English
screenings.

"THE ABSOLUTE DEGRADATION OF THE ARTISTIC IMAGINATION"

Be prepared for a totally disgusting and, for many, literally nauseating experience… a stream of unrelieved and explicit gore. Four or five (it is difficult to determine the sum from the scattered parts) young outdoors adventurers run into a fiendish butcher of humans out in the Texas bush country. The madman in turn runs amok with chainsaw and other instruments of destruction, including a meat-hook. The film is sick, and so is any audience that enjoys it.
Catholic Film Newsletter, Oct 1974

There are films which skate right up to the border where 'art' ceases to exist in any form and exploitation begins, and these films are often the field's most striking successes. *The Texas Chainsaw Massacre* is one of these; in the hands of Tobe Hooper, the film satisfies that definition of art which I have offered, and I would happily testify to its merit in any court in the country.
Stephen King's Danse Macabre, Macdonald & Co (UK), 1981.

… an unpleasant but not unintelligent film. The tone is one of goofy nihilism and giddy disgust… In Hooper's masterstroke, the cannibals responsible turn out to be a degenerate rural family, even 'filthier' and more primitive than Divine's.
J. Hoberman & Jonathan Rosenbaum, *Midnight Movies*, Harper & Row, 1983/Da Capo Press, 1991

It is almost surely the most affecting gore thriller of all and, in a broader view, among the most effective horror films ever made… Kim Henkel's script is mean, spare and smart… Hooper has the eye for the sort of vivid, nightmare image that would fester in the viewer's mind…

Unlike the villains in most other gore films, Hooper's fiends are not sexually motivated. The driving force... is something far more horrible than aberrant sexuality: total insanity... The final image — one of Leatherface spinning in impotent rage after the girl's escape, chain saw clattering over his head — is among the most memorable in horror film history.
David J. Hogan, *Dark Romance: Sexuality in the Horror Film*, McFarland, 1986

This movie *extends* the boundaries of cinematic terror and revulsion to the point where we are now forced to redefine the term 'horror film'... I consider myself a hardened observer of horror films, yet this one reduced me to a pale and quivering hulk. We can cluck our tongue all we want about sadism, violence, exploitation; yet we can't deny it takes talent to make a film so frightening that it practically has us peeing in our pants... In the light of its accomplishments, this monster-piece can be called neither tacky nor sloppy... Considering its subject matter, *Massacre* is not gratuitously gory, yet it never fails to convey the physical impact of the savage crimes it portrays...
Paul Roen, *Castle of Frankenstein* 25, Jun 1975

Above:
Leatherface
and Grandpa.

Just as *Night of the Living Dead* became a cult favorite, *Texas Chain Saw Massacre* bears all the elements of being the new heir apparent to the Throne of Grue-Shockeroo... Ironically, proving once again what humanity has been aware of in this Watergate Era: the most horrible monster of all is, at times, man himself.
Richard Buonnano, *Castle of Frankenstein* 25, Jun 1975

The less said about Tobe Hooper's *The Texas Chain Saw Massacre* the better, perhaps, though I must take my share of the blame for calling attention to the film after its first European screenings at the Cannes Festival in 1975... The fact that it is rather efficiently and effectively done only makes the film more unpalatable.
David Robinson, *The Times*, 19 Nov 1976

... as relentless, merciless, inexorable, and implacable as a sixty-ton semi running

over a matchbox... Its effect on the industry and whoever saw it is undiminished. It is the best (and worst, depending on your point of view) of its type ever... Hooper is one of the few who have successfully been able to capture the essence of insanity on film... the movie is a miraculous combination of planning, acting, and accident which results in an unequalled viewing experience... This is a jaw-dropping, stomach-churning film that is anything but entertainment. It is fifteen punishing rounds with Rocky Balboa that leaves many shaken and strangely enervated... One is left in much the same state caused by a ride on a magnificent rollercoaster. One can admire it for its construction, respect it for its ability to thrill, and just be glad it's over.
Richard Meyers, *For One Week Only*, New Century Publishers, 1983

Nothing but shocks and gore, but the beginning of the wave of such deplorable movies which flooded the world's screens towards the end of the decade.
Halliwell's Film and Video Guide, HarperCollins

... brings genuine horror back to the cinema. Be warned: its Gothic realism reminds us how rarely screen mayhem actually evokes real fear and revulsion in these times when 'murder by numbers' is an everyday news item.
Alexander Walker, *Evening Standard*, 18 Nov 1976

There is no nudity or explicit sex... but you should watch it and compare it with explicit sex films and then decide if you were a censor which one you would want your children to watch. Keep in mind that it is a cult film and is shown in college university towns around the United States with no protest from censors that an X-rated film would immediately evoke... The interesting thing to ask yourself about this film is whether it could have been produced with a maniac chasing a guy instead of a woman? Whether there is explicit sex or not — this story obviously combines sex and violence.
Robert H. Rimmer, *The X-Rated Videotape Guide*, Harmony Books, 1984/ Prometheus Books, 1993

A *reductio ad absurdum* of a horror movie which manages to keep a lady constantly in distress... for over an hour (our time), with no diversions (for her or for the viewer). 'Unrelenting' is a good word to use here... And yet the film *could* have been *more* harrowing: as it stands, there's surprisingly little blood-and-gore evident. Hooper's film has a weird sort of tact. The director trusts to his title and his hardware: you don't see what the awful chain saw does. You don't need to

— all you need to know is how one works. *Hearing* is believing *here*. And yet this is still not exactly a *likeable* movie... Even the occasionally amusing, Clegg-like antics of the crazy family are really no relief — the film is informed by a pristine viciousness.
Donald C. Willis, *Horror and Science Fiction Films II*, Scarecrow Press, 1982

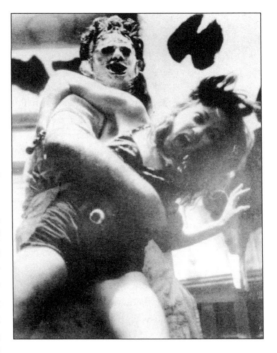

Chain Saw Massacre (and if ever a misleading title sold a movie, this surely must be it) remains, after all the hyperbole has subsided, little more than a cheaply executed and in some respects remarkably old fashioned piece of Grand Guignol... Kim Henkel and Tobe Hooper's script shies away from any causes or social comments of its theme and deliberately avoids any examination of the killers' motives or the victims' feelings... The movie is, rather, a tongue-in-cheek commercial shocker... It is a sign of the hard times that Tobe Hooper should have been awarded a handsome Hollywood contract on the strength of a picture so reassuringly predictable that it successfully dissipates all apprehension.
John Pym, *Monthly Film Bulletin*, Vol 43, No 515, Dec 1976

Above: An 'obese gibbering castrato' and a screaming woman.

The Texas Chain Saw Massacre is a vile little piece of sick crap... It is a particularly foul item in the currently developing hard-core pornography of murder, fundamentally a simple exploitation film designed to milk a few more bucks out of the throng of shuffling wretches who still gather... in those dank caverns for the scab-picking of the human spirit...

It is a film with literally nothing to recommend it: nothing but a hysterically paced, slapdash, imbecile concoction of cannibalism, voodoo, astrology, sundry hippie-esque cults, and unrelenting sadistic violence as extreme and hideous as a complete lack of imagination can possibly make it... We are here discussing something close to the absolute degradation of the artistic imagination.

Obese gibbering castrati grasp snarling chain saws as they chase and kill screaming women... every conceivable impulse, through hysterical necrophilia, is transposed into disgust.

It seems an impossible trip from the rosettes of Busby Berkeley to *The Texas Chain Saw Massacre*, but that sickening ride from an impotent but refreshing sentimentalism to an impotent but monstrous viciousness — dreaming always of Hollywood, Hollywood — has now been made, and made with enough energy to sweep the despicable makers of this despicable little movie into the big time.
Stephen Koch, 'Fashions in Pornography: Murder as an Expression of Cinematic Chic', *Harper's Magazine*, Nov 1976

From its very opening shot of disinterred half-decomposed corpses perched upon their tombstones under the blazing Texas sun, *The Texas Chain Saw Massacre* never lets you forget that its horror is also a crazy beauty. Since the film's action, like its title, leaves little to the imagination, it is free to develop images.

Its progress is the progress of nightmare. For this kind of movie, that sounds ordinary enough, except that *The Texas Chain Saw Massacre* at some level seriously demonstrates it. It follows a rather strict unity of time — less than one full day — and of place and action, and it makes stunning use of such decorum in its final moments. Possibly the most startling image of the movie is the sight of the morning, daylight, after Sally hurls herself out of the window of the modest dining room that was to have been her death chamber.

I can fault the movie here and there — mostly for its inexperienced acting, just once or twice for some uncharacteristic horror-film cheap shots — but I can't deny its power, its humor, its canniness, or the intelligence that calculated its simple action.
Roger Greenspun, 'Carrie, and Sally and Leatherface Among the Film Buffs', *Film Comment*, Jan-Feb 1977

The Texas Chainsaw Massacre is only defensible as a nightmare. The only cerebral reading of the film sees it as a rabid vegetarian tract: the people in the movie suffer exactly the same atrocities inflicted daily upon beef cattle in the name of Ronald McDonald. However, the film is so visceral that there is barely time for an audience to breathe, let alone ponder What It's All About… Hooper's achievement is that he brings back to the movies an awareness of violent death lost through the slow-motion sentimentalisation of Bonnie and Clyde and the contemptible distortion of TV cop shows in which a shot victim has a penny-size red spot on his pristine shirt and time for a five-minute monologue before he goes.
Kim Newman, *Nightmare Movies*, Proteus 1984/Bloomsbury 1988

Ken Livingstone, 31, married and a member of the committee for three years, is adamantly opposed to censorship, but he tells me: 'I would hope that my wife would want to go and see something else. I wouldn't want to inflict the garbage we see on

Left:
'... the worst thing
I've ever seen,'
says Mrs Beryl
Schofield.

other people.' Dudley Barker, 35, agreed. But he claims: 'It's just ketchuping. Nobody could be influenced by it.'

Cllr Frank Archer, deputy chairman of the committee, feels the film could influence no one. A widower, 70 this week, he sits for Erith and Crayford. 'I only go to the cinema very occasionally,' he says. 'The last thing I paid to see was *Emmanuelle*. This chain saw thing was just a souped up Hammer horror.'

I could only find one member, Frank Smith, who expressed serious reservations about the film: 'As far as I am concerned the British Board of Film Censors is far too liberal,' he says. 'Take it from there.'

Reactions from the GLC film censorship committee after seeing *The Texas Chain Saw Massacre*, quoted in 'Who are the chain saw enthusiasts?', Londoner's Diary, *Evening Standard*, 25 Nov 1976

I was watching through my fingers. It was sickening. A scene where a cripple was given a tin to go to the toilet was the worst thing I've ever seen. It was rather sick all along. At one point a hitch-hiker, who is mad, cuts his hands and cuts other people. There is blood.

Councillor Mrs Beryl Schofield, speaking about Southend's ban of *The Texas Chain Saw Massacre* (no date given) — the councillors curtailed the screening before the end of the film. ■

EATEN ALIVE

Eric Lasher: He really is one of the hardest working directors there is — when he's working it's all-encompassing. I have never seen Tobe sit down and just do nothing. The saddest thing is, he does such great stuff and somebody else puts their hands on it. Editors, producers — they chop things up... It's like you have a baby and somebody comes along and says, 'It'd look better with one hand.' The intent is lost, they cut out these wonderful character moments that are important, explaining why people are motivated to do the things they do. If you don't have them, people appear to be doing stuff for no reason. The director's name is on the front of the picture — they don't say the *editor* really fucked it up. The producer works again, because all he is is a guy who finds money...

Richard Kidd: It's what happens when you have the eccentric loner: he wants to do grand and big things but he doesn't want anyone messing with them — as a result he manages to alienate those folks, and by the time anybody's spent much time around him they're kinda pulling their hair out — that's just the kind of guy he is.

Richard Kooris: Tobe has an interesting aspect to his personality — he can be very solitary but when he wants to he can be very entertaining. He's got these little dark eyes that light up — he's almost child-like, almost like an elf — and he gets very excited about things, and his excitement is infectious. He gets so excited about what he's seeing in his head, and what he wants to do, that he's able to communicate it to people, and that's why he's been successful.

Levie Isaacks: I would say Tobe is a master of the camera, there's no doubt about that. I really enjoy working with him — he's somebody I learned a lot from, he's great to work with.

Above:

Tobe Hooper

behind the

camera on

Invaders From

Mars.

Bill Moseley: There are very few of us who are totally dedicated to the genre. A lot of people are just doing it like waiters — making a bit of money before moving on to Mom & Dad movies or starring opposite Bruce Willis. But there are a few of us who are really into it, and there are a handful of directors like Tobe that are really dedicated.

Wayne Bell: Tobe is a good creative guy — and a creative guy can come up with something interesting in almost any medium.

Kim Henkel: You know, Tobe has an ability to involve himself with the worst possible people...

Lou Perryman: He's a dear person underneath — when you know somebody, you know their Shadow, you know their public persona too. And his Shadow is dark, but he's a very kind, warm human being and a born film-maker — Jesus Christ, the most natural film-maker I've ever known. And certainly a very skilful editor.

Robert A. Burns: You know, Tobe is extremely subjective... Film can be a juggernaut, where everything has to be sacrificed once it gets started, as an industry it tends to be that

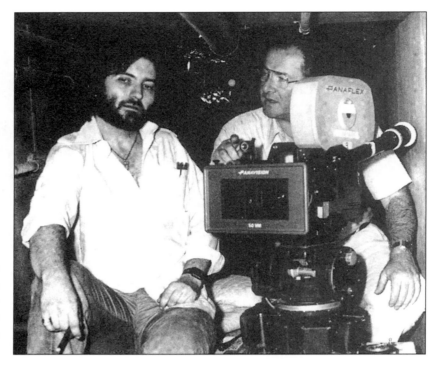

Right:
Hooper with
cinematographer
Andrew Laszlo, at
work on The
Funhouse.

way, particularly in America — 'We're making a film here!' — you know, if you're not with us you're against us… Tobe used to be an extreme example of that: if someone does you a favour, it's not, 'Thanks' it's, 'Oh good, go ask for another,' it's *more* than 100 per cent…

Sallye Richardson: In a lot of cases if you can get someone to do it for nothing, then that's really good — and Tobe's good at doing it because he's a very endearing person, very charming. He's one of the most likeable people in the world. And if he wants you to like him, you will definitely like him! There's no doubt about that… He does have a dark side — be that as it may, I don't think there's any point on dwelling on the dark side — but the part that's wonderful is really beautiful. The only time I can really remember him losing his temper in a bad way is when he saw that he could manipulate somebody by doing it, and it was really a thought-out thing. And when he was shooting *Poltergeist* he felt like he needed to show his authority on the set because of Spielberg's presence, so he'd just throw these little fits to show he meant business. But I think he might have done that one too many times in front of Spielberg, and that's when they had the tiff…

Sallye Richardson: Tobe's dad raised him in a hotel. He lived in the hotel as a kid and that's when he started making movies, he made little movies in the hotel, I guess 'cause he was bored. He was self-taught, there wasn't anything like film school… It was all instinct for Tobe — he learned by watching a lot of movies…

It seems reasonably certain Tobe Hooper was born on 25 January 1943. Few accounts of his childhood and adolescence contain the same facts. Some have him directing his first film at the age of three, being a professional child stage magician, having a father who owned a cinema where he spent all his time, a father with a hotel next to a cinema (where he spent all his time), a father who dealt in real estate and bought a whole block including a hotel and cinema… The common thread is the cinema where Tobe spent all his time, often watching the same film over and over. Hooper says he made his first film at the age of five (or nine), when he began using the family's 8mm camera. Before the age of ten he'd bought his own camera, making anywhere from dozens to hundreds of home movies, still spending as much time as he could watching films. His first film? Possibly an 8mm adaptation of *Frankenstein* as a grade school science class assignment, possibly something else entirely. He's talked about making teenage 8mm Roger Corman pastiches, about being confined to bed for months at a time reading EC comics, about how his vision became so coloured by the language of film that he saw life as if through a viewfinder… Contrary to many accounts, Hooper did not attend the University of Texas in Austin — and as Lou Perryman pointed out, by far the most impressive aspect of his talent is the fact he is self-taught. Every person who's worked with him speaks of his visual sensibility, his unerring cinematographer's eye, his editing talents… Also, his tendency to lose control of almost every project with which he's been involved, his paranoia and his poor business sense.

Following *Chain Saw*, Hooper and Kim Henkel worked together on various scripts (just before *Chain Saw*'s release Henkel told the *Texas Monthly Reporter* 'We want to do a broad comedy. Something very looney tunes and merry melodies'), including an intriguing true crime story.

Kim Henkel: Tobe and I wrote this script called *Bleeding Hearts*, a period piece set in Phoenix and LA in the '30s, loosely based on the Winnie Ruth Judd murders. It was a famous case for many years. At a train station in LA a couple of trunks were discovered that belonged to Winnie Ruth Judd, a passenger. In the trunks were the bodies of two women who'd been chopped up with an axe. She was arrested, alluding to all sorts of background circumstances and proclaimed her innocence. She was tried and convicted, escaped from prison and was not heard of for several years. By fluke she was later discovered living in northern California and brought back but finally released. At the time I wrote the script she was still living in northern California — it was a very sensational case. But it was kind of a wild piece and

Mardi Rustam presents a new horror classic by TOBE HOOPER,
creator of "THE TEXAS CHAIN-SAW MASSACRE"

Meet the maniac & his friend.
Together they make the greatest team in the history of mass slaughter in...

EATEN ALIVE!

Starring NEVILLE BRAND · MEL FERRER · CAROLYN JONES as Miss Hattie
MARILYN BURNS · WILLIAM FINLEY · STUART WHITMAN as Sheriff Martin
Directed by: TOBE HOOPER · Produced by: MARDI RUSTAM · Executive Producer: MOHAMMED RUSTAM
Co-Produced by: ALVIN FAST · Associate Producers: SAMIR RUSTAM · ROBERT KANTOR · LARRY HULY
Distributed by: VIRGO INTERNATIONAL PICTURES, INC.   R RESTRICTED

would have taken a lot of money — nobody was willing to put that kind of money into it.

In 1976 Hooper made *Eaten Alive*, his first 'Hollywood' movie, for schlock producer/occasional director Mardi Rustam, the human being responsible for such classics as *Nigger Lover*, *Psychic Killer* and *Evils of the Night* (these latter two featuring Neville Brand).

Tobe Hooper: It's much more complex than it seems. I tried to establish some kind of motif that carries throughout the show — sometimes that's more important than what you're actually showing. This has a lot to do with lights and shadows: it takes place in a single night, from dusk to dawn. And all the characters bring with them some sort of history, they're not just cardboard characters walking into a slaughterhouse. [*Variety*, 21 Apr 1976]

Describing it in *Variety* as 'a commercial film that I feel good about', Hooper's feelings soon changed. He left the picture before completion, citing gratuitous nudity demanded by the producers, and additional scenes were shot following his departure. There are indeed two noticeably different styles at work: Hooper's characteristically stylish, roving camerawork, and badly lit, static set-ups reminiscent of Herschell Gordon Lewis at his least inspired. The cast looks petrified and, barring a bravura slobbering turn from Neville Brand, performs abysmally, Mel Ferrer delivering a performance so shell-shocked he appears to have recently emerged from cryogenic suspension. Despite Wayne Bell's protestations (see below), the music score is quite effective: one astonishing sequence has the camera hovering above Brand as he wanders around dusting — the stupid kid is crying, parents arguing and country music blares while the jarring Bell/Hooper score bubbles away. While almost every aspect of the picture is fatally compromised, of all Hooper's films it best captures the sleazy, twisted atmosphere of the EC comics he loved, and it maintains a small following (writer/critic Kim Newman and myself among them) though its adherents appear not to include either the director or *Chain Saw* veterans from its cast and crew.

Tobe Hooper: There are a few good moments in it I don't mind admitting that I shot myself; but there were some things in there that were shot without me... Neville Brand did some wonderful things for me in that picture, roaming about this old hotel and talking to himself. That part I'm really happy about... [*Fangoria* 12, 1981]

Kim Henkel: Tobe called me from LA, desperate for me to come out and rewrite this script they had. So I went out there and took a stab at it, but the whole thing was a real mess. I've never even seen the film, the finished product — maybe a small portion of what I wrote is up there on the screen. A lot of the rest of it was done by this character Al Fast and God knows who else... I remember meeting Neville Brand, shaking hands with him — his hand was like a bar of macerated soap...

Wayne Bell: The problem with the *Eaten Alive* score is we didn't have much time, and it's a poorer movie to begin with. And after the success of *Chain Saw* there was less of Tobe to play with — because the essence of the *Chain Saw* music was play, by playing and having fun with it we achieved a better result than, 'Oh shit we've got to get this cranked out.' Also, we were out in LA in sterile apartments as opposed to getting a comfortable feeling at home — and we didn't have all the same instruments. I recall there was also a little primitive synthesizer too which was added to the *musique concrète* style, and I got into trouble with that because the synthesizer stuff, when you start to mix it in, some of its defining edge is lost if it's buried under other things. And what sounded like a musical sound by itself ended up sounding like noise in the mix. But really it's a crappy movie and I don't think we produced very good music for it... And to augment our music there was some celesta added in — they had one at Glen Glenn studios — that part of the score we did not do.

Below:
Neville Brand
hacks up
the scenery in
Eaten Alive.

Marilyn Burns: Oh my God, oh my God — I haven't talked about that in years. The reason I wore a dark wig — I was going to jump into the alligator pool if it got any worse. It was *that* bad at the *beginning*. Everything that could go wrong, did... They had a nurse for Neville to keep him from drinking, which didn't work... Carolyn Jones wanted to be made up as old and ugly as she could look, and then there was Stuart Whitman who kept thinking, 'What am I doing on this picture?', and Mel Ferrer, who *really* wondered what he was doing on this picture — everybody wondered what they were doing on that picture! By the time of the ending — Tobe had walked off and the producers came up to me and said, 'You're going to have to direct the ending'! So when you see the ending and I'm lying on the floor screaming and flailing, I'm cuing the midget, cuing the alligator, bring in Stuart — and I never heard 'Cut' — someone finally yelled it as loud as they could, and they came over to me and said, 'Are you OK?' and I said 'I'm fine, what's wrong guys?'... It was like that... the whole picture...

The producers added a little scene — they were dying for me to take my clothes off — so I gave them the longest bathroom scene ever without letting anyone see anything! They all sat up waiting for my nude shot, and I ended up taking off so many clothes — I still had a chemise, bra, panties and little shorts on! And it still took twenty minutes to get everything I was taking off.

My parents went to see it — the first scene starts and it's, 'My name's Buck and I'm raring to...', it was so embarrassing...

Eaten Alive was retitled and reissued at least half a dozen times.

Kim Henkel: [*Laughs*...] Oh, I think I gave you a hint of how snake-bit that whole deal was — these guys were just that kind of people — I think what they did was decide, 'We got a film here, we're going to release it, and six months down the road when we need another film to release, we'll just put a new title on it and release it like it's new film' — and that's what they did — though I'm just speculating...

Gunnar Hansen: I thought it was Tobe's attempt to continue *Chain Saw Massacre* — that Neville Brand was the Cook: here he is alone, he's moved over to the swamps, but it's the same set-up, but it's just the Cook trying to get through...

Following *Eaten Alive*, Hooper and Henkel spent a couple of years developing projects which failed to materialise.

Kim Henkel: We went out to LA and made *Eaten Alive*, then we got a three-picture deal with Universal — 'course that came to nothing. We actually generated a script, but it was just a mess — that was such a befuddled and clouded period in my history I don't even want to think about it — it was called *Viper*. There were some interesting parts in it — it was centred on a series of murders taking place in

Hollywood by a character who was using a peculiar instrument — he wouldn't kill anybody actually, he'd snatch their eyeballs out, leave them staggering down the street blind and eyeless... The script did get finished, but I wouldn't say properly — it was an abomination in many respects. But no three-picture deal ever involves three pictures unless you do the first one...

After another aborted project, leaving *The Dark* after only a couple of days, Hooper's talent was finally recognised by producer Richard Kobritz, who hired him to direct the excellent TV miniseries adaptation of Stephen King's *Salem's Lot*. While working on his next theatrical project, *The Funhouse*, Hooper was approached by Steven Spielberg, possibly to direct a film about some little kids and a friendly alien. Hooper was busy. So it goes. *Poltergeist*, the picture on which they collaborated, took $76 million at the box office and should have guaranteed Hooper a place as an A-list director. (Hooper said he had poltergeist-type experiences after his father's death, which he felt gave the film an element of truth which was partly responsible for its success.) But the fall-out

Below:
Wayne Doba (left)
and Kevin
Conway in
The Funhouse.

The cinematic Sci-Fi event of the Eighties

THE CANNON GROUP, INC. Presents a GOLAN-GLOBUS Production of a TOBE HOOPER Film
LIFEFORCE Starring STEVE RAILSBACK
PETER FIRTH and FRANK FINLAY
introducing MATHILDA MAY
Director of Photography ALAN HUME   Associate Producer MICHAEL KAGAN   Production Designer JOHN GRAYSMARK
Special Effects JOHN DYKSTRA   Based on a novel by COLIN WILSON   Screenplay by DAN O'BANNON & DON JAKOBY
Produced by MENAHEM GOLAN and YORAM GLOBUS   Directed by TOBE HOOPER
©MCMLXXXIV CANNON PRODUCTIONS N.V.

Right:
Cannon's original
Lifeforce
marketing poster.

from the rumours and controversy generated by Spielberg's on-set presence stalled Hooper's career, Hollywood being happier to discredit him and ascribe the film's success to Spielberg. Exit Tobe Hooper, until Cannon came along. In a classic misjudgement, Hooper was seduced by what he perceived as the 'old style movie mogul' nature of the Cannon operation, failing to register the ruthlessness (and trash factory production line) for which the company was well known. The result was a trilogy of poorly received films: *Lifeforce*, *Invaders From Mars* and *The Texas Chainsaw Massacre 2*, the first of which was butchered by Cannon. (For its DVD release, fifteen minutes of excised footage was finally reinstated.)

Tobe Hooper: One of the things I like about *Lifeforce* is that it involves the genesis of the vampire legend. These aren't blood-sucking vampires, but rather spirit-takers. They take your soul, your spiritual being. *Space Vampires* made the film sound like an exploitation film, and nobody wanted that connection. Secondly, I don't think of these beings as vampires — as I said, they aren't blood suckers. [*Fangoria* 46, 1985]

Tobe Hooper: If twenty-seven minutes had not been cut and it had remained *Space Vampires*, you would have seen the movie in a very different light. When the distributors called it *Lifeforce* they made the film sound pretentious and something that it wasn't. Those twenty-seven minutes were the *Space Vampires* part of the movie. It was a plot point that, when missing, totally restructured the piece. It was an unnecessary trimming. I consider it an incomplete picture.

It was meant to be funny for sure, but the sequences removed made the difference between humour and camp, it laid it wide open… It was meant to have humour akin to the humour in *Texas Chain Saw Massacre*. It was supposed to be a kind of ludicrous humour, but with those pieces removed, without the story points, it was ruined. [*Fangoria* 55, 1986]

Below:
A 'write your own caption' shot from Lifeforce.

THEY'RE HERE... AND THE EARTH
WILL NEVER BE THE SAME!

Invaders From Mars

THE CANNON GROUP, INC. PRESENTS
GOLAN-GLOBUS PRODUCTION INVADERS FROM MARS
of DAN O'BANNON and DON JAKOBY
PRODUCED BY MENAHEM GOLAN AND YORAM GLOBUS DIRECTED BY TOBE HOOPER

Above:

Cannon's

original Invaders

From Mars

marketing poster.

Following his experiences with Cannon, and disillusioned with constantly losing final cut on his theatrical features, Hooper began to work more in television, producing above-average pilot episodes for *Dark Skies*, *Nowhere Man* and, most recently, Steven Spielberg's *Taken*. There was also a detour into pseudo-reality TV with the second in the occasional *Real Ghosts* series.

Levie Isaacks: *Real Ghosts* was one of those quasi-reality shows: we went down to San Diego to the Hotel del Coronado, this famous old Victorian hotel that Thomas Edison supposedly wired himself, a beautiful place. It sits on the beach on del Coronado island — some of the people who saw the ghost were still there, like the elevator operator. Another episode was in a branch of Toys 'R' Us. So we depicted these stories of these 'real' ghosts, interviewed the 'real' people, and tried to make it look like it really happened. It was done for Gil Adler, who produced *Tales From the Crypt*, it would have been 1990 — the first Gulf War started while we were shooting.

With Levie Isaacks shooting, Hooper had also made *Spontaneous Combustion.*

Tobe Hooper: It was just one of those naturals, kind of like the first *Chainsaw*. One telephone conversation with my writing partner (Howard Goldberg) and I had the basic core of the piece. This is the first time I've done a great deal of the writing myself, and I found it much easier to just sit down and write this thing rather than try to communicate my ideas to another writer. And it showed in how fast it came together. We had a first draft script in three weeks and a final shooting script in six weeks.

There was a lot of day-to-day rewriting and restructuring on the film. I would see something in the dailies and adapt the characters to the reality of the situation. I also rewrote the film's ending a couple of times. Initially, the ending was more surreal. I changed it to something a little more realistic. Well… realistic if you consider a man going through a nuclear meltdown something that happens every day.

This picture is not so much about horror or science fiction as it is about science *fact*. Spontaneous combustion has been around for a long time. I'm using this film to take a better look at it and possibly explain it. [*Fangoria* 92, 1990]

Eric Lasher: *Spontaneous Combustion* would have been as big as *Poltergeist* had they not ruined it. It's a shame… It makes Brad [Dourif] look like a bad actor, and he's not, he's a brilliant actor — they cut the wrong takes, if take two was the best, they'd use take one. And Tobe lost control again…

Hooper's comments about another TV movie, *I'm Dangerous Tonight* (based on a Cornell Woolrich short story, and also shot by Levie Isaacks), give an insight into the way he considered the medium at the time.

Below:

UK video jacket.

Tobe Hooper: The little show I just did, *I'm Dangerous Tonight* — I shouldn't call it a 'little show', but budgetarily, it is — got extremely good ratings for the USA Network. You reach so many people that television is really a place to get serious now, as opposed to five or six years ago, when the thinking went that if you got a television assignment you could go in and whip it out, saying, 'It's only television.' The attitude's changed. Pursuing the right projects on television, and reaching large numbers of people, should, if it works, give me the kind of control over my projects that I need to get a pure one out in the movie houses. [*Fangoria* 100, 1991]

Since 1990 Hooper has only directed three non-television films, two of which (*Tobe Hooper's Night Terrors* and *The Mangler*) starred Robert Englund, the Whoopi Goldberg of horror cinema.

Eric Lasher: In *The Mangler* Robert Englund is doing a caricature of Tobe — the cigar, going 'God dammit' all the time… Tony Hooper was the designer — the mangler really works, you can roll sheets through it and it'll fold 'em in the end. He spent weeks designing the folding mechanism. In

Right:

Robert Englund,

owner of

The Mangler,

a laundry press

that eats people.

pre-production he was asked to do a rendering of the machine and he couldn't get it right, so he built a model of it, about five feet long. I took a photograph of it on Tobe's pool deck and blew it up and it got the picture a million dollars, it green-lighted the picture basically. When I saw photos of the machine, it was like they shrunk people and put them around it. The chain that ran it was about 100 feet long. But again, the film had people messing around with it…

Above:
The Mangler
at work.

In 2000 Hooper hooked up with trash producer Boaz Davidson (auteur of Cannon's *Lemon Popsicle* series and *The Last American Virgin*) for the disappointing *Crocodile*.

Eric Lasher: They ruined *Crocodile* too — that was a nightmare from the beginning… We were shooting here in Los Angeles and they had a big strike — the executive producer was making both union and non-union pictures, and they decided to teach him a lesson. Forty-something people lost their jobs, and we ended up shutting down for a month and moving to Mexico. We were shooting nights for six weeks in 100-plus degrees weather… The guy that was actually on-set must have weighed about 400 pounds — he used to get into the director's chair and fall asleep, all the time. Well, that's fine, you're not of any use anyway… He was a joke. We were in a little chase boat following the houseboat when they first leave — this guy wanted to go. The little chase boat is leaning, we're taking on water and Tobe's like, 'Ah, we're going to drown!'

In late 2002 it was announced Hooper would direct *Return of the Living Dead 4* and *5* (both co-scripted by *Leatherface* actor William Butler) as a back-to-back job in summer 2003, but in Spring 2003 his name appeared as director of a remake of notorious '70s atrocity *The Toolbox Murders*. What attracted him to such a project is a mystery, and it's disappointing that at the age of sixty, when his reputation should be consolidated as one of the great genre directors (in March 2003 he was inducted into the Texas Film Hall of Fame), he's lending his name to a remake of a dreadful Z-movie. But there's always time for things to change in Hollywood…

Films as Director:
1959 *The Abyss* (existence unconfirmed)
1963 *The Heisters* (10 minute 35mm short)
1965 *Down Friday Street* (16mm short)
1970 *Peter, Paul & Mary: Song is Love* (1 hour PBS TV show)
1971 *Eggshells* (16mm blow-up to 35mm)
1974 *The Texas Chain Saw Massacre* (16mm blow-up to 35mm)
1976 *Eaten Alive* (aka *Death Trap, Legend of the Bayou, Starlight Slaughter, Horror Hotel Massacre*)
1979 *Salem's Lot* (TV movie)
1981 *The Funhouse*
1982 *Poltergeist*
1983 Billy Idol: 'Dancing with Myself' (music video)
1985 *Lifeforce*
1985 *Amazing Stories* (TV series, episode 'Miss Stardust')
1986 *Invaders From Mars*
1986 *The Texas Chainsaw Massacre 2*
1987 The Cars: 'Strap Me In' (music video)
1988 *Freddy's Nightmares* (TV series, 1st episode 'No More Mr Nice Guy')
1988 *The Equalizer* (TV series, episode 'No Place Like Home')
1989 *Spontaneous Combustion*
1990 *I'm Dangerous Tonight* (TV movie)
1990 *Real Ghosts* (TV)
1991 *Tales from the Crypt* (TV series, episode 'Dead Wait')
1993 *Tobe Hooper's Night Terrors*
1993 *John Carpenter Presents Body Bags* (TV anthology movie, episode 'Eye')

1995 *The Mangler*
1995 *Nowhere Man* (TV series, 1st two episodes 'Absolute Zero' and 'Turnabout')
1996 *Dark Skies* (TV series, pilot episode 'The Awakening')
1997 *Perversions of Science* (TV series, episode 'Panic')
1998 *The Apartment Complex* (TV)
2000 *The Others* (TV series, episode 'Souls on Board')
2000 *Crocodile*
2001 *Night Visions* (TV series, episode 'Cargo')
2002 *Taken* (TV series, pilot episode 'Beyond the Sky')
2003 *Return of the Living Dead 4* and *5* (abandoned?)
2003 *The Toolbox Murders*

Other Films:
1971 *The Windsplitter* (actor)
1986 *Fangoria's Weekend of Horrors* (documentary)
1986 *The Texas Chainsaw Massacre 2* (actor, quick cameo outside Enright's hotel room)
1992 *Sleepwalkers* (actor)
1993 *John Carpenter Presents Body Bags* (actor)
2000 *The American Nightmare* (documentary)
2000 *Texas Chainsaw Massacre: The Shocking Truth* (documentary)
2002 *Masters of Horror* (documentary)

Abandoned Projects:
1975 *Bleeding Hearts* (scripted with Kim Henkel)
1977 *Viper* (scripted with Kim Henkel)
1978 *Dead and Alive* (scripted by L. M. Kit Carson)
1979 *The Dark* (replaced by John 'Bud' Cardos)
1981 *Venom* (replaced by Piers Haggard)
1982 *The Lights* (a contemporary action/fantasy film for 20th Century-Fox)
1987 *Whose Woods Are These* (scripted by Richard Christian Matheson)
1987 *Double Vision* (scripted by Mick Garris)
1985 *Return of the Living Dead in 3D* (stalled in pre-production, switched to *Lifeforce*)
198? *Floater* (for Empire, based on a Gary Brandner novel)
199? *Brew* (for Platform Entertainment)

(Hooper had originally been considered to direct *Motel Hell* for Universal, but Universal felt it was too extreme. The project was finally picked up by United Artists, directed by Kevin Connor. It's terrible.) ∎

"THIS IS THE CINEMA OF EXCESS!"

I t took a long time, but it was perhaps inevitable that a sequel to *The Texas Chain Saw Massacre* would one day emerge. The notion was not new — in the 1970s Warren Skaaren and Bill Parsley had acquired the rights (Kim Henkel: 'We were *persona non grata* so to speak with Skaaren and particularly Parsley') but Skaaren's draft script thankfully remained unproduced.

Tobe Hooper's *The Texas Chainsaw Massacre 2* was the third in a nightmarish three picture deal he signed with Cannon Films, run by cousins Menahem Golan and Yoram Globus, Israeli film entrepreneurs who had virtually single-handedly created the Israeli film industry in the '60s. In 1979 they moved to the US and took over the ailing Cannon movie empire. While producing exploitation trash of every variety, from martial arts to dance craze movies, vigilante violence vehicles for Charles Bronson to teen nerd sex comedies, Golan and Globus desperately yearned for a Palme d'Or at Cannes, leading to a string of 'artier' films in the mid to late '80s. This pipe dream of artistic respectability ultimately contributed to their downfall — and their commercial side, unlike Roger Corman's New World, was incapable of nurturing talent and discovering a Joe Dante, a Jonathan Demme or a James Cameron. And while Tobe Hooper enthusiastically proclaimed Cannon's similarities to the film moguls of old, he neglected to consider the fate of directors who failed to deliver what the 'old style' studio moguls demanded.

Cannon had been uncharacteristically generous with Hooper's budgets for *Space Vampires* ($25 million) and *Invaders From Mars* ($12 million); Hooper had gone over schedule on the latter, and Cannon succumbed to a fit of paranoia with the former, changing its title to *Lifeforce* and editing it by over twenty minutes. The result was a much smaller budget ($5 million), a maximum shooting time of eight weeks (5 May — 4 July) and a post-production period of approximately seven weeks before *Chainsaw 2* opened theatrically on 22 August 1986.

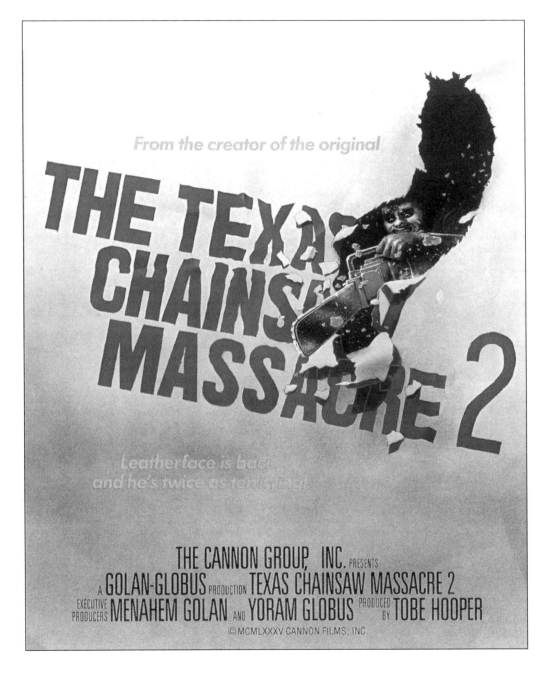

Above:
Behind the scenes
with (left to right)
Caroline Williams,
Dennis Hopper
and Tobe Hooper.

The compromised shooting schedule was only one of the problems to plague *Chainsaw 2*. The lingering hangover from the original film continued when few of *Chain Saw's* cast and crew returned: Jim Siedow the sole actor, though Lou Perryman appeared in the role of poor old L. G., due to have his brains beaten out. From the crew only Wayne Bell returned as sound recorder — his work in the music department would be missed.

Gunnar Hansen: With *Chainsaw 2*, they offered me scale plus ten per cent and said, 'The ten per cent is for your agent.' I said, 'Well, I don't have an agent, but I would want more than that. You've got to decide that you think I'm worth that bit more — think about what that is and make an offer that reflects it.' And all I really wanted was an acknowledgement that I was worth something to the movie — that they should offer me an extra $200 or $300 a week — they came back with an offer that was scale minus the extra ten per cent! They weren't interested in paying.

Unit publicist Scott Holton claimed that Hansen had 'vacillated' about whether he wanted the part or not and therefore lost the option. Holton also reasoned that the

Hitchhiker is dead and played by a dummy, while Sally Hardesty is insane and confined to a lunatic asylum. Holton's claims did little to placate Gunnar Hansen, Ed Neal and Marilyn Burns. John Dugan, the original Grandpa, also felt he had been frozen out of the casting for *Chainsaw 2*; in this case Holton maintained that Dugan had been considered for the role, but lack of time made it necessary to cast an Austin local.

Scott Holton: I don't think the broad-based market is even aware of who the actors in the first film were. If they were Robert Redford and people of that calibre, there would be good reason to think about bringing those people back. But who *are* Neal, Hansen or Burns? [*Cinefantastique*, Oct 1986]

Wayne Bell: They weren't willing to cut Gunnar in, they didn't offer him enough money — one would have wished that Tobe had gone to bat for him, though you never know what kind of latitude a director really has with people like that. That's the dynamic in every movie — the relationship between the maker of the movie and the owner of the movie, the supplier of the money. It varies — and Tobe's relationship was not good, though I don't know it has been in any of his movies…

Below:
Leatherface
with LG's face.

Lou Perryman: Tobe and Kit Carson called me up on a conference call and said, 'Hey, we want to skin you alive!' and I said 'What?' 'Yeah, we're doing a sequel…' The casting director gave me a hard time and made me read in spite of Tobe saying, 'We're using this guy.' But it was interesting — Caroline [Williams] was an interesting choice — and it was the first time I really got to work with Tobe as an actor after being his friend… They initially gave me two weeks, then came back and said, 'We want you for one other day.' But somehow they ended up keeping me on for the duration of the picture…

Bill Moseley: I worked on a ranch one summer, and there was this kid, about fifteen or sixteen, a sugar freak, he'd eat anything sweet and just go nuts, talking a constant stream of nutty stuff from commercials, anything that came into his head.

And suddenly, in this weird, squeaky voice, he said 'Texas Chainsaw Manicure' and that just got me. When we'd finished working I went back to my little cabin and wrote a five minute scenario of a woman going to a beauty parlour for a manicure, the door opening at the back and Leatherface coming out and giving her a manicure with a chainsaw. I went back to New York City, raised about $1,000 and went out to Staten Island, took over a beauty parlour and shot *The Texas Chainsaw Manicure*, and gave myself a cameo as the Hitchhiker. My wife gets the manicure, comes out and shows me — and it turns out to be a beautiful manicure. I had the Ed Neal outfit and the birth-mark on my face, and I go, 'Hey that's great honey, we should celebrate with some head-cheese.' I'd bought a lump of real headcheese — which was a mistake — and hold it up in front of my face, and in one take I actually licked it, which was not a good idea...

But it seemed like everywhere I tried to sell this thing there was a reason they wouldn't buy it. So, falling into despair, I figured, 'Well, that's the end of that...' I was working for *Omni* magazine and they sent me out to LA to cover the making of *2010* and I took along a copy. I showed it to a screenwriter friend I was staying with and he thought it was hilarious. He took it to Tobe Hooper and also got me Tobe's home num-ber — this was probably in 1984. So I went back to New York, called Tobe about a week later and told him I made the short film. He said, 'Yeah, I loved *Manicure* — now who was the guy who played The Hitchhiker?' and I said, 'Well, that was me,' and he said, 'If I ever do a sequel I'll certainly keep you in mind' — so that blew my mind. He said to stay in touch, so I think I sent him a postcard but never heard from him again, so I figured that was the end. But then in about the spring of '86, out of the blue one night, I got a call from someone purporting to be Kit Carson. He asked if he could send me a copy of a screenplay — I think my comment was, 'Who is this really?' It felt like a cruel joke. I had just come in from an NYU student film audition, I'd been for a part as a dead body and didn't get it — one of those days when I wasn't really in fine humour... He asked for my address and I gave it to him thinking, how could that hurt? I got the script in the mail a few days later. He had told me to pay attention to the part of Plate Head, so I did. I thought the script was just brilliant, it was hilarious, wild and wonderful and I loved the part. So I called him back and said, 'I think this is fantastic, I love it.' A few days later I got a call from Cannon's legal department say-ing, 'Do you want to negotiate your contract or do you have an agent?' I didn't, but had met one a couple of months earlier, so I called her to ask if she'd negotiate the contract. She negotiated my deal, called back and said, 'Sorry, I could only get you scale...' At the time, as a writer, I was making maybe $250 a week, so I asked how much scale was — about $1,800 a week! I said, 'I think I could handle that.' They also wanted me to shave my head — she added in the infamous 'bald head payment' so Cannon also had to pony up $5,000 for me to shave my head!

I never auditioned and I never met Tobe until the production was under way. Tom Savini had finished doing the first pass of the Chop-Top make-up, I was in full make-up and Tobe shows up and walks into the make-up room — he has a box of cigars under one arm and a Dr Pepper in his hand and he hands Savini a box of Cuban cigars. Tom says, 'Here's Bill Moseley, he's playing Chop-Top — what do you think of the make-up?' Tobe looks me over and says, 'I think the plate could use a little more pus,' and Savini goes, 'Clear or amber?' and Tobe goes, 'Amber' and walks out of the room. I just thought to myself — 'This guy knows what he's talking about, this is a pro...' And that inspired complete confidence — this guy knows his shit...

Bill Johnson: My agent said, 'They need someone who looks like Baby Huey.' I wasn't as tall as Gunnar but I guess it didn't make any difference... I didn't have to put a mask on — just went in in normal street clothes. I had a couple of call-backs, the last one was with Caroline... I got cast and it wasn't too long, maybe a month before they started shooting. But I was in full costume and make-up for seven weeks before I got to shoot a scene!

Above:

Dennis Hopper

as Enright: 'more

silly than he had

ever thought he

would look in

a film'.

Caroline Williams: The beauty of the role was that I played with two Leatherfaces. I played with the one who swung the chainsaw, and I played with the one who was in love with me. So, I got that dichotomy, that multiplicity of emotional changes, between those two actors, because they were both excellent, and they could do each other's act. The actor Leatherface was Bill Johnson. Bill had this incredible sweetness and comic timing, and [stuntman] Bob Elmore had this incredible viciousness. In the running scenes with Leatherface chasing me, there's obvious malice there. There's something to fear there. Then, Bill would come in to do Leatherface's actual acting, and there was such humanity there, a human-type character. So, that gave me a lot to work with. [*Fangoria* 60, 1987]

And then there was Dennis Hopper...

Mike Sullivan: Dennis once said I had made him look more silly than he had ever thought he would look in a film — the crossed chainsaws, having the two holstered chainsaws was just one step too far, the bandoleers — he didn't want to do it.

Bill Johnson: He was working on pre-production for *Colors* at the time I think... His thought processes are [*pause*] non-ordinary. His sense of humour is — there's left-field and there's a place beyond left-field, and that's Dennis' sense of humour. It's funny, but it's very different. Bill Moseley, myself and Dennis were getting pulled out of make-up at sunup, and Bill was on a roll about something and we were all playing the game and Dennis came up with this comment and it was *weird* — it really stopped the ball rolling... I wish we could have got more of that in the movie. He has an artistic sensibility — and he's really sensitive — he's really attentive and open to non-verbal communication. So we had some really nice interactions and I really enjoyed those kind of connections with him.

The scene where he's reaching down — Caroline's just fallen into the hole, he's trying to pull her up — if you watch really closely he's having to hold back from laughing. I think I may have heard it from Caroline, but he had to restrain himself more than once at the vapidity or the incongruity of what was going on in the scene, he was really restraining himself from laughing out loud. I don't know what was going through his mind, but he has such an aberrant sense of humour — Heaven knows what he's thinking.

Bill Moseley: I never really spent any time with Dennis Hopper — I would see him, but I had to go to the House of Pain (what I called the make-up studio) so early I usually missed him at the breakfast room of the Brook Hollow Motor Inn, where we were all billeted. I would see him every once in a while from afar, he'd be smoking his Marlboros and putting his custom-made leather hand-tooled golf bag in the back of the Lincoln Continental the production company had supplied him with, on his way to Willie Nelson's country club to play golf. The only time I ever worked with him was in the final scene…

Richard Kooris: My company Texas Pacific became the production company for the film — Cannon hired us to provide all the production services. The film processing was done at TVC in New York but we were supplying a lot of the labour, all the production offices, locations, renting equipment, purchasing — all that went through our company here. We crewed it almost completely from Austin — the only people who weren't from Austin were the special effects and make-up people. It was the largest picture crewed mostly out of Texas that had been done up to that point. It was a big, important thing for the industry in this state.

It was interesting dealing with Cannon — I had no idea what they were like. I got into a dispute with them at the end of the picture — they'd paid us through the filming, then they picked up and left town when we finished, owing me about $30,000 — they refused to take my phone calls, so finally we had to sue them. We had a contract that had to be adjudicated in Texas so when the constables served them with the papers in Los Angeles, they called me up and said, 'Oh, we're so sorry

— you mean you've been calling? You mean we owe you money?' — they were such sleazeballs, just horrible people, so I said, 'Yes, you owe me money — here's how much, pay me and we'll drop the suit. And by the way, I want a couple of other things…' One of them was the answer print to the film, so I still have it here…

Mike Sullivan: Richard Kooris suggested they hire me. I did all the pre-production, I started on it months before we began filming. That would be December '85, January '86, whenever the production office was set up, which was in the spare room of Third Coast Studios. I did a lot of the planning on the sets — there wasn't a position for an art director on that film — they just didn't put one in — that's normally what I do, so they asked me if I was interested in being the prop master, which I had never done and I thought well, sure. And they said, 'In addition to doing the props could you also help design the sets?' so I said, 'Sure, I'll do that, it sounds like a fun project.' And so we started looking for locations — I was there right until the end of production.

We realised how big a project it was — it's become known as the 'artsy' *Chainsaw Massacre*, the one that had more art direction to it — and that was pretty much a conscious choice from the beginning, that we were going to do something that had more in the way of production values than the first one, which some people have found as a fault, and other people have found as the strength of the film.

Richard Kooris: I had a reputation in town as being a really good shooter and Tobe and I had been friends — so when he got the chance to do *Chainsaw 2*, he wanted to do it in Austin with Texas people. I think he was kind of burned out on the LA scene a bit and he wanted to come back where he had more control. With *Chain Saw*, even though it was hard, he had done it his way and he was able to put his stamp on the picture. When he came back to do 2, he wanted the same kind of circumstances — he was in a way trying to recreate the feeling he'd had, though obviously on a much bigger budget — I think he felt that one of the reasons he'd sort of lost control on *Invaders* and *Lifeforce* was that he hadn't been able to execute them in the way he liked to make films. So he was trying to return to his roots... And he phoned me up and just said, 'I'm coming back to Texas to do *Chainsaw Massacre 2* and I asked you to do the first and you couldn't do it — are you available?' I wasn't doing features but said, 'Sure, I think that'd be a gas, let's do it!'

In the commercials world I'm a director/cameraman — I shoot virtually everything that I direct, I'm a cinematographer at heart, so Tobe and I got along great. I think one of the reasons he asked me to do it is we saw things in a very similar way. So compositionally, or from a lighting standpoint, we were always on the same page. He's a really bright, creative, interesting individual — professionally and creatively he's a great guy

Above:
Vietnam veteran
Ken Evert
as Grandpa.

to work with. It's kind of a tragedy he hasn't surrounded himself with better people — I think he would have done better things had he done so. He's very hard on himself physically — I think one of the reasons he got so ill was because he lived on Dr Pepper and Cuban cigars! You rarely saw him eat. He usually had a cigar in his hand, and he was always drinking a Dr Pepper. One of the big crises on the last day of the shoot was that we ran out of Dr Pepper — at 4am we had a production assistant out scouring all the 7-11s trying to find some Dr Pepper in bottles, he wouldn't drink it from cans. We had a little basket rigged by the video assist monitor, which is where he sat, a little holster the size of a bottle of Dr Pepper, and it was the job of someone on the set to make sure there was always a fresh bottle in that holster. That's not the way you want to treat yourself if you're on a nine and a half week marathon...

Mike Sullivan: I've been in Austin since '71, I came here to build a theatre at St Edwards University and I've been here doing theatre and cinema ever since. I knew a lot of the people who worked on the first film — Ed Neal was a friend, and I think I'd met Tobe through him. I also knew Kit, I'd met Dennis Hopper before, and I had known Bill Johnson since I was sixteen — he was an apprentice at the University of New Hampshire Summer Shakespeare Festival, I was the resident designer and member of the acting company. When I came to Austin there he was, a student at UT, and when they were looking for somebody I thought, 'There's this big guy who could play Leatherface'... And then I thought, 'There's this weird little guy who could play the grandfather, who works as a carpenter down at the Zachary Scott Theatre, but I bet he could do it.' A guy by the name of Ken Evert, and he ended up being Grandpa — he was a Vietnam vet who'd been a tunnel rat, and when they were talking to him about the difficulty of doing that make-up, how he'd have to be still for so long, he looked at me and said, 'My only problem with this is I hope I don't have flashbacks — I used to sit in the tunnels waiting for Viet Cong to come along. Sometimes I would sit poised with a knife for up to twelve hours.' I was going, 'You know, I think you're the perfect guy for this job.' His nickname was Hellweek among theatre people — he would have these flashbacks to Vietnam — he was very proficient with the knife and with the gun, kind of a dangerous character. He just loved that scene where he got to suck Caroline's finger, he thought that was one of the best things he had ever been asked to do. The last time I saw him he was living on the streets — a guy on the corner with a cardboard sign, that's where he ended up. I haven't heard about or from him in years... He is a strange one — I assume he's still alive...

Bill Johnson: Ken was intense — he carried his KBar [Marine Corps combat knife] with him wherever I saw him. I don't wonder that he might have had a touch of Post Traumatic Stress Disorder like many Viet vets. Tom Savini literally sang Ken's praises for his work as Grandpa — '... he was ancient, he was magnificent...' — Tom was literally rapturous and rightly so. Ken was awake twenty-four hours just about every time he donned that panoply of appliances — at least eight hours of make-up time, and the camera crew hustled to get as much done as they could while the make-up and Ken could hold out. He could only take in nourishment through a straw. That's it. A straw. If he rested it was in some awkward position with little movement...

Initially it took four hours to do my make-up, they tuned it so it only took about an hour towards the end. Grandpa took like twelve hours and they used him for twenty-four.

Bill Moseley: I was always on Forced Call — you're supposed to have a twelve hour turnaround, you have to be back at the hotel and you can't be disturbed for twelve hours. If they do, they have to pay you like a whole day's wage. And they were forcing my call just about every day because the Chop-Top make-up took about three and a half hours to put on and about an hour and a half to take off. So my calls were usually around 4am and I'd have to go down to the House of Pain, where Savini and his henchmen would put on the Chop-Top make-up. I'd be ready by about 7.30-8am, and some of the locations were about an hour's van ride, so I'd get there about 9am or so...

Lou Perryman: My make-up took a great deal of time — I went in at three or four in the morning and they built this slant board so I could sleep while they were working on me. I woke up and

*Below:
LG flakes out
after being
brained by
Chop-Top.*

they were done, it took about six hours. They had made a plaster cast of me over my head and chest and down one leg so they could build the appliances. I couldn't eat because I had the make-up round my mouth...

Eric Lasher: We went in at 3.00am to do Lou's make-up, I went in and photographed the whole thing from beginning to end, it took about six hours. Then they put him in a car and sent him across town to the set which was fun — he was playing to the people they were passing, he's all sliced up — and then he worked for another six hours...

Lou Perryman: And I was running around in shorts — I mean, when you skin somebody, do you really let them retain their drawers, their *knickers*? This guy wakes up, he's been skinned alive, but he's still got his drawers on... Yeah. So I got this pair of boxer shorts with little Texas longhorns on 'em...

Casting wasn't the only contentious area of *Chainsaw 2*. New Line had also been interested in producing the property; it was theorised that Cannon acquired it by luring Tobe Hooper with the promise of big budgets for *Invaders* and *Lifeforce*. Kim Henkel had collaborated on various sequel script outlines with Hooper: when plot elements with similarities to their work materialised in the finished *Chainsaw 2*, Henkel sought financial redress from Cannon. (Describing an early New Line marketing handout for *Leatherface,* based on 'a story synopsis derived from Henkel and Hooper's original blueprint for a sequel', David Schow states in *Fangoria* 88, 'Eventually everybody gets dragged into a tunnel maze beneath the graveyard, similar to the labyrinth seen in the latter half of Cannon's 'Saw 2.' New Line's rationale for using it, even as a pre-production marketing device, is inconceivable.)

Kim Henkel: On several occasions over the years we worked on ideas for sequels. We'd long talked about many of the elements, in particular the whole underground thing was part of the conception we had for a sequel. That was one of the main things that survived and became part of the Cannon script...

Chainsaw 2 was scripted by L. M. Kit Carson (who also acted as associate producer), best known for '60s cult film *David Holzman's Diary* (in which he acted), scripting the remake of *Breathless*, and as co-writer of *Paris, Texas* with Sam Shepard. The father of Hunter Carson, child star of Hooper's *Invaders From Mars*, Carson had known of Hooper since the early '70s, before the original *Chain Saw*. They finally met when Hooper was on his way to showcase *Chain Saw* in Cannes; on his return

Left:
Tobe Hooper
(centre) expounds
while Kit Carson
(right) ponders.

Hooper arranged for a screening for Carson and Paul Schrader. Carson, like Kim
Henkel, had never particularly cared for horror films: he and Schrader claimed to be
so terrified they had the projectionist skip a couple of reels and go straight to the
end. (By the time *Chainsaw 2* was completed, Carson maintained he still hadn't managed to sit through the original.)

Carson and Hooper had worked together on a script called *Dead and Alive* in
1978, which was to have been produced by William Friedkin. A bizarre-sounding
story of two little old ladies stealing souls in a California funeral home, it was never
produced, and presumably still lies buried in a vault at Warners…

Just before Christmas 1985, Hooper approached Carson about working on
Chainsaw 2. Carson was unsure, giving the following reasons in *Film Comment*,
August 1986:

1) Woman-hating slasher sleaze yuk;
2) The curse of sequel-itis;
3) Wipes your name right off the Serious Screenwriter's Map;
4) No way to write-shoot-produce a *real* movie in seven months, etc.

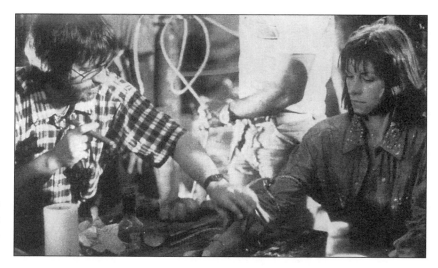

But then, in an episode similar to Hooper's legendary pre-Christmas run-in with shopping crowds and chainsaws, Carson had a traumatic yuppie-hate experience in a shopping mall at Christmas.

L. M. Kit Carson: The first thing I said was, 'You're going to have to find the right victims.' One of the things the first movie had going for it was that people were really sick of hippies and wouldn't mind seeing a Volkswagen full of 'em squashed. So, I went home to Dallas and went to the Galleria, which is an elaborate shopping mall just stacked with yuppie stores. It's like a yuppie feeding ground. I saw all these people buying *piles* of things, you know. Seven sweaters at a time. I called Tobe up and said, 'I've found the victims.' [*Fangoria* 57, 1986]

Tom Savini: The publicist, Scott Holton, brought this guy Barry with him... during a meeting we had while Barry was there, we said, let's kill *him*. He's a yuppie-looking guy. So, we cast his head and we're going to try to kill him... There's a point to be made about them in this film. We're going to wipe out a lot of yuppies. [*Fangoria* 56, 1986]

Mike Sullivan: That was originally one of the good things about it — it actually had a plot instead of being random — and I thought some of the funniest stuff Kit wrote was the take-offs in the yuppie killings. That all went away, it's a chase movie. That's one of the things that's really very similar in Tobe's films and those of Robert Rodriguez — which are basically chase movies too. I worked on *Spy Kids*, and the first thing that Robert had us do was decide what the corridors would be like because of all the chases — I thought, 'We're back to working on a Tobe Hooper film!'

Bill Johnson: Kit's really eloquent, he loves language — when I read the original version of the screenplay I thought, 'This is awesome.' It was an incredible satire: notice beautiful table in sunlight, set for breakfast, designer marmalade — chainsawed! Cut to exquisite clothier, wonderful rows of delightfully textured clothing — chainsaw it! OK, so we were seeing a rebellion here, a class rebellion, economic discrepancies. But the only thing that remained of it was Jim Siedow's speech…

Jim Siedow: It was Tobe's idea to play this one from a more comedic angle.

Caroline Williams: It's a comedy, an incredible black comedy. It's The Three Stooges Go Grand Guignol. And it was fun. It was a lark, it was a laugh. And it was difficult at times. But my motivation every day was to be as useful to Tobe Hooper as I could possibly be, because I could see the love he has for this movie.

In a way, this movie is such a send-up. And Stretch is basically a send-up of your cliché horror movie heroine, an upscale '80s version of your classic horror movie victim. The thing is, she keeps trying to get herself out of trouble, and, in doing so, she gets herself into more trouble. [*Fangoria* 60, 1987]

Carson's idea was to take the chainsaw family to Dallas and plunge them into a culture clash with the ravening yuppies who consume everything in their path. Linking *Chainsaw 2* to the first film, Sally Hardesty became Sally Hardesty-Enright, the niece of Dennis Hopper's ex-Texas Ranger Lefty Enright, who's been tracking the family for the thirteen years. Carson went out of his way to create depth to the 'chainsaw family' back-story (he proposed Enright is their missing surrogate father!), gave Leatherface a love interest and wrote in the empowering of Stretch. In *Chainsaw 2's* most perverse scene, she discovers she is able to use her sexuality to control Leatherface and turn the tables on him, leading to a bout of chainsaw impotence. Carson was subsequently told he'd written a basic feminist rape-counselling text, but denied that's what he was really aiming for.

L. M. Kit Carson: What I was more interested in was taking this woman and running her through a set of experiences that strip away all of the ordinary levels of life until her spirit rises up and becomes as fierce as the things confronting her. [*Fangoria* 58, 1986]

Caroline Williams: One of the things Kit told me is that there is a ferocity in women that comes out at certain times, and it's just there under the surface in many women all the time. That gave me a lot of insight into what I could do with her, how far I could go with her, and I just decided to max out with her, to do whatever I wanted to do. Tobe's direction was, 'If it feels like you're doing too much, you're doing just right.' So, I figured I could be the little kid at the playground, and I could just go do anything I wanted, and that's what I did. [*Fangoria* 60, 1987]

Bill Johnson: I remember hearing Tobe say, 'This is the cinema of excess, that's what I'm going for here!' At first I'd been thinking, 'Maybe this could be my break' — the script sort of called for me to express slightly more perhaps: Leatherface had presumably fallen in love with Stretch, breaking the family code, betraying the family. Tobe really needed actors who knew how to do acting — some directors really understand how actors work, can talk to them in a way that will [*pauses*]. But some directors are really more into photography or lighting and they rely on actors who can act already. When Bill asked Tobe one day, 'Hey Tobe, what shall I do in this scene? What's your direction here?' Tobe said, 'Just do more of that crazy Chop-Top stuff!' I think he has a sense of a vision, and he tries to get that...

Lou Perryman: When it got to my first scene, Tobe said, 'What do you want to do here? What are you thinking?' I said, 'I'm thinking two things — this guy thinks he's Hud, a handsome, slim, studly cowboy...' and Tobe said, 'Ooh, I like that, anything else?' I said, 'Yeah, you know, I wanna spit — this guy wants to spit,' so I started spitting and Tobe said, 'Yeah, I like that.' So the first thing after I'm skinned alive, I sit up and look around and there's that L. G. tattoo on my arm, the first thing I did was go [*horrible snorting sound*] — that's my signature! It *is* L. G.!

Bill Johnson: My character had no language... Tobe did mention one thing he thought would be interesting, but it was hard to get things to develop — 'Hey, why don't you come up with some kind of chainsaw language, OK?' [*Makes chainsaw revving sounds.*] But it just didn't seem to materialise — communication just shut down, people were tense. It felt just like being in a crazy alcoholic family, people were shifty, the production manager always seemed angry and punitive — I felt icky, I just wanted to run away...

Leatherface just does what he's told, he just hangs out until he's told to do something — so I just adopted that stance. Maybe I should have said, 'Hey Tobe, what about me petting the saw and taking Caroline's hand and petting the saw with it, what do you think about that? Maybe *she* can love the saw too!' That would be, you know, going for some real intimacy — maybe the French market would have liked it — 'Ah oui, comme ca!'...

Once again the film was shot in and around Austin. The main locations were the abandoned Prairie Dell Amusement Park, where most of the Texas Battle Land exteriors and some of the tunnel scenes were shot, and the old *Austin American-Statesman* building. Also used was the Cut-Rite Chainsaw Store, the film's bemused proprietor being its actual owner.

Lou Perryman: I was coming back from Dallas, from an audition, and saw this old abandoned kind of amusement park. I don't think they'd seen it — Tobe had moved to California years ago, so he doesn't know the area any more. I told Tobe about it and he said, 'Hey, that sounds great.' So I do take credit for that…

Mike Sullivan: There was a chainsaw store, maybe six or seven blocks away from the *Austin American-Statesman* — the one that's used in the

Above:
'These Acme bootsoles last a lifetime,'
Enright informs Leatherface.

film — that guy who owned that store thought I was like Jesus walking through the door, I bought basically everything in there. It was not a big business but he kept me supplied, every time one went wrong we would take it over, he would put everything else aside, fix our stuff, get it back in shape and return it to us. He manufactured special bars for the saws so we could have longer ones, he ordered doubles and triples, like the silver saw Dennis Hopper uses. The amazing thing was the amount of money spent on chainsaws — there were hundreds of chainsaws…

Bill Johnson: The underground stuff was in the old *Austin American-Statesman* newspaper building where they used to have the presses, so it was like a giant warehouse building that was two or three, maybe four stories high. It had been abandoned for a different location, so it was a giant empty space.

Mike Sullivan: Once we had that *Statesman* building, a lot of ideas just started popping. I'm not sure exactly how the script was structured, but I know there were a number of changes to the script as we found things, that Kit wrote based on what we found.

Tobe pretty much left us alone, and they didn't have a lot of money, so they were grateful for what they got. It was not a big budget production. When we first set up I was trying to figure out how we were going to be able to produce what they wanted in the way of production value with the money they had, which was nothing. It's one of the lowest paid jobs I've ever done, doing as much work as I did. When we set up, I had a guy who'd worked on a couple of other projects with me but never on a film. He'd managed a couple of restaurants — he was a friend of a friend. I said, 'Look, I can pay you $50 a day and what we're going to have to do is find a bunch of people and set up an assembly line for making the props.' His name was Jay Raymond — the two of us took this empty warehouse and turned it into our art department, which is not an unusual thing to do, low-budget films do that kind of thing all the time. We were standing outside one night and this woman was walking down the street, and we thought we were going to get hit on because of the area of town we were in. But she turned out to be this wonderful sculptor who knew a load of art students, and she said, 'How much can you afford to pay people?' and we said, as we needed a lot of people, 'How about $5 an hour?' 'Heck, I can find you hundreds of people for $5 an hour,' and I said, 'OK, you just keep 'em coming and I'll find them things to do.' And that's how almost all that stuff came together.

There was a sculptor in town, Daniel Miller, who later worked for Disney on *Honey I Shrunk the Kids*, he created all the back yard and giant plants — he was a styrofoam sculptor working at a place called the Arts Warehouse, across the street

Below:

Tom Savini,

Nubbins (aka

The Muppet) and

Tobe Hooper.

from the *Austin American-Statesman* building; we arranged to get a section of it, and turned it into what we called the Bone Shop. Daniel, myself and Jay supervised these student artists — we had people working twenty-four hours a day. We went out and collected bones from bone graveyards in central Texas in about a fifty mile radius: anybody who had dead cow bones, we just went and picked them up, put them in the Bone Room and starting making things. We didn't have money to buy furniture, so we went to the dumpsters at the Goodwill Industries and took out broken pieces of furniture they were throwing away — if it was missing a leg, it got a bone to replace it. If it was missing a back then a new one got made out of bones and attached. I still have a couple of pieces I thought were elegant examples — a '30s art deco chair with femurs for legs, a ribcage for the back, that kind of thing... There was probably 500 or 600 pieces. A lot of stuff had to be made using skeletons, so we contacted the Carolina Biological Supply Company — and this is a strange part of the story. We ordered thirty of the cheapest skeletons they had in the catalogue, assuming they would be plastic — when they came, they were bone, they were skeletons from India, actual people. So we hung them up and gave them all names, then we had a casting session and cast them as different characters in the show...

Daniel Miller created all the walls for the smoke house — he did a series of plaster and bone sculptures and then pulled vacuforms from the moulds to make the walls of the smokehouse. The dummy that got made, that's another Daniel Miller creation, and he also did the grandmother — the last I heard of him he was living somewhere in Mexico doing sculpture.

There was an awful lot of craftwork on that film, and there was a load of backyard carpenters we hired — friends of Willie Nelson we'd known from rigging concerts who actually ended up becoming my art department crew for many years after that. They were carpenters, painters — they weren't trained film technicians, they were guys who did work around town, jacks of all trades. We needed to do some kind of passage from one of the elevated platforms to another, and these guys came up with the idea of making a suspension bridge because they'd never done one and thought it would be fun. There was an awful lot of that kind of serendipity when we were doing *Chainsaw 2*: I went out to California to Ellis Mercantile, a big prop house, and they had a stuffed German Shepherd, so I rented it and we put it on a treadmill — it had died on a treadmill — it became part of that quarter mile passage.

Richard Kooris: The sets were incredible — for a picture of that budget to have sets like that... That underground set we did — the tunnel portion was done up at the amusement park. This crazed guy had built it out of these half cylinder, prefabricated metal things that he was trying to sell to farmers to build sheds from — he ended up building this amusement park out of them... We took all the tunnels and turned them into the underground tunnels by spraying them with this stuff that looked like dirt. Then we went out and got every old electric light and lamp — we scoured the junkyards, junk shops and antique shops around Austin for like fifty miles and got everything you could put a light bulb in. And that was the stuff we stacked along the sides of the tunnels. It's a gorgeous set, an absolutely incredible set — it was pretty much my idea to do that, because I didn't want to try to light these things with conventional movie lights, you'd never get away with it. So I wanted to build the lighting instruments and the ambient illumination into the sets themselves. We did end up hiding small movie lights in the set, but I wanted something that would glow on its own. We probably stocked 300-400 feet of tunnels with all these lights and lamps and junk.

Above:
Caroline Williams
does her best
to out-scream
Marilyn Burns
at dinner.

All those running shots through the tunnels — we built a rig that had never been built before: we took a four-wheel all-terrain vehicle and put steadycam mounts on the front and back of the vehicle. So when we were running before or behind the actors through the tunnels, the camera was on a steadycam mount on the vehicle and was either chasing or being chased by the actors. We could actually float the camera six inches in front of someone's face while they were running at full speed... It was a pretty neat deal.

Mike Sullivan: I don't consider you should do a close-up of everything I do, but a lot of things that were done in *Chainsaw 2* artistically ended up not being featured. The tunnels in the family's hideout, those took weeks to do, and it plays as just very quick moving shots, you don't see a lot of the art that went into those strange sculptures lining the walls of that space. It was well over a quarter of a mile of tunnel, and we did sculptures along that entire length of hallway. The Alamo mural that gets kicked in and the blood and guts come out, that was a major task.

Eric Lasher: The scene where Dennis takes the chainsaw and sticks it through Daniel Boone and all the blood spills out — if you look at the face, that's Ronald Reagan! They couldn't get to it whenever they were supposed to shoot it, and all the blood and guts were real, from slaughterhouses, they sat in barrels for two weeks — they shot the scene and nobody would go back in after, the stench was so horrible, you'd actually have passed out if you walked in.

Mike Sullivan: That thing was created almost forty miles out of Austin, so the people who made it had to travel an hour just to get to work. That's not a usual situation. That stuff was all done at a strange location around Jarrell, outside of Austin. A guy was trying to turn it into a roadside attraction, it had failed as a number of things — it had been a restaurant and a roller skating park — the guy had built it out of polyurethane foam covered with ferro cement. It was abandoned when we got there. There was a covered roller skating area that had all these long tunnels and those became the tunnels leading to the wall where it was broken in. Then the room where the grandmother is was at the top of the Matterhorn, a mountain of foam covered by cement... We made the letters that go on the top and the giant figures. At one point the entire art department was either on top of that building or securing those giant statues as a tornado was coming through — we had like gale force winds and people were standing on top of that styrofoam structure holding on to those letters so we didn't lose the set!

Left:
Stretch discovers
Granma.

The corridor with all the lights was done up at the Matterhorn. We combined about four or five different locations into the one that becomes the family's lair. Some of the corridors leading into what we called the Banquet Room were at the Matterhorn. The interior of the radio station was on the second floor of the *Austin American-Statesman* building. We took the existing walls and turned them into the radio station. The opening scenes in the hotel where the Cook is winning his award and L. G. is making his french fry statue — that was in a real location. The other hotel scenes were a set.

Richard Kooris: Then the rest of the set was built in this enormous room, the old press room in the *Austin American-Statesman* building. And that room was gigantic, about 175 feet long, probably seventy-five to 100 feet wide and about eighty feet to the overhead. [Production designer] Cary White went in and built this multi-level set, and brought in tremendous amounts of dirt and built all these ramps and ladders — it was a maze of little caverns and nooks and crannies. Then we moved a lot of the lights from the amusement park down to this set and re-dressed it with them, in addition to a whole lot of other things...

Mike Sullivan: I don't know how many miles of zip cord were used to light that space with those Christmas lights, but they had every electrician and anybody who even knew anything about electricity in this town ringing the entire *Austin American-Statesman* building with makeshift tables — they had these strings of lights put together — and I would estimate some days there were twenty or thirty people out there running Christmas lights...

Most of the big set, where the smoke house is, the slide and the suspension bridge and the banquet, with all the Christmas lights, that was in the old press room. All that space used to be taken up with printing presses. The amazing thing about it was we had a whole bunch of riggers — carpenters, painters, a lot of different craftspeople — who would go up to the top of that room. Over the years the space was covered with ink, it had been thrown up into the air and floated down and covered the beams — these guys would come down and they were literally black from head to toe. They'd go up in just a pair of shorts and boots and come down totally black...

Richard Kooris: When we went into the old printing plant, we had to rig the whole room with electric cable, so we would send the electricians up on cherry-pickers to rig the cable in the overheads — when they came down they would be totally black from head to foot, jet black... All the old printing ink was sitting on the rafters up there, so these guys would come down and all you could see was two eyes and a mouth — they were literally coal black from head to foot, it was the weirdest damn thing...

Chainsaw 2 was fraught with problems from the outset. Besides Hooper having to direct the film when he'd initially only intended to produce, the day before principal photography began Cannon cut a week from the shooting schedule, necessitating some quick on-the-spot rewrites and the delegation of some material to the second unit, which proved to be another disaster.

Tobe Hooper: I was just going to produce it and I couldn't find a director. Literally, I could not find anyone my budget would afford, a director whose work I knew, so I ended up running out of time and directing it myself. In doing so, I amplified the comedy and, I think, gave the general audience exactly what they did not want. I think they expected more of the same. But at least I got a chance to make a comedy — a very grim comedy — that is receiving an acknowledgement for its stylization. In the past four or five years, it's

Below:
Leatherface gives his new best girl a present.

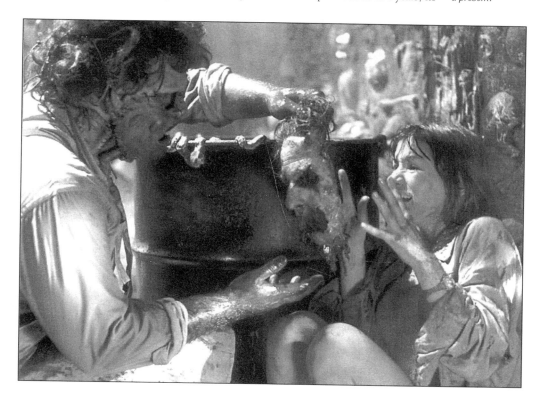

Above:
Stretch in
LG's face.

being seen for the first time. [Interview with Keith Phipps, *The Onion* a.v. club, Oct 2000]

Richard Kooris: The original budget we had was about $7 million, but Cannon were unrelenting and said, 'You have to cut it back.' The original shooting schedule was nine weeks — we ended up shooting for nine and half — they made us cut it back to seven weeks and we said, 'We can't shoot this picture in seven weeks,' and they said, 'We want a seven week schedule,' so we said, 'OK, fine, here's a seven week schedule but we can't do it in seven weeks!' So we then proceeded to extend it and extend it until we got back to where we started... We didn't do it on purpose — there was a lot of material, the amount of effects and make-up was just so enormous that you just couldn't do things quickly — it wasn't like two people sitting down having a conversation, it was very, very complicated.

Bill Moseley: Cannon had this date — I think it was 4 July, and it was like, 'This is the end of production no matter what you have.' I think Tobe had gone over budget and schedule on *Invaders From Mars* to the point where it freaked out Cannon, because they're certainly not a 'deep pockets operation'... And I think that probably gave them a chip on the shoulder, so when there was even a hint of that with *Chainsaw 2* they started throwing all the scary guys they could at the production.

Bill Johnson: They had a deadline to exhibit it, it had to be on the screen by a certain date, so they were in a very fast boogie to have it done. I was told one of the producers, Golan or Globus, arrived in a limo, went over to the script and ripped out a section and said, 'OK, you're back on schedule,' got back in his limo and split!

My sense of Tobe was that he's an intuitive director, and it takes time for people to bond in a way that intuition can pass between them non-verbally. I got a sense we were starting to get that happening. In the first *Chain Saw* film he didn't have outside pressures on him, or at least not people turning up in a limo and really causing him a lot of embarrassment — that was really stupid, that should have been done privately... If they're worried about profit, they're screwing their own profit by doing that, and if it's a power play it still has the same bad result...

From the sets I've been on, the special world of the movie seems to pervade the set, but *Chainsaw* was a crazy place, it was very weird, unstable, there were questions about who's doing what... I felt like the son locked in the cupboard, who every now and again gets taken out to show the neighbours everything's OK and then gets sent back. There was unrest and nervousness, I didn't know if that was the way Tobe worked or not — there was definitely an uneasiness, a tension, a pervading sense of anxiety.

Richard Kooris: Tobe loves to craft things and do them his way — unfortunately on *Chainsaw 2* it was totally the opposite, he just got killed by Cannon. He started editing the film a month before we ended shooting — we finished shooting on 4 July and he'd started in June, brought the editor in and set up a cutting room. The story I heard was that Cannon had an opening date for September in Japan — the US opening was in August, but the big money date was evidently a presale to Japan, if they missed that date they would lose about $4 million.

Bill Johnson: They had an editing room on the set — between times when he was shooting Tobe would go and do some editing. I did ten weeks on it, and Tobe needed to go longer but they pulled the plug, saying, 'Go with what you've got, get it edited.' I was looking forward to doing more — we'd actually got into a rhythm, a flow of some kind, getting used to the special world...

Bill Moseley: There were sometimes two or three revisions to the script per day — the original script I had ends about page seventy — so Kit would do a lot of rewrites during the night and there was a lot of rewriting, a lot of improvising. For instance, I did a scene in the radio station where my character is introduced — almost half that scene was improvised. There was a bunch of stuff that in the moment just popped into my plated head. Kit would sit there and tape record everything we did and after we finished the scene, he would play back the scene and type up the new one after we improvised it...

Bill Johnson: Kit Carson had this little tiny portable typewriter and he'd be just outside the door of the set where we were waiting to go in and

Below:
Leatherface up
to no good.

he'd be typing and ripping out the page — 'Here, memorise this in the next three minutes!' Jim Siedow had a hell of a time with these last minute re-writes.

Mike Sullivan: That's true. I saw him do that — they'd be looking over his shoulder sometimes! I think that actually helped the show. There was an awful lot of funny stuff in there — I don't think Tobe necessarily knew what to do with some of the script. It took him by surprise and he didn't have enough time to think about it, which is one of the dangers of creating it on the spot. I felt that the Cook and Chop-Top were both very inventive people.

Richard Kooris: That's true, that's true — but it shouldn't have been as hard as it was. And there's plenty of blame to go around. Cannon certainly deserve plenty of it, but Tobe deserves some of the blame too. Tobe did not like to make that many decisions in advance — he's a more spontaneous, seat-of-the-pants film-maker and he likes to get in there and be on the set and make decisions there. He would make certain decisions in advance, but a lot of things that could have saved time and energy, he didn't make in advance. That's not really a criticism, it's just a description of the way he works, and when you work that way, it takes longer... The larger the picture gets, the less option you have to do that, that's the way a personal film-maker operates — you can get away with it on a small picture with a small crew and no effects, without a lot of things interlocking... In 1986 a $5 million picture was still a pretty decent sized film, and when you get on a picture with that many moving parts — there were about 135 people on the crew — you are more like the manager of a manufacturing operation than you are the director of a small, personal movie. If you insist on operating like the director of a small, personal movie when you're on something that big, it doesn't work very well. There are too many things that have to be coordinated, that have to be managed in order for it to work... Unfortunately Tobe did not have the best assistant directing and production management support on that picture, and I think that came back to haunt him.

Bill Johnson: Kit had a lot more interesting things going on than what we ended up doing... It just became really crude, the lowest common denominator. He seemed to be deeply involved with the quality and was doing what he could within the changing rules — and the rules kept changing — it was just hard to keep tabs on what was going to happen. Kit was really articulate and seemed to understand what actors need to hear in terms of understanding or portraying their character — he was sharp, he had an artistic sensibility, he understood actors — it would have been great if he could have collaborated more.

Bill Moseley: But we were really into it, there was a momentum that happened during the course of the production that was unstoppable. Obviously there were problems with the budget and with Cannon — Cannon would send these thick-necked Israeli hit men-types to scare everybody into shaping up. I wasn't really aware of exactly what was going on, but I would see these characters on the set.

Mike Sullivan: There was an undercurrent through the whole production that there was a rift between Tobe and the producers, but I tried to avoid it and keep him supplied with Dr Pepper... It sounds like there was a certain amount of chaos in the first film, but with ours I think the chaos was more in the shooting aspect of the production than it was off-camera. I tend not to want drama — the drama happens in the film, maybe with the actors, but I don't particularly like dramatic crew people. I tend to gravitate towards guys who can hammer nails and paint flats, the craft people...

Below:

Leatherface

deals with LG.

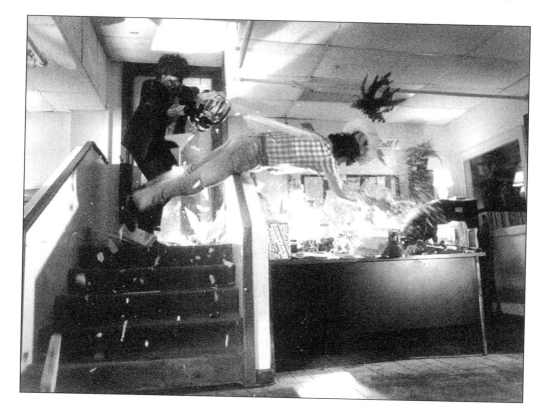

Above:
Enright discovers
Franklin's
mummified
remains.

Eddie Surkin was a pretty amazing special effects guy — we had so much broken glass to do that he went ahead and built a glass-making table in one of the rooms in the *Austin American-Statesman*.

In a short time the tight schedule and inhospitable working conditions began to take their toll on the cast and crew.

Wayne Bell: A lot of the time we were in this huge warehouse where the newspaper had been. They had just built their new offices across the river and the place we were in was going to be torn down, so the art department got to build all sorts of fantastic stuff in there. But the building had been abandoned for some time and there was evidently a lot of mould in the basement and we all got sick at some point, I was out for a couple of days...

Bill Johnson: The *Austin American-Statesman* [building] was made of metal, with no insulation — unfortunately for us — and it turned into an oven. They trucked in about a hundred tons of dirt, trucks of bones, about a million light bulbs of varying sizes and wattages... It was at least 100 degrees in there all the time — people were passing out. So they brought in a portable forty ton air conditioner with a giant hose about three feet in diameter, which they shoved in one of the doorways and between takes cranked in air. But it was really hellacious — the air was always full of something, they had skeletons from somewhere out of the country, probably covered in toxic cooties, there was smoke and Fuller's Earth, which is this superfine powder. A lot of films fill the air with frankincense — it gives a smoky atmosphere, gives mood and helps with depth perception — and they had dry ice, the frankincense going... And this stuff was getting trapped in my mask — they'd also used hairspray to spray down my costume — it had something to do with light reflection. And I'm having to run so I was sweating, then getting cold — I eventually got pneumonia. Tobe got it, quite a few people got it. Bill Moseley stayed pretty cool, he took care of himself, he's wiser than I... I had the worst case of walking pneumonia the doctor had ever seen, I was out for about a week, I almost died one night it was so bad. If my wife hadn't been there swabbing my body down with ice-cold compresses I probably would have died. It was pretty lousy.

Bill Moseley: I loved what I was doing — physically, I had the stamina — I don't know, everybody was dropping around me — there was a lot of smoke, we were in covered sets with air conditioning, outside it was boiling, so a lot of people were getting sick from the smoke and the temperature changes. But for me — something just sustained me — I was working probably eighteen to twenty-hour days...

Richard Kooris: Tobe got sick for a week, and the picture kept shooting. Tobe was flat on his back in bed, they were shooting him up with antibiotics so Kit and I directed the picture for a week... I'm a pretty healthy guy and I stayed healthy through the whole picture — I didn't get sick and my wife didn't get sick. A lot of people did though, a lot of the actors. I'm convinced it was something that was growing in that horrible building, it was a perfect growing environment... The air

Below:

Behind the mask is an actor with pneumonia.

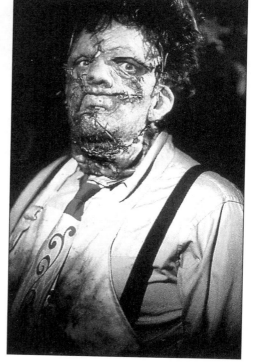

Right:
The Muppet.

smelled bad, there were leaking pipes, it was 120 degrees, the building hadn't been occupied for a year — it was just ideal for awful organisms... There were no working air conditioners in the building — the only air conditioner we had was a rented portable on a big trailer which we had to leave on twenty-four hours a day to chill the place down at night. When we arrived in the morning it would be very cold, then we'd turn all the lights on and the sun would come up and the temperature would rise throughout the day, by the afternoon it would be 120 degrees — we measured it a few times — that's why people got sick.

Mike Sullivan: You know, if the crew had been conscientious and cleaned up after themselves, the illnesses, that kind of legionnaires' disease, wouldn't have been an issue. I finally got really tired of the whole mess — everybody complaining and bitching and moaning and never cleaning up after themselves — so we cleaned out that space, we filled two dumpsters completely full of leftover lunches and things like that. It was no wonder the place was infected. Everybody was working so hard that nobody could be craft service — there wasn't a craft service on that film —

and they normally would be the people to clear up after everyone. I think it was more a result of us not taking care of ourselves than it was the building.

But we used a lot of Fuller's Earth, and we also used a lot of erosion control netting which has a fibre that's meant to break down in the environment — you lay it down where you have fresh construction and it holds the earth together until whatever you've planted can come up... You start using wind machines, which is what these portable air conditioners are, and you're going to get that stuff in the air...

There was fire in that space too, and the fire chief who showed up (who also happened to be called Mike Sullivan and lived across the street from me), said, 'You know Sully, you really shouldn't have used a lot of this material, it could catch fire, you guys were really lucky.' I said, 'Well Sully, this conversation really shouldn't go any further than you and me,' and he said, 'I'd be a little bit more careful if I were you.' I said, 'Well, we sprayed fire retardant on it,' and he said, 'Well, yeah, but this is a disaster waiting to happen.' We only had one more day to shoot so I said, 'Come back tomorrow and do an inspection — any time after noon will be fine.' That was 3 July, and we finished shooting at noon on 4 July.

Eric Lasher: At one point, when Stretch comes out of the smoke house and goes up the little ramp, Jim's talking — 'Your brother's sawing down his own house' — and he hits something and you can see a little spark go up a piece of string or something that's hanging from the ceiling — within twenty seconds the entire place was full of smoke and they had to call the fire department, and this guy Josh took a twenty-step ladder, ran up and grabbed the burlap off the ceiling and jumped down with it. He saved the set basically — the whole place would have gone.

Richard Kooris: It shouldn't happen — it wasn't like we were shooting in the middle of Africa or on Everest — there was no reason why this film shouldn't have been done on a proper and humane schedule — but you know, people figured out a way to make it hard. Part of it was poor planning, poor pre-production, the script was being rewritten as we shot — Cannon had rejected the original script — even up to the day we started shooting they were still changing things. My wife was the script supervisor and she said she has never had so many different revision pages on a script. She's a real trouper though, she just went along with it and she put her foot down when she had to. She's got a great ability to watch a scene and when we'd go to the next take, to remember what everybody had done and which hand they had whatever it was in — she was deadly on that. So the job is continuity and making sure we're using the most current page of the script and replacing pages — it's a demanding job... It was physically hard on her too. The jobs that we had mean we get the earliest call in the morn-

Right:
A minor
misunderstanding
between brothers.

ing and we go home last at night. The DP is working on every single set-up — as soon as a scene's finished everybody goes to the craft service table to relax, I walk immediately to the next set-up and start lighting it. So the DP is working for the entire day, never sits down, and the script supervisor is pretty much the same thing too.

Wayne Bell: The very last day was another twenty-six hour wonder, just like the first *Chain Saw*. It was on 4 July — rather, it started on 3 July and ended on 4 July! [*Laughs*]

Mike Sullivan: And on 4 July they still had lots of stuff to shoot, so it was a bizarre scene at the *Austin American-Statesman*. They still had one shot to do of the exterior of the radio station, which was just a flat standing on a lot across the street — I think it had two sides, maybe part of a third, but it had nothing in back of it once you went up the stairs. It was a regular fake movie building. So we had a full crew shooting in the banquet room, another crew shooting Joe Bob Briggs being killed by Leatherface in a stairway, we also had Leatherface in the van crying over his chainsaw. That was being done 'poor man's process' — you take a lamp, or maybe more than one lamp, on a stand, and you wind the cord around the stand and then you unwind it so it feels like cars are going by, though you're not moving. And then a couple of crew guys gently shake the van — and Bill Johnson was inside the van for that, crying over his chainsaw. That was the third camera shooting. Then I walked around the corner and Kit Carson was sitting there with his little portable typewriter and a pair of earphones on, typing away. I said, 'Kit, what are you doing?' and he said, 'I'm writing the script.' 'You're writing the script — it's the last day of shooting, it's ten o'clock, we've got to get everything pulled in two hours, what the heck are you writing? A new scene we're going to shoot today?' He said, 'No, I'm writing yesterday's scenes' — he was writing the dialogue which he had on a cassette tape, he was writing the script from yesterday! I sent my two assistants to the store to get a case of champagne — at noon Cannon pulled the plugs and we started popping champagne — it was the most bizarre last day of shooting I have ever been associated with.

Richard Kooris: It was a very, very, very hard shoot — it was physically one of the hardest things I've done in my life, and it was very hard for everybody who worked on it. The schedule was just brutal. We shot six-day weeks for nine and a half weeks, fifteen hour days — I was so tired that I slept for the next three weeks when it finished. On the last day of the shoot, I think we worked twenty-seven or twenty-nine hours straight. We had a morning call on 3 July — we had a whole bunch of material we had to get done, two crews working, Tobe was running back and forth between the two crews — we were trying desperately to finish. We shot all day, all night and into the morning — Cannon had said, 'You have to pull the plugs on 4 July,' but they didn't say when, so we kept going until we got everything done. People were so tired at that point they were bursting into tears, having nervous breakdowns — it was like the end of the Bataan Death March...

Bill Moseley: The last scene was when the grenade goes off — that was a pyrotechnical scene and they were some crazy guys, I think they were from the Israeli army, they had made this big explosive: flash powder and debris blowing all over the place, and I was supposed to chase Stretch then run up these stairs. There was a camera shooting over me at the top of the stairs — the camera needs to see me *and* the explosion behind me that's supposedly the grenade going off. Cannon was about to pull the plug, so we did a twenty-four hour day to end the shoot — the last scene, at the end of twenty-four hours, was where I had to run up these stairs with no railing with this explosion behind me. I was kind of paranoid or deluded at that point and I thought Cannon had planned it so they would have gotten all the scenes out of me and they would then kill me for publicity! So I was frightened and that gave me just enough adrenaline to run up the stairs — the explosion went off and everything seemed to be fine. Then it was determined that the camera didn't see the explosion, it needed to be bigger! So the crazy Israelis decided — their jobs were on the line, they were more concerned about *their* skins than mine — they packed in just about every piece of explosive material they had left. And then I thought, 'I *am* right — I'm not deluded, they really are trying to kill me!' I think I might have even prayed, you know, 'Please God just get me through this, just don't let them kill me.' When they said 'Action' I really shot up those stairs, there was a big-ass explosion and I could feel the heat on the back of my neck — those guys were fighting for their future pyrotechnic careers! But I obviously survived…

Lou Perryman: I had a hand grenade as a souvenir, but I gave it to my daughter's boyfriend — he's a bit more sensible than I am — I was afraid I'd get tempted to drop it somewhere around the Governor's mansion when Bush was running for President. That should have made the international papers… So I just said, 'Here, take this motherfucker off my hands before I do something crazy.'

A major cause of on-set distress was the presence of production manager Hank Kline and second unit director Newt Arnold. Occasional director (*Hands of a Stranger*, *Blood Thirst*) and a veteran of dozens of films, including several with Sam Peckinpah, *Blade Runner* and *The Godfather Part II*, Arnold's presence inflamed Hooper, while Kline's inflamed everyone else.

Wayne Bell: The production manager was a Cannon guy and I think he was sometimes working at cross-purposes from what Tobe was trying to do. He was trying to keep a lid on the expense — it was just product, he had no sense of what we were trying to create. It got behind and they brought in a second director to shoot 'B' unit stuff and I found myself going back and forth between the two units — I had one of my assistants on one of the sets, then if it got serious, like important dialogue, we'd switch and change units. The guy they brought in was just a hack

Left:
Leatherface with
The Muppet.

of some sort — Newt... They had no idea what Tobe was doing — just get it knocked out. But I don't know if even Tobe really knew what he was trying to do — it's an odd picture that doesn't hang together too well...

Bill Moseley: The second unit director was Newt Arnold, and he was one of these characters that Cannon was sending down — it wasn't doing something for Tobe,

Above:
The living members of Chainsaw 2's Family.

it was doing something *to* Tobe... So Newt came down — he was another old time guy — and he was in *Goonies*! He's taking a shower in *Goonies*!

Mike Sullivan: The production manager was Hank Kline. The first day I went in and talked to him about budget and said, 'The amount you've got budgeted for what you want is ridiculous but we'll try to do it.' I'd also made my living as an actor, and most of the time I'd played Jewish characters — although I'm Irish I grew up in a half-Irish, half-Jewish neighbourhood, and learned how to do that dialect as a kid. And he came out of that meeting with me and talked to some of the other guys on the film and said, 'It's very nice of you to bring in one of my people on this film.' And they're going, 'One of my people? What does he mean?' And he's like, 'You know, that Jewish kid you hired to do the props.' 'You mean Sully?' 'Yeah!' And they thought it was pretty funny. But I said, 'Don't tell him, don't tell him I'm Irish — I'm playing this for all it's worth, I'm getting as much out of this guy based on my being Jewish as I can, 'cause this guy is going to pinch pennies like you've never seen.' And somebody said, 'Isn't that a little anti-Semitic?' and I said, 'No, it's just survival.' And he was the hatchet man sent by Cannon — every time they wanted to cut some money off or they thought Tobe was being too extravagant or he was going to go over budget, they would send Hank out to do his mad dog routine with the entire crew. Everybody got affected by that except his one Jewish buddy! I asked for something, I got it! And I used that with him right to the end of the movie!

Eric Lasher: There was all kinds of stuff going on — Hank was a spy, he was the one who everybody hated — everybody knew he was a spy. Something would happen and the next day there would be flak about it — and it's got to come from somebody! It was detrimental to the project because Tobe used to spend time in negotiations instead of working on the movie.

He was responsible for some of the problems I had too. I was sending films back from Austin to Cannon in Los Angeles, and getting complaints back — 'Who's this girl you're photographing?' Well, it was Caroline... 'Where are the monsters?' This was two weeks before they started shooting anyone in full make-up — and I got fired! Tobe hired me the day they fired me, Tobe was going to quit actually, and I told him not to. He was really mad about being used. So he hired me back — Gary Farr is the credited photographer. He was a really nice guy, did a lot of Oliver Stone films, he died of a heart attack about three or four years after *Chainsaw 2*. He was sent out there, just trying to do his job, but no one would cooperate with him because they all really liked me.

Richard Kooris: Tobe's relationship with Cannon was very strained. That's why they sent that production manager down to work with us. There was a lot of bad blood. He was a hatchet man essentially — he gets sent in to cut the budget and crack the whip on the crew. He was an *idiot* — everybody hated him. He cut everything short, none of the departments could get what they needed, the food got horrible, there was no water on the set, he wouldn't supply drivers to take the crew to and from the location — we had a location that was forty-five miles from Austin, and it was a night shoot, people were falling asleep on the road trying to drive back in the morning and he wouldn't give us drivers! I ended up paying for a driver for the camera crew because it was so unsafe. The guy was just a monster... Towards the end of the picture there was no craft services. It was 120 degrees inside the set we'd built in the *Austin American-Statesman* and for the last three weeks there was no drinking water!

Tobe Hooper: It was the lousiest second unit direction I've ever seen. The guy went off on his own tangent. In my mind it had been very well talked out and he knew exactly what to do. For instance, there's a scene where yuppies are massacred in an underground parking lot. The scene was shot but was terrible, and it was something any good second unit director could do. But the guy tried to add his own interpretation to something that was already laid down in history. There was this scene with Leatherface breaking out of the back of the catering van. Well, I went wild when I saw the footage. The doors slam open and there's this blinding light like Leatherface is standing in the *Poltergeist* closet. Then all the yuppies have a sheepdog expression come over their faces and he just steps out and hacks them to bits. The second unit director believed the yuppies should be under his spell; well, I invented Leatherface and I didn't realise he had those powers. It was totally in conflict with my concept, and I didn't have time to go and reshoot those scenes. So that was the first thing I tore out of the movie. Then Cannon tore out Dennis Hopper's back-story that told you about his character... Enright had used her mother as bait to entrap Stretch's uncle in a drug bust, so when he sets her up as bait for the maniacs the whole situation has come full circle, and there was a terrific symmetry to the story. In addition to this, it becomes clear that Enright is not right in the head; he's drinking lots of mescal, hallucinating after eating the worm, you know, chainsaws coming out of the walls and surrounding him... [Interview with Philip Nutman, *Shock Xpress*, Winter 1987]

Eric Lasher: There was a sequence with Dennis that was cut, the hallucination scene in the hotel room, before Stretch knocks on the door — there's chainsaws coming through the walls everywhere — that's all gone. The whole yuppie scene that was cut in the underground garage — this guy John Ivey gets backed up against the wall and the chainsaw goes through his head and he falls forward into the camera. The yuppie stuff was cut for time in a way. You went away from Stretch — she was originally supposed to be hung upside down, trapped, and he puts the mask on her and a bag over her head and leaves her — that all changed. She was trapped there and they went off on this killing spree. They decided it was pulling away from the main character, so that's basically why it was cut. The dialogue in the Rolling Grill AGoGo on the way to kill the yuppies, all that is now laid in over the scene when she comes out of the smokehouse, so you get the pertinent points in the story, but they're in a different place.

Bill Johnson: I don't know what the deal was, no one told me squat. I know Tobe was upset about something — he had a fit one time, it was pretty amazing... The second unit was shooting at the same time, close by, and the noise they were making was disturbing what we were doing — and Tobe went over to the door of the set and screamed over, cursing a mile a minute, asserting his rightful rank, 'This is the first unit, we take precedence!' But Newt seemed really relaxed and self-assured...

Richard Kooris: Oh yeah, Newt, the one-eyed wonder, oh yeah [*laughs*]. He had an eye patch — he was another old-style guy who thought he was God's gift to movies... I don't know where Cannon dug these guys out from... He was one of those old grizzled veterans, he'd been to the wars... You have to remember that this was like a real culture clash — you had guys like Newt and Hank Kline trying to mix with Tobe Hooper and Kit Carson, and it was an odd confluence of generations and abilities — very, very strange. That tension went on throughout the picture — especially in the light of the previous two films that were box office flops. Cannon's attitude was that they needed this picture to be completed on budget, on time and be distributable, and they needed it to make a lot of money — which ultimately it ended up doing, it ended up making a great deal of money for Cannon. But they did not trust Tobe, didn't trust him as far as they could throw him. ■

Above:

One of these

figures is

Dennis Hopper.

The Texas Chain Saw Massacre 2

"WORTH CUTTING FURTHER"

Tobe Hooper had spent over $40 million of Cannon's money on three films. Box office returns for *Lifeforce* and *Invaders From Mars* were poor ($11.6 and $4.8 million respectively), both failing to recoup even half their production costs. *Chainsaw 2* would go on to make a healthy profit, but it was the beginning of the end for Cannon. Audience disinterest in late '80s Golan and Globus celluloid atrocities and SEC (Securities and Exchange Commission) investigations into their financial records led the company to declare bankruptcy at the end of the decade.

Chainsaw 2 met with a varied reception, many feeling Hooper had failed to achieve the correct balance between gore and comedy (too much of both). The film's visual qualities (it's still Hooper's best looking work) were compromised by lapses into narrative incoherence and a cheesy music score by Hooper and Jerry Lambert, the installer of Hooper's satellite dish... Caroline Williams won a Best Actress award at the 1986 Sitges film festival, but on the whole *Chainsaw 2* was consigned to the 'misfire' category. The years have been surprisingly kind to it, especially with the advent of a widescreen DVD release (still lacking narrative restoration), but some may still find 100 minutes of hysteria-level shrieking and screeching coupled with a tinny, grating score a slightly painful experience.

Its high violence and gore content led to *Chainsaw 2* being released unrated in the US, restricting the number of theatres in which it could play and the amount of advertising it could receive — which more likely accounts for its lukewarm box office performance than its lukewarm reviews. (Although its initial $8 million gross was quite respectable given its limited release.)

In spite of deciding to up the on-screen blood-letting to appease the gore fans, who he felt required more than the original film had delivered, Tobe Hooper was characteristically bewildered by the rating.

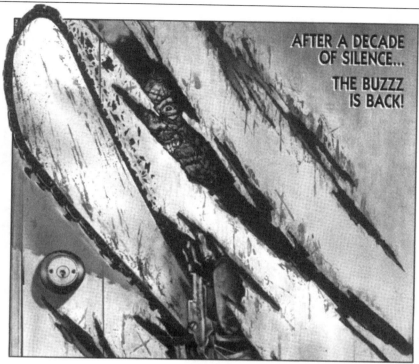

Tobe Hooper: I guess it was down to the L. G. character having his brains beaten out with a hammer and when he was skinned. Of course I didn't show him having his face removed, just put back on, but Tom Savini's make-up job was kind of gory so I shot the scene with an amberish glow to diminish the nastiness. Nevertheless, I still think it should have got an R rating. [Interview by Philip Nutman, *Shock Xpress*, Winter 1987]

Richard Kooris: Going out unrated cut its chances down enormously — it didn't even open in a lot of cities, we couldn't get newspaper advertising because it wasn't rated. When it opened in Los Angeles the only advertising was on billboards and at bus stops — no newspaper in LA would carry the ads. You can't release a picture without newspaper advertising — no one knows where to find it, where it's going to play — and it got no newspaper advertising in its initial release. The significance of the Japanese release is that Cannon was already getting into financial trouble at this point — even though they weren't letting on, they were under the gun money-wise. The picture cost $5 million and some change, they were going to get $4.5 million from the Japanese release, so they had a gun to Tobe's head. They gave him thirty days to cut the movie, and said, 'At the end of that time we're taking it away and finishing the cut because it *will* be in the theatres when we say so.'

Cannon took over the cut and if we'd shot anything with blood, gore or chainsaws they just threw it in, and in order to make it come to the proper length they had to throw the story away — that's the real tragedy…

Tobe Hooper: I'll be honest: I feel that that film came out of my frustration at the comedy in the first film not being appreciated or understood. And so I amplified the comedic aspects of it, but at the same time Tom Savini made everything so anatomically correct, that, you know, the film ended up not even getting a rating. I like the film as this wacky, crazy, bizarre, over-the-top dark comedy, but it missed its mark in doing what the audience expected it to do, which was to scare the hell out of them and give them a little more of what they had experienced in the first film. One of the flaws in the film is that unfortunately too much time was spent with the chainsaw family. You got to know the family and their insanity too well and it demystified the potential horrific elements. I like that film, too, but I have to say that it certainly isn't the quintessential sequel. It was part of a deal commitment, and I had fun doing it to the detriment of the film itself. Sometimes we do things for the wrong reasons. [*The Austin Chronicle*, Nov 1998]

Bill Moseley: I thought the movie was great — I did not have a problem with it. Given a little more time it could have been better, but that's something for people to talk about after the fact. I'm sure for every movie there are stories about the famous lost shots and we didn't get this and it's too bad that happened. But as far as I was concerned I thought it was a lot of fun and I loved the movie. I really loved Chop-Top, I had an empathy there, for better or for worse! Ask my kids about that! And I loved working with Jim Siedow, he's just the best.

I was so happy to be a part of the *Chainsaw* family, that legacy, I just thought it was fantastic — I'd seen so many crappy horror movies and I'm such a fan of the

Above:

Skinned but

still wearing his

drawers, LG cuts

Stretch loose.

original. It was like Tobe and Kit were handing me a very important assignment to carry this thing on to the next stage. The *Chainsaw* legacy didn't so much oppress me as it did inspire me — it was like bum's luck! You can't even get a job as a dead body and then you get handed the keys to a Ferrari — following arguably one of the greatest horror movies ever, really. And it was a new character — it wasn't like I had to be someone who'd already been played by someone else. Though I certainly owed a lot of my inspiration to Ed Neal, he did such an amazing job in the first film. Being in this film inspired me to bring to the table all the things I would like to see in a horror movie.

Eric Lasher: Why would you greenlight a film, put all this money into it, to ruin it? The film still survived; unfortunately it's not the film they intended to make originally… It turned out to be what it is, which is a cult classic in a way — I'm amazed that I was involved. Looking back, I know where I was on every single shot — this is still my best film experience and I've done like forty films. It was the most amazing… just being there, wandering around. It was an unreal environment…

Bill Johnson: I was reasonably satisfied. I wish that there could have been more freedom for the creative aspects — I don't know how much influence the producers had. I know I don't like feeling pressured and I'm sure Tobe didn't. He had his own organic time line, and we seemed to be getting into it when we had to shut down… I would have liked to have done the satire it seemed like Kit was originally aiming at, I would have liked it to have been unstoppable Academy Award material, but that was outside of the curve for anything that could happen in that short a time — and in that genre… There have been some really great horror movies — and how often are they nominated…? There's a danger in the aberrant members of society wanting to get their fifteen minutes of fame! I think I wanted a little bit more as a movie fan — a bit more bottom, maybe back story…

Mike Sullivan: I rather liked the original script better than the final version. All the humour that Kit had in the original was gone, and I think the film morphed into a chase movie. As for the look of the film, I think Richard Kooris' cinematography captured most of the good qualities of the art direction. A lot of the detail was lost, but I think that is true of almost every film. The only visuals I wish had made it more into the film were the dioramas we created in the tunnels at the Matterhorn.

There were a lot of people who had to invent on that show because we didn't have the money to buy or rent things, so it had to be created in the cheapest way possible. So the use of the imagination in a lot of areas — make-up, props, sets — you had to be inventive. In some ways I think it's probably the most inventive I've ever been on a show. I've worked a lot on historically-based films where you do what we call 'the matching game' — you find historical photographs and then you use them as research material. With *Chainsaw*, there was nothing to use, it was like *Spy Kids* — everything had to be created out of whole cloth, you didn't have something you could refer to, it had to come out of the imagination.

Jim Siedow: I enjoyed them both very much but I enjoyed the second very much more, because it paid so much more! I could only spare a week for the first one, this one took around three months. We all had a really good time. My character was much more fun to do as well. And — compared to the first one — we had our own air-conditioned trailers and everything! It was much more comfortable.

Left:
Bill Johnson and
Tobe Hooper.

Above:
The Family in
'Breakfast Club'
mode.

Richard Kooris: I was very happy with what we had done visually — I think the film looks spectacular, especially given the circumstances we had to work in — I was very happy with my work. The picture that I saw through the viewfinder and the dialogue that I heard — that picture never came out. There are an enormous number of scenes and a lot of character background that got cut — particularly surrounding Dennis Hopper's character. So the script I originally read, and the script we shot — that was not the picture that got cut. I was very disappointed in the cut I saw because I think they basically turned it into a slasher movie, and that was not what the picture was originally. The script I saw was a wonderful, mordant satire on materialism, yuppies, consumerism and the American way of life — Kit did a brilliant job, sort of extended the *Chainsaw* myth in all the ways it should have been as a cultural satire, it was very Swiftian. All that stuff wound up on the cutting room floor — that was my main disappointment, and I think Tobe's too. There was a whole back-story about Dennis Hopper's character — we shot these incredible scenes in his hotel room where he's having all this psychological conflict about things which have happened in his past, he's depressed, almost suicidal…

When you cut all that out it really cheapens Hopper's character — the Texas Ranger becomes a sort of cartoon figure who just wanders through the film with his holstered chainsaws, it just eviscerates the film. It would be wonderful if whoever owns the original material would let Tobe go back and cut the film that he wanted — there really is a great satire buried in there, and we shot most of it…

Caroline Williams: Cannon Films treated Tobe horribly. They were constantly second-guessing him, looking over his shoulder, pulling money, giving money. The film that was written and shot was a wonderful satire. Then they got hold of it, and just fucked it up. [*The Guardian*, 28 Sept 2001]

Bill Moseley: For the most part, my scenes didn't suffer from the editing that went on. One scene I did do that I remember was when Leatherface, the Cook and I were doing an A unit scene with Tobe, then we got put into a van and driven to an under-ground parking garage. Newt was directing this scene where there's a battle between Texas and Oklahoma students. The Rolling Grill AGoGo pulls up and there's a bit of a riot, the students are trying to ransack the truck and Leatherface swings a chainsaw at a Texas student who's making the 'hook 'em horns' sign. Leatherface slices off his hand, it flies through the air, lands and slowly turns into the middle finger… So there was the garage scene, there was the scene with Joe Bob Briggs where we come to a radio station and Leatherface starts chopping up the yuppies and yuppettes… And there was a thing I did, where I'm sewing up the muppet's head wound, 'cause the muppet gets shot at the beginning, and I'm humming 'People Are Strange' while sewing up the hole in my twin brother's head. And I think that was cut out — that was the penultimate scene we shot.

Jim Siedow: I know there were scenes they made him cut that were wonderful scenes… But I don't know why, I really don't. There was one with Chop-Top and me — they were funny as the Devil, don't know why they cut 'em, they were good scenes.

Elite Entertainment's original US laser disc release added ten minutes of deleted scenes (minus sound effects), while a 1996 video release claimed to be a 111 minute 'Director's Cut'; MGM failed include any of the missing sequences on their budget DVD release.

Chainsaw 2 fared even worse in Britain than its predecessor. In 1984 (naturally) the country had succumbed to a wave of anti-horror film hysteria created by the tabloid press and opportunist politicians. The resulting government legislation against so-called 'video nasties' and James Ferman's obsessive desire to protect the

... charmante famille!

MASSACRE
A LA
TRONÇONNEUSE
2

population from the insidious corruption of the film medium ensured it remained unseen for fifteen years, denied even the local certification which allowed its predecessor to be seen in parts of the country.

Chainsaw 2 was first seen by the British Board of Film Classification (a friendlier face than Censors) on 8 October 1986. The examiners were divided between rejection and releasing it as an 18 certificate with serious cuts. Following a second BBFC viewing on 10 October, the examiners were still divided between rejection and release with major censorship cuts. They remained undecided after a third viewing on 15 October, and by 23 October the BBFC could still not reach a decision whether to reject or cut heavily.

On 29 October, Steve Southgate, Technical Manager of Columbia-Cannon-Warner Distributors wrote to the BBFC detailing some of the cuts made in the print they were submitting (referred to as the Northern European Cannon Cut). It's almost impossible to imagine how the film would play in this version:

'The opening scene with the boys in a car when they are attacked, now only consists of one shot of an open head wound.

'Scene in radio station where L. G. is being hit on his head with a hammer now has been reduced to only three blows. (The scene with the girl sitting with her legs astride with Leather Face in front of her with chainsaw remains the same.)

'The scene with Dennis Hopper going into the underground cabin for the first time, where he discovers blood and entrails coming out of a wall has been shortened.

'The complete scene where Leather Face uses an electric knife on L. G. removing flesh from legs, chest, and face has been removed, and also Leather Face placing skin mask on girls face has been removed.

'The scene where Leather Face has chainsaw put through his chest has been shortened to establishing shot only. The scene with Chop-Top cutting his throat has been shortened. The scene with Chop-Top slashing girls back with cutthroat razor has been reduced.'

By 21 May 1987, after *Chainsaw 2* had been resubmitted several times, the BBFC still felt it was 'worth cutting further'. At which point Cannon gave up, and the film languished in the vaults until BBFC director James Ferman retired. The BBFC's Annual Report for 1987 stated: 'No feature film was refused a certificate outright in 1987, although one film, *The Texas Chainsaw Massacre II*, was found to be far too violent for certification. The film's distributors submitted a number of abridged and re-edited versions, but none has yet met the Board's objections to the brutal excesses of the uncut version.'

In 2001 it was finally certificated 18 uncut on video (July) and on film (Aug), receiving its first UK screening at the Frightfest horror film festival in late August.

Bill Moseley: I think Gunnar set the standard but I think Bill was awesome. One of the things which Bill did which was just incredible was the scene where he first meets Stretch and they have their 'sex scene' in the storeroom of the radio station. When she starts challenging him and he ends up putting his saw between her legs — basically, I just thought he did such an amazing job. There were a couple of scenes in *Chainsaw 2* that required a certain kind of, I don't know, sensitivity, if you will, out of Leatherface that I don't think *Chain Saw* required. Not that Gunnar couldn't have done it, I think Gunnar is awesome. I just think that Bill did a really cool job, adding say another little sensitive dimension. Who would ever think of Leatherface as a romantic character? [Interview on amazon.co.uk]

*Below:
Leatherface prior
to his bout
of chainsaw
impotence.*

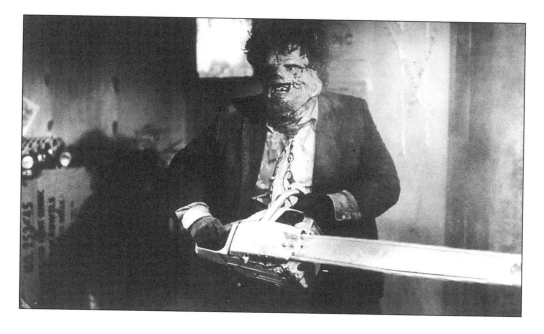

Right:
Leatherface poses
amongst the
records at the
radio station.

Gunnar Hansen: People think of Leatherface as this sort of chubby, loveable guy, but he isn't — basically, Leatherface kills whatever moves... The only people who could possibly think of him as loveable are his family because he does what they tell him — there is no love thing going on!

Bill Johnson: The scene where Caroline is in the tub of ice and Leatherface is running the saw up her inner thigh — I thought, 'I dunno, it doesn't seem like

Leatherface to me...' I thought, 'Man, that's reaching way out' — I'm trying to find a way to justify that as an actor... It just seemed too twisted — who's going to get off on that? My thought is I would want to introduce her to my chainsaw first before getting into that foreplay — you know, 'If you want to make friends then maybe you and saw-saw can kind of get together a bit.' But there was that drive going on — I'd had no experience of offering my point of view, and it didn't seem safe, I didn't know what to do, so I decided I'd better just go with the flow — I just wanted to be accepted, I wanted to be loved!

Gunnar Hansen: What's odd to me is that there have now been five Leatherfaces and I'm the only one that people clearly remember. It's very strange... I met R. A. Mihailoff and went out to dinner with him — I think he thought I was going to be pissed off that he played my role! He's the sweetest guy in the world (he wouldn't want you to know that because he's a biker!). My feeling is the reason people associate me with that role is because I was the original. I had the tremendous advantage of being the original — I got to define the character — so when you see Bill Johnson playing Leatherface in *Chainsaw 2* you're not going to like it, not because he didn't do a good job, but because he couldn't physically recreate the character. If Bill had done it in the first film and I the second, even if I had done a good job (whatever that is) people would still say I hadn't done it right...

Bill Johnson: I have the highest respect for Gunnar — what he did was pretty amazing — he should have got an Oscar nomination! He really gave himself to that character and it was really complex and intense — there was a kind of innocence, like if Calvin had been pushed too far for too long and he'd got a really big body and learned how to use a saw... It was innocent but there was no restraint on sadistic impulses — which were nurtured not to be recognised as sadistic, but as necessary to stay secret and safe — secrecy and safety are the basics: first is survival, and then you can start to develop your higher self — they were still working at the survival level... And any chance at trying to break out of that mould in the second film — here's a stranger, we're not going to eat her, I [Leatherface] have an inclination of some kind that doesn't want to hurt her at all — was certainly squashed: can't have that, no, no...

REVIEWS

The first *Chainsaw* was gruesome and depraved, yes, but it also had an undeniable artistry, and it truly was frightening. *Part 2* has a smirk on its face, and would rather

giggle than scream; at the end, we haven't seen a nightmare — we've just seen a lot of latex face masks and red dye.

His original *Texas Chainsaw Massacre* caught people by surprise with its cast of unknowns, its low-budget documentary feel, and the presumption it was based on reality… The movie had a raw, naked force… In the years since it was made, *Chainsaw* inspired hundreds of films, including the Dead Teenager movies and all of the special effects extravaganzas with rotting flesh and decaying organs.

… Another mistake is to equate screaming and mayhem with suspense. This movie goes flat-out from one end to the other, never spending any time on pacing, on timing, on the anticipation of horror. It doesn't even pause to establish the characters; Dennis Hopper has the most thankless task, playing a man who spends the first half of the movie looking distracted and vague, and the second half screaming during chainsaw duels.
Roger Ebert, *Chicago Sun-Times*, 25 Aug 1986

Mainstream values are pushed beyond the lunatic fringe to reveal a vision at once ghastly and hilarious. Fans of the genre may find the sociological musings an unnecessary distraction, but there's still enough blood let to satisfy their wildest dreams. Director Hooper is back on the Texas turf he knows best and proves there are still a few thrills and chills left to be found.

Performances of the family are fine, especially Siedow and a crazed Moseley, but the real star here is carnage, highlighted through Cary White's production design and Tom Savini's makeup.
Jagr, *Variety*, Aug 1986

… some sickly humorous moments and relentlessly vicious moments, but overall does not seem destined to duplicate the success of the original despite a smart, albeit grotesquely macabre screenplay by L. M. Kit Carson and the return of the original director Tobe Hooper.

Saw 2 does resemble Hooper's earlier films, picking up elements not only from the original but also some of the bizarre humour and surrealism of *Eaten Alive* and a final setting that has strong echoes of Hooper's *Funhouse*. What the film lacks is the relentless oppressive atmosphere of horror that made the first film so unique.
Dennis Fischer, *The Hollywood Reporter*, Aug 1986

... not first-grade chopped steak. The recipe of Tobe Hooper, who directed both movies, is to toss in pinches of humour while the saws roar and the blood and guts flow... Mr Hooper's direction is a little sloppy. You can see that the hammer that is supposed to knock Stretch out never touches her. And his timing is off. Scenes go on too long; Leatherface keeps waving his chainsaw in the air to little effect, and Chop-Top doesn't have much to do except scratch his head for lice, hop around and yell crazy stuff about Vietnam and napalm.
Walter Goodman, *The New York Times*, Aug 1986

... this film was made under every possible adversity... Under these circumstances, it's amazing that the film arouses as much tension and unease as it does. It's too aimless and over-wrought to qualify as a good movie, yet several scenes... remain the most unnerving situations found in Hooper's work after *The Funhouse*. The film is given extraordinary support by Caroline Williams, whose performance builds from believable country girl ambition to a level of hysteria that Shelley Duvall only hinted at in *The Shining*.
Tim Lucas, *Video Watchdog*

... if the original *Texas Chain Saw Massacre* was wrought with a dark and troubling intensity, then part 2 is a laughing clown with a knife poised behind its back: it might make you laugh but it gets you in the end, regardless.
    The Texas Chainsaw Massacre 2 does have its flaws. On its own, it seems a little lost and something akin to a punchline without a joke. Couple it with the first movie however, and the joke suddenly makes a whole lot more sense.
David Kerekes, *Fantasy Film Memories 3*, 1991

Less follow-up than parody... a far more elaborate production than the cheapskate but intense original... The Savini effects that remain in the film... are impressive in a *Fangoria* magazine sort of way, but seem to signal Hooper's admission that he is unable to do without splatter and rely on suspense and imagination as he was able to in his first film.
The Aurum Film Encyclopedia: Horror, Ed Phil Hardy, Revised Edition, 1993 ∎

Opposite top:
Chainsaw chilli
mixture!

Opposite below:
Japanese poster.

Leatherface: Texas Chainsaw Massacre III

"JUNIOR LIKES THEM PRIVATE PARTS"

The *Texas Chain Saw Massacre* was a unique phenomenon, but a unique phenomenon that makes a great deal of money doesn't remain unique for long. And so it was that three years after the slightly disappointing reception to Tobe Hooper's *Chainsaw 2*, New Line Cinema licensed the property for their attempt to duplicate the success of a unique phenomenon... Having made four financially successful entries in the generally atrocious *Nightmare on Elm Street* series, New Line must have assumed they could transfer *Nightmare's* cash cow 'gore and rock' formula to Leatherface and his pals. There was never a chance *Leatherface* could be successful on those terms (although there is a heavy metal theme song over the end credits).

Somewhere in the early stages of pre-production, Tobe Hooper took a story outline for the new instalment to New Line with a view to producing it, but his possible involvement ended once *Spontaneous Combustion* got underway. Writer David J. Schow was contracted for script duties in January 1989, with principal photography planned for June. At this point Kim Henkel was briefly involved.

Kim Henkel: Obviously the Cannon thing hadn't worked too well, so when we were making the deal with New Line, I felt that some input from our end would be valuable — I naïvely assumed that if we had an agreement to do it [*laughs*] there would be some real consideration given... A joke is what I would call it. Theoretically I was supposed to be a consultant. I walked into the single meeting I had with them, and clearly they had already made up their minds about exactly what they were going to do and how they were going to do it, and I was wasting my time. As soon as that became abundantly clear I just shut up. There's no point in beating your head against a wall — obviously they had no intention whatsoever of hearing anything I said. But you know, the whole *Chain Saw* business is just a fluke

— but we were very conscious about what we were doing, it wasn't a hare-brained venture. What the people attempting to follow up on that wanted to do is to imitate its characteristics without any sense of what was going on at the core...

David Schow's credentials were hardly dumbed-down horror-sequel friendly, his reputation largely stemming from dark, violent short stories — but he had written a script for the *Freddy's Nightmares* television series... Perhaps with Hooper producing, Henkel as consultant and Schow writing, the film might have turned out rather differently. By May it was still without a director, and original producer Jeff Schechtman was fired. Numerous potential directors were contacted, amongst them John McNaughton, Peter Jackson, Jerry Olson, Jonathan Betuel, David Blyth, Jon Hess and Jeff Burr. Betuel was chosen but was unable to take the job for contractual reasons. In the meantime New Line executives had viewed *Stepfather II* (coincidentally featuring *Chainsaw 2* star Caroline Williams) the latest film from young director Jeff Burr, and after Betuel was forced to drop out, Burr was hired in mid-June.

But even before Jeff Burr was appointed director and the second draft of the script was completed, Schow had run into trouble with New Line's executives for an excess of violence and offensive material.

Robert Engelman: David Schow's first rough draft of the screenplay was there. I worked with Mike DeLuca, New Line Cinema's Vice President of Production/Development, and made changes, making it less bloody, less graphic, taking it in some different directions. Our film is more graphic [than the original] but without the gore. It is high tension with no letting up. The goal is to underplay the gore, not to focus on it. Though we do have the payoffs, that's what makes this different from the typical slasher or gore film. But, you will need a shower after seeing it! [Press notes]

Mike DeLuca: We set out to make a straight horror film that was relentless and very disturbing. What makes *Chainsaw* so effective is its reality, you can believe it could happen. When we first spoke to David we decided to go back to the tone and feel of the original. When we described what we wanted to David, he took it to a level we weren't quite expecting. We had to pull it back in subsequent drafts, but we were happy with the tone and feel, and we felt it was very much like the first one. [Press notes]

A good cast was assembled (amazingly for New Line: no obnoxious teenagers) including Viggo Mortensen, Ken Foree, Joe Unger and William Butler. By this time

Mortensen was establishing himself as a leading indie/weirdness movie kingpin following major roles in *Salvation!* and *Prison*. Foree was a horror film favourite following his pivotal role in George Romero's *Dawn of the Dead* and Stuart Gordon's outrageous *From Beyond*; Unger a well-established character actor in film and television, while Butler gleefully prided himself on having been butchered in all eight horror movies in which he'd appeared. Kate Hodge made her feature film début as heroine Michelle, and particularly notable was Jennifer Banko as the 'Little Girl', one of the more interesting and disturbing characters added to the *Chainsaw* series over the years. R. A. Mihailoff, a six-foot-five biker whose roles usually consist of truckers and, um, bikers, provided a genuinely menacing Leatherface.

*Above:
Ken Foree
as eccentric
survivalist Benny.*

With Jeff Burr on board the script rewrites continued, Burr objecting to Schow's introduction of Leatherface's new family and his desire to move the film into new areas. Multiple revisions by the scriptwriter can be confusing enough — once the revisions go through the hands of several dabblers the results can be pure chaos. The final insult was the imposition of a 'happy' ending, a sequence not shot by Burr, where Ken Foree, last seen with a chainsaw embedded several inches into his skull, emerges from nowhere to save Kate Hodge...

R. A. Mihailoff: Halfway into filming, the President of New Line Cinema, Bob Shaye, decided that he liked the character Ken Foree played so much that he wanted him to live so he could come back in a sequel. They were scheduled to make parts 4 and 5, and I had a contract option to return as Leatherface in parts 4 and 5. I gladly would have played it. But it was my understanding that at the time *Leatherface* was filmed and readied for release, there were individuals inside New Line who wanted to take the company away from the exploitation of horror films. And even though Bob Shaye did own the company and was a fan of horror, he did not end up with the final say. [Interview by Royce Freeman]

The special effects were executed by the KNB EFX Group, formed by Robert Kurtzman, Greg Nicotero and Howard Berger, and the stunts were coordinated by Kane Hodder, who'd established himself as the best-known Jason in the *Friday the 13th* film series. The production designer was Mick Strawn, veteran of New Line's *Elm Street 3* and *4*, *The Hidden*, and *Critters 2*, who worked in close conjunction with KNB. Between them they endeavoured to give the film a suitably grim, oppressive look, with what should have been some startlingly gruesome effects, including the vertical bisection of Toni Hudson's Sara and an explicit brain-bashing for William Butler.

Nicotero and Strawn worked together to produce the Leatherface mask, sculpted using latex, with Howard Berger's father as the face base. One of Schow's original ideas had been to unmask Leatherface, revealing a mangled, noseless visage hinting that Leatherface had himself been skinned at some point. Ever the optimists, New Line decided to postpone the unmasking for a future episode. The film's opening mask-construction sequence (using slabs of baloney!) is highly effective, while the unmasking scene is noticeably absent despite an obvious lead-up.

Mick Strawn: Originally it was a one-piece mask, which doesn't work. We didn't want to copy what had been done in other films. The final design came out of the concept that it is supposed to be a bunch of pieces of skin sewn together, twisted and torn, and that's what worked in the end. Of the three movies, I think it is the most evil looking. [Press notes]

The major constructions for *Leatherface* were the body pits, the farmhouse and the 'Texas-style' gas station (in spite of the odd cowboy hat and armadillo, *Leatherface* exudes little Texas atmosphere). Schow based the body pits on those found under the house of serial killer John Wayne Gacy. The first appears at the beginning, a four-foot trench filled with human melt-down slime (adipocere), worms and maggots supplied by the production's animal trainer — the worms were specially bred and the maggots came from road kill ('It's unhealthy to breed them'). The numerous skeletons plus four bags of assorted body parts came from material 'lying around' the KNB workshop. Although not overly clear, the idea was the first body pit was on the site of The Family's previous abode. (Caroline Williams visited the set on the night of shooting and appears in an uncredited 'walk-on' as Butler and Hodge arrive at the pit site.) The second pit, in which Ken Foree's final battle takes place, was dug out and lined with gunite, a concrete substance designed for swimming pools, then filled with heated water and more body parts.

James L. Carter: The look of the body pit scenes is much brighter. Like an old Universal horror film, it has that very theatrical look to it. Part of the reason for that is if you make this stuff too real, it doesn't work, you have to take the edge off somewhere. However, some of the night scenes on this one are really dark... we try to keep it that way... a lot of the frame is black, and you see hints of people. We try to make it natural so people will be afraid because it could really happen. [Press notes]

With a budget of around $3 million, principal photography finally began on 17 July 1989 and ended on 27 August, extended from 25 August, shooting over twenty-seven evenings on exterior locations in or around Indian Dunes Park near Valencia (and Magic Mountain theme park), about forty miles north of Los Angeles. (Indian Dunes Park was where the *Twilight Zone — The Movie* helicopter crash took place resulting in the deaths of two Vietnamese children and B-movie stalwart Vic Morrow in 1982.) *Leatherface* was a snake-bit production in every sense: the set was besieged by rattlesnakes, bees, hornets and fog, which drifted in each night around 1am to frustrate the film-makers.

Jeff Burr: The film is over eighty per cent night shooting, and there is just a certain pace a crew can work because it is unnatural working at these hours, that's just human nature.

Below:
Could this be the end of Benny...?

Shooting all night always slows a production's pace down, not intolerably, but it does slow it down. Instead of getting twenty set-ups, you get fifteen, if not fifteen, then twelve. This has been the most affecting movie, to me personally, that I've done because it has been so gruelling. Not only because of the subject matter, but also putting the actors through all this stuff, I feel it with them, and it can be really draining. [Press notes]

Robert Engelman: Exterior nights are always tough, and what made this the toughest was the time of year we picked in that the nights are shortest. We had a seven hour window of darkness with a crew meal in that period. That's what made it extremely difficult. But, we had a great crew that pushed for the absolute very best. [Press notes]

Principal photography completed, *Leatherface* was subjected to three months of post-production trauma. It opened in the US on 12 January 1990 to unenthusiastic reviews and a box office performance deemed disappointing, though its theatrical gross was ultimately over $5.7 million. New Line's editorial interference, re-shoots and the many cuts required to appease the MPAA resulted in a product which pleased neither director, critics nor fans. It's certainly flawed, giving the impression of a film made by a committee who fail to agree on anything, but the acting's fine and there are more than a few moments where sparks of Schow's original, vicious script shine through. While Burr has continued to work in the fantasy and horror genres, *Leatherface* remains one of his better efforts, studio butchery and script tinkering notwithstanding.

Jeff Burr: All this stuff got truncated — and that's way before we even started submitting it to the ratings board. When we ran into all the ratings problems we had to submit it many, many times to get an R. We were cutting the negative because they wanted it to play in theatres right away — so the negative kept getting cut and they never did a protection negative of those scenes. It was a nasty movie, a very nasty movie. The theatrical version made me look incompetent... It was literally incoherent... The last thing I said to Mike DeLuca — 'I want my name off the movie, I want my name off the fucking movie!' And then he hung up... [*Texas Chainsaw Massacre: The Shocking Truth*]

New Line's DVD release includes a 'making of' documentary, many deleted scenes (including the original ending) and commentary from Jeff Burr, David Schow, Greg Nicotero, Mark Ordesky, William Butler and R. A. Mihailoff.

As usual for an entry in the *Chainsaw* series, *Leatherface* was refused a certificate in Britain. Writing to the Managing Director of its distributor Enterprise Pictures on 22 May 1990, James Ferman stated:

'... It is the general view that the film has little purpose other than to exploit the pleasures of pain, fear and butchery, of brutal torture, sadistic violence and mutilation, to the extent that it is a dehumanising experience unsuitable for distribution in the British cinema.

'We have considered carefully whether or not cuts could render this work acceptable for the 18 category, but do not believe it would be possible wholly to remove such elements as the involvement of a small girl and a crippled mother in the game of humiliation, terrorisation and death, with all its air of relishing the corruption of innocence. Nor could it remove the glee with which the film savours the prospect of cutting up the 'private parts' of women, or the agony of the young woman gagged and nailed to the chair. In short, this film seems to glorify cruelty and sadism, especially towards women, in a way which encourages callousness. Nor has it any merits which would justify such a painstaking process of re-editing. Once it gets into its stride, it proves for the most part a humourless, deadening experience, which cuts would do little to alleviate.

Above:
A victim.

'The Board has never given a film or video certificate to the original *Texas Chainsaw Massacre* or the first of its sequels. Please bear in mind that features which have as their primary purpose the selling of killing or maiming as a source of pleasure, or which portray their characters not as feeling human beings but as victims ripe for humiliation, terror and violence, sexual or otherwise, are likely to encounter similar difficulties. We must, therefore, refuse a classification certificate to *Leatherface — Texas Chainsaw Massacre III*.'

Summing up their decision, the Board's Annual Report for 1990 stated:

'The one film refused a certificate in 1990 was *Leatherface — Texas Chainsaw Massacre III*, the third in a series all of which have now been rejected on grounds of violence and terror, particularly towards female victims. This latest in the series was by far the crudest, with its emphasis firmly on torture, cruelty and mutilation, and with a young child encouraged to revel in the atrocities of his cannibalistic family. Cuts were considered but judged to be so extensive as not to be practicable.'

It remains unreleased in Britain at the time of writing, though New Line's DVD will almost certainly be certificated in its uncut form.

AN INTERVIEW WITH SCRIPTWRITER DAVID J. SCHOW

How did you become involved? Were you happy to become part of the Chainsaw *'family'?*
It was my very first feature screenplay gig, so I was fairly ecstatic. It would not have happened had I not been championed by Mike DeLuca, then a development guy at New Line. *Leatherface*, in fact, was Mike's first official credit as producer. Mike originally called me in to New Line for meetings based on reading my short fiction, and it should be pointed out that finding a studio person who actually *reads*, as in 'for pleasure', is virtually unheard of. At that time New Line was on the brink of its fifth Freddy film, *A Nightmare On Elm Street: The Dream Child.* I submitted a treatment titled 'Freddy Rules' and we were all ready to go when the studio said, 'Now, all we need is to see another screenplay you've written,' and I was busted — because I didn't have one. I was practically the only person in Hollywood *without* a script in their back pocket. So I did not get that gig. Subsequently, I pitched to Jeff Freilich, who was producing the *Nightmare* TV show (cumbersomely titled *A Nightmare On Elm Street: Freddy's Nightmares*). I wrote an episode titled 'Safe Sex'. Within twenty-four hours of delivery of that first draft script, Kevin Moreton of New Line signed me to do their next horror project, which was *Leatherface.*

Below:
Leatherface and
his monster truck.

Left:
Leatherface
behind the wheel.

And, just for closure's sake, *Nightmare* 5 trickled down through four other writers during this time. While they were shooting the movie I was engaged to do several dialogue polishes — there was literally a runner taking pages from my house to the set. Then, as frosting, I got to play Freddy — well, part of him, anyway — his right hand, for the trailer to that film.

How difficult was it to avoid references to previous films? Did you go out of your way to do so? Were you told to?
I worked principally with Mike DeLuca and the original line producer, and their only mandate was to be scary and edgy; remember — New Line wanted to rebuild *Chainsaw* as a franchise, based on this movie. Typically, studios will tell you to go 'all the way' or 'over the top' — nothing is too outrageous a proposition until the script is delivered, whereupon, sometimes, you *then* hear, 'Ahhh... not *that* over the top, please.' I wanted to reference the original film in subtle ways, by echoing the little astrological elements, by exploiting what we called the 'Conelrad' radio-interference noise, by updating and trumping aspects of Leatherface's familial group, which I purposefully transformed into an 'adopted' family of new characters. 'The Saw is Family' tagline is actually from the second movie, and its echo here was on purpose, too.

Above:
Benny and
soon-to-be-
butchered Sara.

Were you given complete freedom with the script or were there certain elements you were asked to include?

Part of the process is that ideas generate notes which generate more ideas, but at the first draft stage this interplay is not apparent. One idea that helped sell the script was the inclusion of what we semi-punningly referred to as the 'monster truck' or the 'terror truck', with a hood bra made out of tanned human flesh. The character of Tinker was originally named Tinkerbell, and I think Legal gave that a no-no because of Disney. But Tink's place was as family patriarch. This was to lead to a reveal whereby we discover that Tink, who had a huge chroming vat, had replaced some anatomical attribute of each member of the new family with a substitute made out of electroplated human bones, which is what Leatherface's leg brace was originally made out of. I very consciously made the montage at the beginning — close shots of Leatherface assembling a new leather face from bits and pieces of assorted victims — mirror the beginning of *A Nightmare On Elm Street* (Freddy assembling his bladed glove), to speak to New Line's need for a franchise and imply a relationship between the two films.

How many drafts before a shooting script was arrived at? Was it subject to much change as the shooting progressed? How closely were you involved with the film as it progressed? How

long was your involvement — from starting the script to the end of shooting/whenever...?
As I recall this was pretty tightly scheduled, and most of the hardcore work was done on the 'draft and set', which means the first draft, then revisions, then a polish. Interim revisions and tweaks absorbed the rest of the time, and major changes weren't really worked until Jeff Burr got on set and added his spin to the whole enterprise. I was there through most of the shooting, because frequently you are called upon to invent filler bits of business on the spot.

It's always been said the film was subject to much editing to avoid a US X rating — true? Was that material you wrote or effects that they just got 'carried away' with?
I think it's safe to say that New Line was a bit mortified at the initial assembly — but remember, that's because they knew the MPAA would raise a shitstorm that could possibly hamper the release. It pretty quickly became obvious that cutting footage was no solution, because the MPAA can object to a movie based on amorphous qualities such as 'tone'. So you set out to make an intense movie, then you have to reel the intensity back and back and back in order to appease some censor who can prevent the release of your film. If you cut a movie enough, it just bleeds to death. New Line was really stuck between a rock and a hard place, because when you cut enough footage, suddenly your running time is in jeopardy and you have to make the very hard decision to either re-think the whole endeavour, or shoot new footage to Band-Aid the missing stuff. And remember, all the time you've got a scheduled release date staring you in the face like a loaded gun.

So it was not so much a question of getting 'carried away' with the effects, because it turned out that a lot of the effects initially suggested were not even shot due to lack of time. Here's an example: The death of Sara (Toni Hudson; the movie's 'prior victim' and the one who warns Benny that there are weirdos in the woods), began with her slumped against a tree. Leatherface jams the chainsaw into the tree at the base, between her legs, and saws *upward*, bisecting her. But all you were supposed to see of this hideousness was a silhouetted POV from *behind* the tree. Cut to a close-up of Leatherface

Below: Part of Leatherface's new Family.

as the sawdust from the tree swirls around him. The sawdust turns red. Then cut back to the POV from behind the tree as the two halves of Sara drop away in different directions. The sequence was not the forensic butcher-shop gorefest you might imagine it to be. KNB EFX actually built the dummy of Sara, and I think you see it in one brief shot, but in the film you see a close-up of Leatherface, ramming the saw, and that's it. Months later, Joe Bob Briggs notes that this is a chainsaw movie with no real 'chain-sawing' in it (that is, on-camera butchery), and it's nearly impossible to disagree with him.

As far as your script went, what aspects did they particularly object to?
It wasn't a question so much of objection to the script as objections logged on the first cut of the film. As far as my involvement went, most objections were after the fact.

Above:
The creepy
'Little Girl'.

There's the creepy 'Little Girl' — the BBFC in Britain were not happy about her — but don't you think she's a staple of the horror genre?
God, I hope so — children can be particularly malignant and sadistic, especially in moral terms, where any activity devolves to the level of scruple-less play. You can't win. You deliberately avoid showing children getting victimised (a huge no-no, despite the fact that kids get victimised all the time in the real world) by empowering them to do the victimizing, then some censor screams that it's imitable behaviour and, 'Children wouldn't do that, except in your sick movie.' Believe me, children *would* do that sort of thing. And given Jennifer Banko's 'family environment', as it were, her behaviour, while not socially acceptable, is perfectly in context for her situation.

How do you feel when the morality arbitrators try to dictate what is 'acceptable' in art?
The galling aspect of that hot-button issue is that generally the people who attempt to Mommy/Daddy the tastes of the whole world are not, and never were, the *audience* for a movie like this. I think the sickening proliferation of bare baby butts in TV commercials looks like, at best, a smorgasbord for paedophiles — but I can't ban that, because it's sold as cute and acceptable, and besides, what do I know — I wrote a frickin' *Chainsaw* movie!

Another thing that riles me — 'critics' of the series bleat about 'violence against women'...
Okay, let's stop right there. Total bullshit. Proof that the people criticizing the movie
are not the audience for the movie in the first place. Rarely have any such people even
seen the movie — they're objecting on the principle of even *doing* a movie like this.
Anybody who watches horror films — especially series horror films — can tell you
that not only do the women prevail in most cases, against terrible odds, but they're
usually the last person standing. Horror films have done more to advance the concept
of the heroine than any other genre. Without the original *Chain Saw*, you never would
have gotten to *Aliens*, if you follow. Horror films, quite unintentionally I think, have
done more to empower women than anything on Lifetime — you know, all those
movies with titles like *Not With My Daughter, You Don't*.

I feel the violence in the Chainsaw *films is actually less sexualised than in most horror films
(apart from the obvious scene in* Chainsaw 2 *which is quickly turned around) — it strikes
me that the* Chainsaw *films contain 'violence against everybody'...*
Leatherface was consciously structured as a film about family values. Granted, the
family values are a little twisted, but they're *there* — a definite hierarchy, mutual
respect, and a role for every member within the family dynamic. The only sexual
aspect is that Leatherface occasionally propagates with some of his victims. Why?

Below:

'Shall I carve?'

Leatherface

prepares

for dinner.

Right:
Tex gets romantic
with Michelle.

To enlarge the family, which is where the little girl played by Jennifer Banko came from. The next generation, the fruit of his loins. All very acceptable and cuddly, except that here we're dealing with a vicious family of predators. At the same time, you may think it's brutal or over-attenuated, but it's no more brutal in sum than the behaviour of a wolf pack.

*If ever there's been a series where the violence is utterly nihilistic and the outlook totally
bleak, it's this one. OK, I'm ranting here — can I have your thoughts?*
I love bleak, nihilistic scenarios, because in fiction they permit us to acid-test human
values by proxy. You will probably never face a situation this dire, but if you did, what
would you do? Would you roll over and become somebody's dinner, or would you
bootstrap yourself up to the challenge and survive at any cost? Everybody talks a lot
about 'just grab that gun', but in real life, could you muster the spine to actually shoot
somebody? How far does the ante have to go up before you would submit to debase-
ment in order to prevail? Horror fiction is about turning that knob up all the way, and
the question it asks most often is, 'What would *you* do?' Which accounts, I think, for
its longevity.

*Got to ask — what was Viggo Mortensen like? He was in a load of pretty impressive
exploitation films before you know what. Was he into it or was he biding his time, waiting
for a big break? Do you think he still talks about films like this or do you think they're now
a blot on his CV?*
We shot *Leatherface* right before Viggo did *The Reflecting Skin*, which was the first
film of his that really impressed me. He was completely committed and did not
'think down' to the material. His memory of this movie may be different, but I like
to perpetuate the gentle lie that New Line was the crucible of major soon-to-be stars.
What was the next movie I did there? *Critters 3*. Not of much note, except it was Leo
DiCaprio's first feature credit. After that, *Critters 4* — bang, Angela Bassett. Do you
see a pattern here? Besides, Viggo was pretty hot as a blonde, don't you think?

How was the atmosphere on the shoot?
I'd charitably describe it as tense, since there was so little time and so many gaps for
Jeff Burr to fill on a moment's notice. We were stuck in Valencia for most of the
shoot. 115 degree days. A lot of people don't know the farmhouse set was practical
— that is, if you entered that house, you were standing on the sets for the interior
of the house — and our set was dead between the sets for *Tour of Duty* and *China
Beach*, and Hueys were constantly flying over — it was like shooting in the middle
of the Vietnam war.

Was it on the whole an enjoyable experience? Were you happy with how it finally came out?
I loved it to death. I have to; it's sort of my first cinematic 'child', despite its birth
defects. Despite the mantra of 'if only' and 'more time, more time'. I'm still in touch
with a lot of the principals. They all remember the movie fondly. In fact, if you go
to my website, you'll see a picture of me and R. A. Mihailoff and Ken Foree the day

after the last day of shooting. Then you'll see a shot of us all, thirteen years later, in the company of a guy named Robert Meyer Burnett, whose first real movie job was as a PA on *Leatherface*. Then he wrote and directed *Free Enterprise*.

How do you think Leatherface *ultimately compares with the other films in the series?*
I was very concerned with how Tobe Hooper might react, because I like and respect Tobe, and his attitude was completely professional and non-judgemental. He did like some of the notions I concocted which, for one reason or another, were not incorporated into the movie. The second film, the first sequel, seems far more compromised to me. I haven't seen the others.

Incidentally, there's a 1939 Hindi film also called *Leatherface*, featuring a guy in a leather mask. I haven't seen it.

REVIEWS

... a toothless, sadistic horror film that ranks at the bottom of the barrel among recent, pointless sequels. Providing zero fun for gore fans is the fact that the killings take place off-screen, presumably due to cuts needed to get the film its R rating in place of the original X that delayed its release from last November. Acting is shrill, and the attempt to create some sympathy for the disgusting cannibals... is ridiculous. Leatherface...

Below:
Leatherface
revs up.

shambles along with a gamy leg in a brace and is therefore a cornball, old fashioned monster.
Lor, *Variety*, 17 Jan 1990

Director Jeff Burr acquits himself adequately and David Schow's script manages a sick vein of humour throughout. But what distinguishes it is the lighting and the editing which insures that the adventures of Michelle and Benny have a real adrenalin-soaked edge to them.
Farrah Anwar, *City Limits*, 27 Sept-4 Oct 1990

Superior to both *Part II* and the subsequent *Next Generation*, the film's frenetic energy and haunting visuals convey the story with punch and style. Although it initially went unnoticed, it's one of the better Bs of the decade, offering an equal share of chills and thrills.
Mike Emery, *The Austin Chronicle*, 2 Nov 1998

This second sequel to Tobe Hooper's 1974 cult hit is a hell of a lot better than 2... Despite his vociferous complaints, the script by splatterpunk author David Schow

remains faithful to the backwoods weirdness of the original and there are some nasty touches with a brain-bashing machine and a homicidal little girl. Director Burr gives the film a classy look, with one of the most atmospheric swamp sets since *Son of Dracula*.
Stephen Jones, *Shock Xpress 1*, Titan Books 1991

... this is a listless sequel. Leatherface limps unmenacingly with a leg-brace... Shot in California with cowboy hats and armadillos, this has none of the Texan atmosphere of the original. Novelist Schow's screenplay has a few memorably brutal lines... but little else.
The Aurum Film Encyclopedia: Horror, Ed Phil Hardy, Revised Edition 1993

Mostly a remake of the first film: cannibal clan battle three would-be dinners. Severely damaged by pre-release cuts designed to reduce gore but which only make the film incoherent.
Leonard Maltin's Movie & Video Guide, Penguin Books ■

"THERE'S NO WAY YOU CAN GO OVER THE TOP!"

Paul Partain: Getting a film shot, edited and distributed is a tremendous task. Not a venture for the faint of heart.

Shot in roughly six weeks in late summer 1993 on a meagre $600,000 budget, the fourth instalment of the *Chainsaw* series was written, co-produced and directed by Kim Henkel, who was less than enthusiastic about the project, especially directing. The prime mover behind *Return of* was producer Robert Kuhn, who, together with Henkel, licensed the property from Charles 'Chuck' Grigson, trustee for the owners of the original *Chain Saw*. Motivated by a combination of lingering unhappiness concerning the financial fate of the original and the desire to generate some cash with a new, they set up River City Films and Ultra Muchos as production companies, hoping to make the film independently then market it to a major for distribution — a standard device of independent production. What no one could have foreseen was the sudden rise to fame of *Return* stars Renee Zellweger and Matthew McConaughey, virtual unknowns at the time of shooting. Both had appeared in teen zombie movie *My Boyfriend's Back* (also featuring Edwin Neal) and Austin director Richard Linklater's *Dazed and Confused*, with Zellweger also receiving attention in the low-budget crime film *Love and a .45*. By the time *Return* found a distributor, it had become obvious the two were destined for Hollywood big-name status. In most cases such a factor should attract business from curiosity value alone, but this being a *Chainsaw* film, complications were bound to arise…

Robert Kuhn: There is a trustee [Chuck Grigson] who has the authority — but doesn't actively try — to promote it [the estate of *The Texas Chain Saw Massacre*], so between

Kim and I, if we see anything, we try to make a few bucks out of the deal. And of course we licensed this sequel in the hopes that we would get the franchise back rolling.

Brian Huberman: Kim seemed kind of weary of it even before it really got started. I think he might have been aware of what was going to happen — my sense was that he did not willingly go down that path, that it was not something he actively sought out, that it was something that was offered to him — I think Bob Kuhn was behind it, that Kuhn had urged him for many years to do it.

Levie Isaacks: I think the influence that Bob Kuhn exerted on Kim was basically through the writing of the script — he wasn't a hands-on producer, on the set all the time. What he did was he brought down a guy, a former teacher from UT, who watched us — he was like Bob's rep on the set. He left us alone, he was there to watch out, he was paid by Bob to look after his interests, he was kind of Bob's spy — but he was certainly not harmful…

Kim Henkel: Bob was involved with the original as an investor. Also he's an attorney and had done some legal work… Bob Kuhn started trying to get me to do it some time before I finally agreed to, but he was very eager. I *was* interested in directing, but I wasn't interested in directing *this* particular film, it just didn't interest me to direct that *kind* of film. But we weren't happy with any of the other prospects…

Levie Isaacks: It was early '93 and I was working on the *Tales From the Crypt* series when I got the call from Kim asking if I'd come out. My schedule was open so I thought, 'Why not?' I'd stayed in contact with Tobe, Kim, Lou, who's one of my best friends, and Eagle Pennell… He was another strange bird, an interesting guy, but terribly flawed to the point where alcohol took his life.

It was pretty low budget, and Kim wanted somebody who was strong in camera — that's why he called me — so that between the two of us we could do something that would work. He gave me a lot of leeway — I picked the locations and oftentimes staged the scene, made lots of suggestion in terms of how to stage it. I was working with a totally new crew, some of whom weren't very experienced. Focus is always a problem — I didn't have an experienced guy — keeping the movie in focus is hard, but I seem to remember that most of the movie's in focus [*laughs*].

What's phenomenal about that picture is the cast — Matthew McConaughey and Renee Zellweger, caught just prior to becoming shooting stars. And they were both really good in the movie, maybe more her than Matthew. He said to me, 'You know, in this kind of role there's no way you can go over the top!' He just let himself go…

Production got underway in August 1993, following a two-month drought. As with the first *Chain Saw*, temperatures regularly topped 100 degrees, resulting in heatstroke cases on the set.

Above:

Jenny fights back.

Levie Isaacks: It was very muggy — one of the things I tried to do was give it a real hot, humid feel, so I used warm light for the moonlight to try to make it feel more sticky and icky... We ended up shooting the car [interior] scene at night in a warehouse using poor man's process. With the lights and all it was easily 110 degrees — we had to close all the doors and make it dark so we could do it. It was close to being dangerously hot — people could have had heatstroke.

Mostly we shot at night so we had some relief from being out in the sun all day, but that part of Texas can get pretty humid, so there were a lot of hot, muggy nights. We were shooting out on somebody's ranch and there was lots of poison ivy — people ran through it because you can't see where you're going at night, I can't tell you how many people came down with poison ivy. That was probably the most debilitating part of the shoot.

Kim Henkel: August in Texas — it was brutal. It wasn't quite as bad as the original in that we didn't have any of these thirty-six hour marathons, but we had long, long night shoots that seemed to go on for weeks — they were completely disorienting.

Part of it was shot in Pflugerville, that's where the house was. The stuff in the woods was around Bastrop, east of Austin. There's an area out there called Lost Pines, a dense pine forest, in an area where there are no pine forests — it covers thousands of acres but it's still relatively small, all things considered. We shot things like some of the sequences in the car in a warehouse… It took about twenty-two days to shoot altogether — but it's not unusually short for low-budget movies.

Lisa Newmeyer: It was a crazy shoot. Very long. One thing that was interesting about it was that it was shot in sequence… The first couple of weeks were really fun, you know? It was all the easy stuff. And then, as it went on, we were doing mostly night shoots, in Bastrop, so we'd shoot from say, seven in the evening until seven — sometimes ten — in the morning, the next day. So it got pretty gruelling. And it became more violent. It just kind of progressed. It became more exhausting — and more disturbing — as the material got more physically demanding. It was fun, up to a point. [Interview by Marc Savlov, *The Austin Chronicle*, Oct 1997]

Levie Isaacks: It was pretty much shot in sequence — it was the kind of script where you could — it's always something that actors like, because they can build their performance. We ended up reshooting or adding a shot, the death scene at the end — we couldn't get Matthew McConaughey, we had to shoot around him 'cause he couldn't be there. It was just pieces to fit in — they had no money, and we were doing a big stunt with a crop duster and didn't have much to work with. We had to shoot some blood on the wing to make it clear that the crop duster came down and took out Matthew McConaughey.

Robert Jacks: We were all so emotionally damaged by the end of the third week or so that Renee and I called a meeting with the director and the producer because we were so beat up and so bruised up that we just couldn't take it anymore, you know, mentally *or* physically, which is unheard of. What you see in that movie is exactly what we went through. There isn't anything in there that's fake. It's all real. [Interview by Marc Savlov, *The Austin Chronicle*, Oct 1997]

Levie Isaacks: Unlike Tobe, Kim had never really made a film before. But he was pretty good, he was very credible — particularly in terms of performances — he had a good grasp of the characters and what they were supposed to do.

Below:
Vilmer stomps on Darla.

He did have a lot of trouble with Tonie Perenski — her problem was that she's pretty! I remember, here we are, we're doing a scene where Matthew has got her down, has got his foot on her neck and is beating the crap out of her and in all the moving around for the set-up she'd gone off and made herself up again perfectly. I'm looking at her saying, 'You look great! You're not supposed to look like that!' She just couldn't bear herself to look haggard or beat up. She told me later, 'You should see me do a comedy — comedy I can do!' But I thought she turned out really well in that — at the time I know Kim was concerned, but in the end I thought she did a fabulous job.

Robert Jacks: My first night on set I had to use a chainsaw for a couple of minutes. I had to cut through these saplings to get to Renee — and I had to do this sort of viciously, and then run myself out of camera. So I started to do it, I was hacking through these tree limbs, and suddenly everybody in the entire company leaves their posts because they thought I had gone insane. To this day, half of them still think I really went crazy and the other half think, 'Wow, this fag can really do this.' That was pretty funny because I hadn't heard of anything like that happening on a movie set before. [Interview by Marc Savlov, *The Austin Chronicle*, Oct 1997]

Kim Henkel: Robbie's a big guy, and he's usually a very gentle, soft-spoken character... Once he put on that mask and he got that chainsaw in his hands and we turned him loose, he was transformed. He was truly frightening swinging that thing around... People were just scattering and diving behind trees and into the bushes right and left. [Interview by Marc Savlov, *The Austin Chronicle*, Oct 1997]

Lou Perryman: Robbie Jacks was a real character, a really big guy, very heavy. His place was like a salon, there'd always be people there hanging around, talking, smoking... He had a massive collection of toys — models from movies, monsters, stuff like that. He was a funny guy, very popular...

Robert Jacks died a day before his forty-second birthday, on 8 August 2001, of an abdominal aneurysm. Jacks was another much-loved Austin character, involved in theatre, radio shows (including one with Butthole Surfer Gibby Haynes), writing, singing (his duet with Deborah Harry — a lifelong ambition for Jacks — is featured on *Return of*) — just about everything, one of his many ventures being writing and acting in *Boy Trouble*, a musical/play about the '80s Austin punk scene.

While not strictly a remake or re-imagining, *Return of* does mutate a few sequences from the original film and re-run them in a slightly off-kilter manner. More interestingly, though not always entirely successfully, Henkel chose to play a few games with the characters and the viewer's expectations by adding some quirks and a new, more ominous sexual element. Besides the writing of Leatherface as a transvestite, a more satisfying addition was Darla, played by Tonie Perenski — a predatory, slightly unhinged female 'family' member with an aggressive sexual appetite.

Kim Henkel: There's the strange sexual things that go on — not only Darla and Vilmer of course, but Darla and Jenny as well... The confused sexuality of the Leatherface character is complex and horrifying at the same time. [*The Return of the Texas Chainsaw Massacre: The Documentary*]

Tonie Perenski: There's something about the violence that's really exciting and dangerous and really sexual... [*The Return of the Texas Chainsaw Massacre: The Documentary*]

Left:

Leatherface,

Vilmer and Darla

whoop it up.

Kim Henkel: Darla was based on Carla Faye Tucker, who was executed in Texas a few years ago. When she was a very young woman she was involved with a boyfriend in some sort of drug deal that went wrong — they wound up killing two people, very violently [with a pickaxe]. I had remembered reading about this woman, who had a horrendous history, one of those God-awful childhoods you read

Above:
Heather screams. about in pulp magazines and you can't believe are really true. And she had described the murders and the sexual nature of her response to them; she was very explicit about it. Ultimately a lot of that got cut, but there was a scene with that character witnessing the last battle between the heroine and the bad guy…

A key scene in *The Return* occurs at the beginning, with Zellweger's character Jenny menaced by her stepfather in her bedroom while preparing for the school prom. The purpose here was to draw parallels between her oppressive family background and that of 'Chainsaw Family', providing her character with extra strength and motivation to fight back against the sexual menace of Vilmer and cohorts. This important sequence was cut by Columbia TriStar for unspecified reasons when they released the film as *Texas Chainsaw Massacre: The Next Generation*.

Brian Huberman: Columbia's idea to call it *The Next Generation* was just appalling, a betrayal of the original idea. And the removal of the abuse is just — that scene is really key to the film.

Robert Kuhn: And all in the name of art.

Kim Henkel: There was also a further confrontation with the stepfather, a sort of Hansel and Gretel motif that was part of the original, but I cut that out because the damn thing just ran too long. There was a bit about a character who comes up on a motorcycle at the prom scene that got cut out, which had to do with family, the family dynamic and children moving away from the embrace of the family. Most of what's on that screen is what I could get and not what I wanted, that's just the way it is, especially with these low budget deals... You make do with what you can get.

While some of the original concepts were cut from the script of *Return* for one reason or another, Henkel did succeed in making Jenny a much more powerful heroine than Sally Hardesty. While Sally had attempted to fight back in the original film, she had never quite successfully turned the tables on her pursuers.

Kim Henkel: In *Return of* I tried to push that even further: Jenny takes over, she pulls a shotgun on them, she tries to manipulate things…

Return of really takes a departure from the norm with the introduction of Rothman, a sort of Illuminati character who holds forth on the purpose of Jenny's torments and the existence of the Chainsaw Family: that of showing victims the true nature of horror. McConaughey, with his line 'Vilmer's whole gig is that he despises the straight kill' in Huberman's documentary, certainly appeared to grasp the concept.

Kim Henkel: Well, I just wanted to play with the notion, but for some reason the way it came off was not quite the way I anticipated or expected. There's a scene where the Darla character talks about a conspiracy, even the Kennedy assassination — people tend to take that literally, that these people were involved in that, whereas my take on it was that anything out of this woman's mouth should be suspect, not looked at as in any way straightforward. And that's the way I looked at much of what was going on, to suggest that there are other possibilities — possibilities that range beyond the confines of the house, but what are they exactly? Who knows?

The true nature of horror — I guess that was a thing that doesn't really come through, but the background to that particular character's thinking is that what has occurred over time is the way which people die, the way in which people approach death, has been radically changed. We no longer experience death as we once did, we are removed from the reality of it, the horror of it, because we're medicated, advances in medicine isolate and insulate us from it — and what he wanted to institute was a real confrontation with the horror of death, because he believed it was essential to the complete journey, to complete the life cycle.

Above:
Vilmer in
the kitchen.

In spite of the attempt to depict the true nature of horror, *Return of* lacks the graphic violence that got the previous two pictures into trouble…

Kim Henkel: Well, I was probably a little squeamish — we probably should have done it. I don't mind doing it, the making of it, the writing of it — and I don't mind it in something that I've done, but I wouldn't go in to watch somebody else's horror film…

There was a pleasant surprise in store for fans of the original who watched the last sequence closely. Marilyn Burns (billed as 'Anonymous'), Paul Partain (as a medical orderly pushing Marilyn on a hospital trolley) and John Dugan (the cop questioning Renee Zellweger) make cameo appearances.

Paul Partain: It had been a long time since I had turned away from acting in the late '70s. Had a career choice to make and no regrets at choosing a different path, but still every now and then I would listen to the recorded production hotline at the Texas Film Commission. There I learned that Kim was producing and directing a sequel so I grabbed an old résumé, went downtown to his production office and basically just said I wanted to play. Kim had been working on writing a scene for Marilyn and John and it was very nice that Kim did decide to include that scene and expand it a bit to let me in. Working with Kim and the gang again was very good and it did get some juices flowing once more that I had missed.

The fun for me was in the shooting and in the interaction between the old *Chain Saw* gang and the new kids — well, the only one left by the time we were on set was Renee. She was a doll. At that time she was in her mid twenties, college grad, just getting started. She looked like she ought to be seventeen years old at the most. I asked her if she was old enough to be here and she immediately broke out the greatest smile, one that the world knows now, and said she had just found her new best friend.

The film speaks for itself. It has some terrific acting by Matthew Mahogany or whatever his name is, and by my buddy Renee Zellweger. But Tonie Perenski steals the show as Darla. In my opinion, it is worth going to see just for those moments.

One mistake we made: the credits should have just said 'Franklin, Sally and Grandpa.' Didn't think of that until way too late.

Marilyn Burns: I like Kim, and he asked me if I wanted to do something in the movie, like a nurse with three lines or something. But I'm Screen Actors Guild — so I called them, and they said, 'OK, you can do this small part but someone has to dub your lines.' I don't want someone dubbing me! So I'm pictured briefly on a gurney running by some crazy woman, which is Renee being questioned by John Dugan, and I'm being driven by Paul Partain and I'm unrecognisable. But I've never seen it — I've never even really considered myself in that movie!

Lou Perryman: Kim asked me to do a part, at one point he wanted me to do the Rothman role, but I had to say no because of SAG, I could have gotten into a lot of trouble, they can fine you a huge amount if you appear in a non-union picture. I even phoned SAG to ask about it, and ended up talking to Harry Medved on the phone!

Perryman's presence would certainly have livened up proceedings, though it's hard to imagine him in the Rothman part... Wayne Bell scored the picture, though much of his work was dropped in favour of music by Texas artists.

Left:
Vilmer continues
to amuse himself.

Wayne Bell: It was decided before I got there that a lot of rock music would be used... I have a piano without keys, just the frame with the strings from inside, like a harp — you'll hear some of that in *Return of...* But much of my work on that is pretty crappy — there are a few cues that I am proud of — there's a little sounder when we first see the house, and there's a cue where Renee Zellweger is out on the road, basically a load of red herring stuff that ends with her being frightened by a plastic bag or something — musically I was pretty happy with that. And the title music is pretty good. There's no electronics in it — what sounds like electronics is actually cymbals played with a violin bow. But with a lot of the chase stuff I fell into the traps a lot of people fall into... And like Tobe and Jerry Lambert, who became slaves to the sampler with their score for *Chainsaw 2* — the sampler was quite new at the time — I became a slave to the power of the computer on *Return of*, linking up exact synchrony between synthesizers and the time-coded picture. And that was a mistake. I should have used the same technique as Tobe and I did in the first film — I'm sure Kim would have preferred it, I'm not sure if he knew how we did it — and created a library of material with general ideas (this sound goes with that kind of scene) that can be drawn on for different dramatic purposes...

Below:
Darla takes it out
on Vilmer.

Production completed in 1994, Henkel and Kuhn began to look for a distributor for the finished film. *Return* seems to have hung in limbo for some time. Reviews began to appear in spring '95, but at that point a distributor still hadn't been found. A weekend of test screenings took place in August '95, and *Return* was finally sold to Columbia TriStar in October. It was never officially released in the US under its original title in its original version.

Robert Kuhn: It never had two separate releases. What we did was we hired a company to do a test marketing: we opened it in several theatres scattered across the country over a weekend, with very little advertising other than just normal listings, no promotion at all. That was under the original title of *Return of...*

Kim Henkel: We took it out and did some test marketing but it didn't have a release — it never had a proper release in the original version. After the test screenings we got a call from Columbia TriStar and they made us an offer that we felt was the best way to go. New Line had had an opportunity to pick it up for distribution, but they didn't express an interest. They didn't own the rights to the title — at that time they had no entitlement to it at all. They never *bought* the first one — we've always retained the rights. They behaved like it belonged to them [*laughs*] but it didn't!

Robert Kuhn: This thing with Columbia TriStar — if it wasn't so sad it would really be funny, it's half funny the way it is...

It soon became apparent that the deal with Columbia wasn't working out the way the partners had anticipated. With McConaughey and Zellweger about to become major stars with the releases of *A Time to Kill* and *Jerry Maguire*, 1996

should have been a good year for Henkel and Kuhn. But despite Columbia trailering the film as 'Coming soon to a theater near you' in early '96, nothing happened.

Above:

Leatherface

with his

Robert Kuhn: The only reason I went with them was because they guaranteed me a theatrical release. In their contract they agreed to spend no less than $500,000 on prints and ads for the theatrical release, and it was going to be a 1,000 print release nationwide. They didn't, but kept telling me they were going to. They were originally going to release it in July '96, then they decided to wait till after *Jerry Maguire*, they put off the release. And then they just went away — next it was 'the first week in January' — then I didn't hear anything, so I wrote their lawyer about March '97: she wrote me back and said they intended to follow the contract. We finally sued them and they did this little token release.

'sludgehammer'

(see last review

on page 219).

At some point during the period of its languishing in non-release, those involved in the making of *Return* became convinced that Columbia TriStar were holding it up at the behest of Creative Artists Agency, who represented Matthew McConaughey. In an interview, McConaughey has since denied any involvement, saying he enjoyed making the

Above:
Jenny jumps
for it.

film and that his performance was one of his favourites.

Levie Isaacks: There were new movies with Matthew and Renee coming out and I guess CAA just didn't want them associated with a horror movie... Bob filed suit — I don't know if anything came of it.

Brian Huberman: Maybe they [Zellweger and McConaughey] were afraid it was going to be used to inhibit the advance of their careers.

Robert Kuhn: I'm not positive about it one way or the other but I'm fairly convinced that Creative Artists did at one point stop it being distributed. Whether at some point Columbia decided 'to hell with it' and didn't want to do it anyway I'm not certain. But they were going to release it in July '96 and I was talking to Clint Culpepper, the vice-president who did the deal with me [named one of the 100 most influential people in Los Angeles in 1999] damn near on a daily basis, because they were getting ready to release it and I was interested in what they were going to do, how much they were spending, and he told me that Creative Artists was holding us up, and that he was trying to fight it through. He called me one day and said, 'Well, we're going to do the 1,000 print release': they'd finally decided they weren't going to pay any attention to what Creative Artists said. And so we waited, and eventually he called to say, 'Well, we decided it'd be foolish not to wait to get the benefit of *Jerry Maguire*, that's two big stars and I know we'll do well, we'll wait till January.' But in November they just shut it off, I never heard from anyone again.

After changing its title and, more importantly, removing the opening scene where Zellweger's Jenny is shown to be the subject of abuse, Columbia finally released *Texas Chainsaw Massacre: The Next Generation* to a mere twenty-three theatres nationwide in August 1997. The date was changed on the opening credits from 'May 22 1994' to 'May 22 1996', though the end credits still retain the orig-inal title! Besides removing the abuse of Jenny, a cou-ple of scenes were edited by a few seconds and restructured, but no other major cuts occurred.

Below:
Video jacket for
the unreleased
version.

Brian Huberman: Columbia just did lip service to a release, they did the minimum — it's really cruel.

Levie Isaacks: It's the way in Hollywood — it hap-pens all the time — they have all the advantages and you have none.

Robert Kuhn: They say they changed the title and edited it because it would sell better in the video stores, but that's all bullshit: nobody re-edits and changes titles just to do a video release. And I don't know that their title was any better — it was *different...* What I should have done — I had talked to Blockbuster and told them I would give them a six-month exclusive and they said they would buy 30,000 copies of the tape for $60 apiece. I had 10,000 of them made and then I did the deal with Columbia TriStar and of course they changed the title! I've never seen the other version, I've never had any real interest — it makes me nauseous to think about it...

"★★★★
...terrifying & brilliant. This is the best horror film of the 90's"
JOE BOB BRIGGS- The Movie Channel

THE RETURN OF THE TEXAS CHAINSAW MASSACRE

Matthew McConaughey
...in his first starring role ★★★

Above:
Vilmer continues
to taunt Jenny.

Columbia TriStar also failed to publicise *The Next Generation*, hardly surprising given its twenty-three theatre release...

Robert Kuhn: The only publicity that thing ever got was all the hurrah about Columbia *not* releasing it — other than that nobody would ever even know it existed. They literally had it buried.

Kim Henkel: They didn't put any money into publicity — but *we* didn't have a whole lot of good stills either [*laughs*]. Oh lord, that's another story. I'd kept on and on at the production manager about how the production should have some stills, and she kept going on about budgetary considerations. I told her flat out to get someone out there — I later found out she tried to get some person who was doing stills to go out there with a camera without any film in so I would *think* there were stills being taken... That's independent film-making — you've got people who are supposed to be on your team working against you!

Suing Columbia TriStar wasn't as simple as it sounds, nor was it the whole story. (The whole story is almost as hopelessly complicated as the original film's tangled finances.) In early 1997 Kuhn and Henkel had been sued by Chuck Grigson for breaching the distribution agreement they'd made with Columbia TriStar. The agreement had been such that the estate of *The Texas Chain Saw Massacre*, as represented by Grigson, would receive a percentage of *Return's* percentage. (In other words, the percentage Henkel and Kuhn owed the *Chain Saw* estate for licensing the title.) Their problems with Columbia TriStar obviously meant Grigson (representing the *Chain Saw* estate) wasn't receiving his due. Presumably once he'd been convinced there would be no income until Kuhn and Henkel resolved their problems with Columbia TriStar, Grigson dropped the charge in late 1997 and joined forces with them to sue CAA and Matthew McConaughey.

Robert Kuhn: First we tried to sue Columbia in Texas and that ultimately got dismissed — we were claiming that they'd breached the contract and therefore we weren't bound by the terms of it — but the Federal Court didn't buy that, so we ended up having to do this Rent-a-Judge thing in Los Angeles.

When we were taking the depositions they were saying, 'We never intended to do a theatrical release, we bought it because you wanted the video release' — that's kind of an interesting position. But Ben Feingold, who was president at the time of that division [Feingold is currently President, Columbia TriStar Home Entertainment; President, Columbia TriStar Motion Picture Group, Home Entertainment and Acquisitions], said that people from Creative Artists did call him and talk to him (or maybe came to visit him, he wasn't sure) about not doing a major release because of their concern about Matthew McConaughey. And he said, 'But it didn't affect me — I take care of my producers, I don't worry about any-body else.' And the film was immediately canned! I guess they did it for some other reason… So they now claim they changed the title and edited the picture just to do

Below: Leatherface emerges from the gloom.

a video release and they never intended to do a theatrical release. Who knows where all that will end up... Well, if they paid for all the time and effort we've expended, it would be considerable, I'll say that.

Columbia TriStar's twenty-three theatre release took $141,000 gross at the box-office, a sum that would barely cover a week's executive lunches.

PRINT COMPARISON, PREPARED BY CRAIG LAPPER

I ran the two tapes (*The Return of The Texas Chainsaw Massacre* and *Texas Chainsaw Massacre — The Next Generation*) side by side on two monitors. The *Return* tape was copied from a Japanese laserdisc and the *Next Generation* tape was the UK released VHS version (certificate 18 uncut).

The only fundamental difference (apart from the change of on-screen title) is in the opening scene. After the opening titles of the UK version (which is identical in all respects to the R-rated US DVD release) we see Jenny applying lipstick, then looking at herself in the mirror. This is followed by her and a friend having their photos taken at a dance. After the titles of the Japanese version (*Return of...*), we see Jenny applying lipstick and looking in the mirror, followed by an extra sequence of her stepfather entering her room and sexually menacing her. This scene, lasting one minute seventeen seconds, is not present in the UK or US releases of the film. The Japanese version then resumes on photos being taken at the dance as per the UK and US versions. Other than that, the Japanese release contains (i) an additional three seconds of some people walking towards a house, (ii) a few extra frames of Vilmer getting into his car. The only other difference is that a couple of sequences have been re-ordered (although no footage has been removed).

Firstly, the scenes around fifteen minutes have had their order changed. In the UK version, we see the kids in Darla's cabin, then the kids leaving the cabin and then Vilmer chasing and running a victim over repeatedly. In the Japanese version, we see the kids in Darla's cabin, then Vilmer chasing and running his victim over and then the kids leaving Darla's cabin. This doesn't really achieve anything plot-wise. The second slight reordering is that a scene of Jenny stopping on the road (around twenty-six minutes) cuts short before moving onto the next scene. In the Japanese version, she stops and squats in the road (unseen at this point in the UK version). However, in the UK version the shot of her squatting in the road occurs later on (after Leatherface's attack) and continues with her standing up and hailing a car with her torch — this is present in both versions, around thirty-six minutes.

REVIEWS

... we FINALLY have a decent sequel to *The Texas Chainsaw Massacre*... All along we thought that Tobe Hooper, the director of *Saw*, was a genius. And he is. He really is. But we completely overlooked the WRITER of *Saw*, Kim Henkel, who not only wrote that movie, but wrote the SECOND greatest movie to come out of Texas in the last twenty years, *Last Night at the Alamo*.

And now Kim has finally done what he probly shoulda done years ago, and he's become a director himself, and his first effort is *The Return of the Texas Chainsaw Massacre*, a flick so terrifying and brilliant that it makes the other two *Chainsaw* sequels seem like After-School Specials.

This one has so many completely unpredictable twists that I don't wanna give it away, but it definitely satisfies the first rule of great drive-in filmmaking: Anyone can die at any moment.

There are a couple of scenes in this baby that were almost too intense for ME to watch — and I've seen 47,000 of these things.

This is the best horror film of the nineties.

Eight dead bodies. Two breasts. Neck-breaking. Sledgehammer to the head. Bimbo on a meat hook. Stuffed state trooper. Woman on fire. Face-licking. Head-stomping. Four motor vehicle chases, with four crashes. Evil stepfather Fu. Meat-locker Fu.
Four stars.
Joe Bob's Drive-In for 15 May 1995

... the film is a knowing horror picture that builds on our knowledge of the three *Chainsaw* predecessors but also keeps its tongue firmly planted in its cheek at all times. Writer-director Kim Henkel penned the original *Chainsaw* and this effort shows that he has a felicitous grasp of the things that cause us to shudder in dread. The performances here are uniformly fun... Bits and pieces of the story will, on occasion, leave you scratching your head to keep pace with the new business at hand. Even though *The Next Generation* moniker makes the film sound like it ought to be a *Star Trek* sequel, there's no mistaking this film's lineage.
Marjorie Baumgarten, *The Austin Chronicle*, 20 Oct 1997

I think it's safe to say I wasn't expecting much from this one, but boy, was I pleasantly surprised. ... Henkel puts enough of a spin on things to keep it interesting, and it's certainly one *twisted* piece of drive-in cheese. Definitely worth renting...
Scott Phillips, 'Alibi', *Weekly Wire*, 9 Mar 1998

McConaughey, as a madman with an electronically operated false leg, seems to have

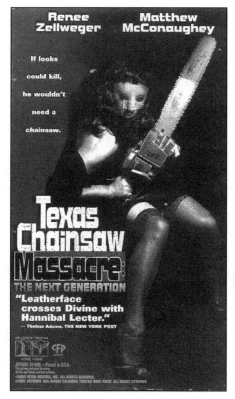

Above:
Video jacket
for the released
version.

studied the worst performances of Woody Harrelson and Dennis Hopper; he sweats, cackles, pops his eyes, lacerates his flesh, and wraps his meanest drawl around lines like 'Do you think all ah wanna do is keel you?!' The movie recapitulates the absurdist tabloid-redneck comedy of the great, original *Chainsaw* without a hint of its primal terror.
Owen Gleiberman, *Entertainment Weekly*, 9 May 1995

... a slightly above-average slasher film that's only partially redeemed by small but endearingly loopy shreds of black humour. The two stars are terrific... Zellweger's plucky heroine is likable and sympathetic, while McConaughey's over-the-top turn as a redneck psycho shows that if he continues to hone his craft and choose his scripts wisely, he could have a future as a character actor in low-budget slasher films.
Nathan Rabin, *The Onion* a.v. club

... cruel and superfluous... The original *Saw* was a seething, paranoid, near-apocalyptic nightmare... But twenty-five years later, the same material looks tired and dated...
Maitland McDonough, *TV Guide* Online

... the whole demented atmosphere and ultra-sadistic mood manages to scare and upset yet again... Henkel adeptly maintains the charnel-house tension with sustained sequences milking the audience's feeling of inevitable dread. This is a far better movie than Leatherface-lovers had a right to expect with Henkel matching the wide-awake nightmare quality of the first cult outing.
Alan Jones, *Starburst* 218

... the new *Texas Chainsaw Massacre* is not innovative enough, scary enough or funny enough to sustain itself... avoids unnecessary bloodshed, even flirting with some pertinent socio-sexual issues. But you can get all this stuff on any afternoon soap. What we want from *The Texas Chainsaw Massacre: The Next Generation* is a giddy mix of gruesome horror and campy humour. What we get is less massacre than mess.
John Anderson, *The Louisville Scene*, 12 Dec 1997

To their credit, the cast — including Tonie Perenski as Vilmer's gal Darla and Robert Jacks

as the cross-dressing Leatherface — throw themselves into the proceedings with enthusiasm. There's a lot of screaming, eye-rolling and wallowing in filth. Some of it even captures the over-the-top humour that made Mr Hooper's original stand out from grim, run-of-the-mill slasher trash.
Margaret A. McGurk, *The Cincinnati Enquirer*

"A giddy mix of gruesome horror and campy humor."
-- John Anderson, LOS ANGELES TIMES

… the original felt like somebody's dark obsessions playing themselves out in front of you. It was fascinating to watch, but you didn't necessarily want to meet the filmmakers over coffee. The new version, fun though it is, feels oddly, comfortably familiar.
John Peavoy, *Filmmaker*, 5 Dec 1997

McConaughey is disgustingly convincing as Vilmer, a tortuous psycho with a remote-controlled leg brace. It's a meek echo of the original *Chainsaw*, but not without its own sick charm. Considering visual eccentricities like Leatherface in drag and the concept of a fraternity of horrormongers, the film has a few redeeming qualities, but not enough to make it truly memorable.
Mike Emery, *The Austin Chronicle*, 2 Nov 1998

Repulsive horror yarn in which a sadistic quartet of rural psychopaths (led by Matthew McConaughey) torture and murder teens on prom night with only one survivor (Renee Zellweger). Writer-director Kim Henkel's sick sequel to its 1974 and 1986 predecessors borders on the depraved with its continual display of jokey graphic mayhem. Excessive violence, a flash of nudity, much profanity and recurring rough language.
Film and Broadcasting Review (formerly the *Catholic Film Newsletter*)

Above:
Poster for the
released version.

last but not defintly least was part 4 which tottaly SUCKED ASS!! i mean leatherface is a total faggot crossdresser who screams like a tottaly quier/girl. plus in all of the movies his family are cannibls exept for part 4 where they eat pizza. leatherface also isnt the main family member, that stupid vilmer is, and also leatherface only killed one person and that was with a sludgehammer not his chainsaw. the rest of the deaths are from vilmer again. so like i said the texas chainsaw massacre movies are my favorite exept for the ripoff number 4.
Engelmeyerfan, 'discussion' on gnovies.com ∎

"A UNIQUE WAY OF GROSSING PEOPLE OUT"

Robert A. Burns: It's not something you can re-do — why on earth they've chosen to remake it is beyond me...

Kim Henkel: Well, very early on Tobe and I were talking to the guy we licensed the rights to and we were supposed to do it — but all of a sudden we got cut out of the picture. So the saga continues... We were actually hired to write a script — what happened was we got paid for writing a script but there was never any intention to even look at that script. In fact, we didn't get paid for writing the script until they were already in pre-production. So we had to produce a token script, which we did — it's a curiosity which we produced... And by the time we delivered it they were probably already shooting — it was a joke.

Bill Moseley: The casting assistant lives downstairs from me in my building and when I found out she was doing that I gave her a picture of Chop-Top and said, 'Jeez, I'd love to at least come in on it,' and she looked at the picture and said, 'There's no point in me giving it to them, there's really nothing in it for you.' That was a slap in the face, but it reminded me that there probably isn't. It didn't make me angry, I just thought, 'Yeah, alright...' I asked her about the plot and she said, 'They don't really want a family, they just want to concentrate on Leatherface — it's going to be kind of like *Se7en*.' With Leatherface... I said, 'Well, OK...'

Gunnar Hansen: For the current one — it's a retelling of the original story, so they've got a new script following the original storyline. I guess they decided I'm too old to play Leatherface, so they asked me to play the part of the trucker, who they're calling Big Rig

Jack. He's got a line in the movie, and he drives off with the Sally character and she freaks out... What I love about this sequel — is it a sequel or is it a remake? — is, why are they remaking a great film if they think it's that great? Well, I think it'll be a piece of shit. I'll tell you why: the casting associate said to me, 'This time it's a dark psychological horror movie, not a bloodbath like the original'...

Lou Perryman: I had these guys from the new movie in my cab — they were like line producers or something — and I was taking them over to the new offices and said [*in a silly voice*] 'Hey, I got to be in this! I got to do a cameo!' Not a chance! They were keeping *everybody* away from it. Except Daniel Pearl...

Daniel Pearl: This will be scary, but with a higher style. Will this be grimy and gritty like the first one? No, I did that already; I don't think I should do the exact same thing twenty-nine years later. I'm approaching this almost as if I didn't do the original. This movie has different things, it's for a different audience. [*Fangoria* 216, 2002]

Marcus Nispel: When I asked Daniel Pearl — well, begged him — to do the movie, I thought, 'What would make it worth it for someone like Daniel, who has done it before, to do it again?' I felt only for something completely new and different. We looked at the original story that *Texas Chain Saw Massacre* is based on, the Ed Gein story, and we went much deeper into that. [*Fangoria* 216, 2002]

Toby Emmerich: My sense from [producer Michael] Bay is that he will not so much look at the previous *Chainsaw* movies as look back to the original, real stories that informed it. [*Variety*, 22 Mar 2002]

Mark Ordesky: The idea is to make a really frightening film. An R rating is not some ghetto where films go to do marginal business. *Silence of the Lambs* was R-rated. [*Variety*, 22 Mar 2002]

After the lesson of *Leatherface*, one might have hoped New Line Cinema would have the sense to keep away from the *Chainsaw* franchise. Not a chance. Film is an industry motivated largely by greed, geared to sell product. So what better way to 'market' cinema than to turn it over to the hands of people who have made their fortune shooting MTV videos and high concept action no-brainers whose budgets could pay off the national debts of most third world countries? And what better way to re-market a remake than to 're-imagine' it? Underterred by the millions wasted (and abuse heaped) on such celluloid effluent as Gus Van Sant's *Psycho* or Tim Burton's *Planet of the Apes*,

New Line decided to employ music video specialist Marcus Nispel to direct the 're-imagining' of *The Texas Chain Saw Massacre*. Producer Michael Bay is an erstwhile music video director (including Donny Osmond's comeback single) turned purveyor of bloated Hollywood action epics (*Armageddon*, *Pearl Harbor*), and returning from the first film is director of photography Daniel Pearl, now perhaps the world's foremost director of music videos. New Line returned to Austin and its environs for the fifth installment, and principal photography finished in mid-October 2002, the production budget coming in at around $15 million.

It was announced in October 2002 that the music score would be written by the 'controversial' rock star Marilyn Manson — and while some sources credited Wayne Bell with the 'original theme', Bell said he had been contacted 'exactly zero times' by New Line about any involvement. The bigger budget supposedly signified a bigger name cast, but barring veteran actor R. Lee Ermey (also in New Line's 2003 film *Willard*, another '70s horror remake — why waste time with original material when there's a wealth of cinema to be remade/re-imagined?), the young cast are unlikely to be recognised by anyone other than followers of American television series, though Jessica Biel appeared in *Rules of Attraction* and Erica Leerhsen in *Book of Shadows: Blair Witch 2*. Actor/bodybuilder Andrew Bryniarski plays Leatherface, hopefully portraying him in a similar manner to his excellent Butterfinger in *Hudson Hawk*.

Andrew Bryniarski: If there's more Leatherface work in the future, I wouldn't say I'm not going to do it. [There's a] difference between beating a dead horse and milking a golden goose. [*Entertainment Weekly* 716/717, 2003]

The cast of tanned, buffed, worked-out and gorgeous young television actors and actresses seemed to enjoy the experience and were surprisingly enthusiastic.

Jessica Biel: ... what made the original so great is that it was kind of like a documentary, like someone just took their video camera and went around. We worked really, really hard to make it incredibly realistic. So hopefully the audience will think it could happen to them or that it could be your neighbour who could, you know, be a psychotic maniac. I don't even know if there is less gore. I would say we have a good amount of it... But it's not going to be blatant. It's kind of a unique way of grossing people out. And it's going to be beautiful at the same time as it's horrifying. [*MTV News*, 27 Mar 2003]

Eric Balfour: Daniel Pearl is one of the most brilliant directors of photography I've ever seen... It starts with five kids on a road trip. Very beautiful, first part of the film, landscapes of Texas. It's gorgeous; they're young. As the film goes on, you just see it start to degrade, become more decrepit, darker, even the film itself starts to look different. By the end of the movie, it looks like *Se7en* or something. It's very cool. And Marcus Nispel, he's a great director. When I talked to Michael and Marcus, they wanted to make a definitive film. They didn't want to make some teen-horror thing... [the cast] wanted it to be the horror movie of our generation, the way *Poltergeist* was or *Exorcist* was or *Halloween* was. We didn't want to bastardize the genre. [Interview by Kate O'Hare, Zap2it, 6 Jan 2003]

Scott Kosar's script appears to re-imagine elements from both *Chain Saw* and *Chainsaw 2*. The new film (complete with voiceover introduction by John Larroquette) takes place in the '70s, one day after the original. A van-load of photogenic youngsters on their way to Mexico pick up the sole survivor of the previous night's massacre. They seek help from R. Lee Ermey's sleazy Sherrif Hoyt, a man with his own agenda following the butchery of his daughter some years ago, who uses them as bait to lure Leatherface out of hiding and finally terminate him. Ermey certainly had fun with his role...

R. Lee Ermey: In *Texas Chainsaw Massacre*, I play the most perverted person I've ever played... Just totally perverted in every aspect of life. New Line's raving about *Texas Chainsaw Massacre*. I won't look at it until it's ready and then I'll make my decision whether it's good. But they're raving about it, so hopefully, it's a good show. My character is an old sheriff. There's one scene where he's inside of a van wrapping up a really sweet, good-lookin' young lady's body with Saran Wrap. He's got one of the kids in helping him and he tells the boy, 'You know, back in my days as a younger man, I used to love doing this, because I could kinda cop a feel every now and then.' And I reach up and squeeze her boob, right? Then after that, he's wrapping down below and he says, 'Wooooo-we! She's awful wet down here. You boys have been having some fun with this sweet little girl, haven't you!?' Then he takes his hand out of her crotch and runs it under his nose! He wipes a little of that wetness on his upper lip and says, 'I used to do this, and you know, it lasts the entire day!' Oh, he's perverted alright! [G. Noel Gross, *CineSchlock-o-rama*, Mar 2003]

Filming had its share of problems, including a change of Leatherface after the first week and a threatened walk-out by special effects crew over safety concerns. Further tension may have been caused by the aesthetic differences between making a feature film and shooting music videos. And, in a stroke of genius guaranteed to irritate all but the most sycophantic journalist, visitors were barred from seeing Leatherface, the publicist claiming they were trying to build a 'buzz' similar to that surrounding the unveiling of Spider-Man. Let's hope the buzz around this re-imagining is something other than the sound of flies around a corpse. ■

Documentaries and Associated Films

"THE TEXTURE OF HUMAN BEINGS AT WORK"

There are currently three documentaries covering the *Chainsaw Massacre* series (though New Line's *Leatherface* DVD will contain a previously unseen 'making of'): Brad Shellady's *The Texas Chain Saw Massacre: A Family Portrait* (1988), Brian Huberman's *The Return of the Texas Chainsaw Massacre: The Documentary* (1996) and David Gregory's *Texas Chainsaw Massacre: The Shocking Truth* (2000). Each is essential viewing, and all three are quite different. Shellady's deals specifically with the first film and Huberman's the fourth, while Gregory's covers all four, though the majority of its running time is devoted to the original *Chain Saw*.

THE TEXAS CHAIN SAW MASSACRE: A FAMILY PORTRAIT

A particularly good 'talking head' documentary, nicely illustrated by relevant clips from the film. Because of the relatively few participants each receives ample screen time, allowing for longer anecdotes and an opportunity to build up a picture of the actors' personalities. *Portrait* features lengthy interviews with John Dugan, Gunnar Hansen, Ed Neal (unfortunately slightly out of focus, but the only place to access a decent Neal interview) and Jim Siedow, with a short burble over the end credits from the legendary Forrest J Ackerman. The DVD issue features trailers for other MTI product, some trivial trivia questions but no new interview footage. Here's an interview with Brad Shellady:

Family Portrait *first came out in 1988 — when did you start work on it?*
It was completed in '88 but I had contacted Gunnar Hansen as early as '85 to shoot a short piece titled *Leatherface: Unmasked*. Gunnar was nice and appreciative of my interest but stated he wasn't really interested. I put the project on the back burner while continuing through college, but came back to it in another way in early '87. I proceeded,

over a period of about four months, to track down John Dugan, Jim Siedow, and Ed Neal. Once they had agreed to appear in a *Chain Saw* documentary, I again contacted Gunnar stating, 'You can't turn me down now. I've got everyone else.' He proceeded, good naturedly, to tell me how underhanded and sneaky I had been, but then consented to be part of the film. I'm happy to say that the greatest thing to come out of it all was an ongoing friendship with Gunnar in which we have collaborated on a number of projects.

How long did it take to make? Was it pretty much a one-man project?
Principal photography took roughly three months, editing about a month. The shooting crew was comprised of myself and my best friend, Bob Enlow, who assisted with camera and sound. We travelled by car (a very cramped one full of camera equipment) to Maine, Texas, San Francisco and Los Angeles. Tired, unkempt and hygienically challenged were the order of the day.

How did you make contact with the various actors? Were they easy to track down and talk to back then? Are you still in touch with any of them?
The way I initially contacted everyone was through good old-fashioned detective work. Ed was the only one who was actively working in film, and had an agent I could contact. John was working as a waiter, Jim retired, and Gunnar (who by then, I had known since '85) was an established writer. Ed Neal was instrumental as he had contact numbers, some out-dated, but they gave me places to start. I had original-ly contacted Gunnar through a friend who swapped Christmas cards with him — I start-ed writing him and the rest is history.

Above:
John Dugan in
A Family Portrait.

   I'm still in contact with everyone, but talk to Gunnar more than anyone else. We all get together if possible and whenever we are near each other we stop by for a visit. I truly wish I could see everybody more but we are pretty spread out geographically.

I saw Family Portrait *played at a festival last year — is there still a fair amount of interest in it?*
It played at the Illinois Filmflam festival on Halloween 2002 and gets played at conventions from time to time. It has aired on TV in Los Angeles and been shown at numerous overseas conventions. There is still a wealth of interest in it as I suspect there always will be as long as there is interest in *Chain Saw* itself.

Have you continued to follow the series? Can't say I'm too thrilled by the prospect of the new one...
I have continued to follow the sequels (or is that STINKquels?) and am always hopeful they will have merit, but, alas, they always blow. I will concede that while none can even hold a candle to the original, I did find sequences to delight in from *Chainsaw 2*. Hey, at least it's Tobe and there is no way it's near as bad as the dreck that followed it. Assuredly the forthcoming remake will put all to shame regarding ineptitude, and the continued tarnishing and whoring of a legend.

THE RETURN OF THE TEXAS CHAINSAW MASSACRE: THE DOCUMENTARY

Top and above:
Gunnar Hansen
and Jim Siedow in
A Family Portrait.

Robert Kuhn: There was also — I have never actually seen this — but there was a documentary done. He got mad at me and didn't put me in the film. He did an interview with me and then decided to throw it in the trash, so I never did see it.

Currently the only 'making of' in the *Chainsaw* series. Director Brian Huberman is an Associate Professor of Film in the Art and Art History department at Rice University in Houston. With his then-partner, now-wife Cynthia Ann Lost Howling Wolf (really) as sound person, Huberman shot over twenty hours of High-8 footage on seven separate set visits, later edited down to an hour-long film. Besides depicting the inevitable frustrations of low-budget film-making (Levie Isaacks' exasperation with an untrained assistant, only one sheet of glass available for a special effect), Huberman was on hand to film some good stunt work and to capture the cast and crew having fun (a word infrequently associated with the making of *Chainsaw* films). Also notable are some real blows delivered and received by Zellweger, Perensky and McConaughey.

In something of a missed opportunity, the documentary is not included on Columbia TriStar's DVD release of *Texas Chainsaw Massacre: The Next Generation*. But after their treatment of Kim Henkel's film, that's hardly surprising.

Brian Huberman: I met Kim making *Last Night at the Alamo*, a film by Eagle Pennell. Kim co-produced it with Eagle, wrote it and had a small part — ironically, as he's the man who puts all the words into people's mouths, he plays an almost mute individual, no one can get him to say much… *Last Night* was shot in Houston, 1982 — I was cinematographer, though I'm really more of a documentary film-maker and it was the only time I did anything like it.

I hadn't kept up with Kim though. By the time I heard *Return of* was being made I'd worked on and made several documentary films. I'd finished a piece in '92, *The Making of John Wayne's The Alamo* — except that it was made thirty years later — which had been added to the director's cut video release.

So I put it to Bob Kuhn and Kim Henkel that I'd like to do the film — and in this case, instead of being there after the event, the events would actually be unfolding, which would allow me to work in a way I think is far more appropriate for the medium, to have history unfolding before the camera. I think what clinched the deal was I didn't ask for any money!

I made it with the woman who became my wife — it was the classic observational two-person crew: camera and sound. I didn't know what was going to happen — I was happy, once I'd got access, in contrast with the *Alamo* piece, to just be there while it was happening. I tried to stay in touch with the production department and get a sense of what they were doing and try to structure my visits around that — of course it was hopeless! The schedule was constantly changing… *Return of* was virtually all shot at night, so it was quite a challenging film to work on, just physically. I tried to put quite a lot of emphasis on the stunt work — there's a lot of action, and action is obviously interesting to film, though on one of the visits I did get multiple takes of people wandering through the woods in the dark…

As Kim says, one of the key themes in horror films is the abuse of women. The obvious film to illustrate that is *The Exorcist*, where a whole army of guardians of the patriarchy gang up on that little devil child, simply because she's coming into puberty, she's becoming a woman — and that can't happen! And the *Chainsaw* series deals with what a writer called 'The Last Woman' — basically, there's always a

Below:
Renee Zellweger
and stunt double
Jody Haselbarth.

last woman, who stops running and asserts herself. A good example is the remake of *Night of the Living Dead* — and there she's basically androgynous once she changes into the combats... So I kind of piggybacked on that — because for me the strongest character was Jody Haselbarth, the stunt woman doubling Renee Zellweger, the current 'Last Woman'.

It's a kind of self-structuring event — it's the making of a film and you know that at a certain point the film is going to end — and my narrative was defined by that. So my job was basically to gather evidence, hopefully themes — in the observational approach, out of the chaos experience the film emerges — I went in with quite the reverse of any preconceived notion.

The production's like an ant hill — everyone engaged in some sort of business, dragging things around, all of that mess and noise — and most of the stuff I was filming was where people were engaged in fairly physical bits of business.

I like picking up the little fragments that one gets using observational style — little bits of gossip and stuff flying by — there were a lot of interesting characters on the film, which helped... There were some nice scenes with Leatherface/Robbie Jacks doing stuff — he was a funny guy, sort of a gay Leatherface — and I already knew Levie Isaacks, the DP, who'd I'd met through Eagle, he was part of that Austin film-making scene. And there's this joy of being behind the scenes — you get to see what others don't! One doesn't need to reproduce what the public is going to see, so you take people around the corners — one is drawn to the maker, one is drawn to the stunt people and the whole illusion of film-making.

I particularly liked the carpenters — I have one little scene where they're making a fake roof. It comes after Jody has announced that she used to have a penis — it's a joke to Renee Zellweger, about some rigging they used when she was jumping off the roof onto a wire, terrifying. In the film it's doesn't look much, those things never do, it seems so ordinary somehow, but when you're actually there... Anyway, that's what it looked like. They're joking about it together, which is just putting the lid on the whole 'woman as the dominant figure' thing. Then one of the carpenters starts singing, some sort of Monty Python-type song about roaming the sea with men, filling the sink up with hair and never having to lift the toilet seat up again...

I'm kind of drawn to those little things, the texture of human beings at work, a group of people drawn together, or who hate one another or don't care about anything... And that's key to the observational tradition: you go in on this very human level and you're aiming for the big picture, but you're not going for the big questions, you're going in more obliquely, and through the evidence of ordinary people involved in the little bits of business that one has to be involved in to make a movie, gradually the issue emerges through the gathering of all these bits and pieces, one gets a glimpse of the whole project, the whole project as a product of people.

After I'd done a first cut I showed it to Kim. He's a cautious character, that's just his way… He has a very clear idea of what standards he's going to accept — so once he figured that the documentary was at least working in a way he found interesting, he sat down and talked, and I filmed a big interview with him. I hadn't really been able to get much out of him during the location filming, he was just completely taken up… So he talks throughout the documentary — and I thought he was very forthcoming in revealing what he was about, what he finds interesting — he's very candid and direct once he gets going, there's no mumbo jumbo about it.

I think it feels like a bit of a portrait of Kim, the director at work — I had no intention of doing that initially, although as he was the general I was following him around, and he did tend to be at the centre of any activity. So it wasn't difficult for him to become the main character. What emerged to me, though I don't think I was ultimately successful, was the film was about family, and the film crew is like a giant family, the director is like the great father with all the wayward children, all the different tribes of the family — the lighting tribe, the camera tribe…

I have to say that that the one person I had the least success with was Renee Zellweger — it seemed like she had the least to offer as a human being of any of the other people — and it's puzzling to me as she's obviously been the most successful. She wasn't unfriendly, she just didn't have anything to say. McConaughey was pretty cheerful — I thought he was the star actor, though at the time they were just ordinary people. From seeing him on the set he was clearly a powerhouse of energy, he's just one of those guys that has the ability to project danger — characters like De Niro, you do not know which way they're going to go, there's an unsettling quality about them, which of course makes them very interesting.

TEXAS CHAIN SAW MASSACRE: THE SHOCKING TRUTH

An almost perfect example of documentary film-making from the now-defunct Exploited Films. The majority focuses on *Chain Saw*, with shorter sections on *Chainsaw 2*, *Leatherface* and *Return of…* Interviewed are Tobe Hooper, Kim Henkel, Wayne Bell, Marilyn Burns, Robert A. Burns, Jeff Burr, Allen Danziger, Gunnar Hansen, Ted Nicolaou, Paul Partain, Jim Siedow, William Vail and Caroline Williams. Hooper is on better than average form, coherent and less prone to the occasional flights of fancy he has embarked on in recent years, and Jeff Burr's outpouring of bile at the fate of *Leatherface* is particularly entertaining. An otherwise faultless film is only marred by an inappropriate, idiotic and distasteful sequence

equating James Ferman and the British Board of Film Classification with Hitler and the Nazis.

The Shocking Truth uses some of stills photographer Eric Lasher's behind-the-scenes footage of *Chainsaw 2*, though no 'making of' was ever properly completed.

Eric Lasher: I used Tobe's video camera, which was cabled to the actual recording device — you had to carry it around with you, so I was wearing a VCR. It was a lo-res camera, so when you have low light you get trails on the film. When the *Chainsaw 2* video came out I took a bunch of the better moments and cut them together: I'd use, say, four versions of the scene with Dennis Hopper's stunt double jumping off the table before it cuts to Dennis, then show the finished take where it's all edited together, but there was a copyguard on the video, so that footage fades in and out. The day I finished it I gave it to Tobe to watch and I never got it back!

The Shocking Truth was added to the 2003 British and Australian DVD releases of *Chain Saw* as a second disc, together with the unedited interviews with Tobe Hooper and Kim Henkel.

Producer/director David Gregory has moved on to further 'making of' documentaries (with notable entries on *The Wicker Man* and *Two Evil Eyes*), closing his company Exploited Films (who also issued *Deranged*) to concentrate on work for Blue Underground.

LEATHERFACE SPEAKS

Shot during a one-day 'American Nightmare' event at the National Museum of Photography, Film and Television in Bradford, produced by Tony Earnshaw and photographed/directed by Jim Moran in June 2000, this short documentary focuses solely on Gunnar Hansen as he talks about his role as Leatherface, the making of *Texas Chain Saw Massacre* and its cult and culture. Moran is a photographer for *The Yorkshire Post*, who also makes documentary films for the Museum, the latest being *The Actor's Director*, about Richard Attenborough.

Jim Moran: We tend to do onstage interviews for the Museum archives, but this was a project we put together ourselves, a very informal talk in the restaurant bar, under a poster of *Chain Saw Massacre* — there's a clatter of plates going on… We made a nineteen minute documentary which was very well received at the Festival of Fantastic Films in Manchester in 2001 and Edinburgh's Dead By Dawn festival in 2002.

Gunnar's a very charming man, he gave us a lot of insight into the making of the film and how he enjoyed making it, how they put together the gruesome bits of hanging the actress on the hook, which was very interesting. It was funny — at the end he said 'Cut' and drew his finger across his throat… The interviewing was done by Tony Earnshaw — we also did David Hess from *Last House on the Left*, though that one hasn't been edited yet, there he's just chatting to someone, leaning against the wall.

HEADCHEESE

Headcheese is a twenty-two minute short film, basically a two-man project from young Texas film-makers Duane Graves and Justin Meeks. The story is loosely based on a chapter from Luke in the New Testament, and concerns a journey undertaken by the deranged Legion (played by Meeks) to a deserted Texas town to rid himself of his inner demons. It was shot in and around many of the locations from the original *Chain Saw*. Meeks wrote and stars in it, Graves photographed it, both co-directed, co-edited and co-produced it. Kim Henkel is also credited as co-producer, which might act as a seal of approval for those who need it. It's available on a Shock-o-Rama DVD packaged with *Freak*, a horror film by Tyler Tharpe, with an insert booklet featuring notes by Henkel. Graves has won several awards for his full-length documentary *Up Syndrome*, about a childhood friend (who appears in *Headcheese*) who suffers from Down's Syndrome. Here's an interview with Duane Graves:

How long have you and Justin been working together?
I met Justin Meeks in a video production course at Texas A&M University in 1997. While screening our first projects that semester, we immediately noticed similarities in our macabre content and style. We also shared a passion for horror films and our personal movie collections were virtually identical. So we began collaborating on our projects for the next — and last — two years of our TV/Film degree there. We worked so well creatively that we kept the team together beyond graduation. Luckily we both wound up in Austin in 2000, and from there have done many horror and comedy shorts and even a feature length documentary on digital video titled *Up Syndrome*.

Above:
Legion on
the cross.

Headcheese *is one of the early titles for* The Texas Chain Saw Massacre — *what gave you the idea of using it for your film?*

Our screenwriting professor in college was Kim Henkel. I actually decided to go to A&M based solely on the fact that Kim was teaching at the university. *Chain Saw* had been a lifelong favourite of mine, so it was impossible for me to pass up the opportunity to have Kim as a mentor. I had known from various books and documentaries on *Chain Saw* that the original title was *Headcheese*. Originally our short was titled *The Voyage Home*, which was the poem by Justin Meeks the short was based on. But since we had filmed many of the scenes at the *Chain Saw* locations, I thought it would be a nice way to complete the underlying homage to name it *Headcheese*. We agreed that, aside from the nod to Kim and *Chain Saw*, it was a fitting title given the inner strife the main character was experiencing.

It's shot in black and white — is that your preferred medium? You're working on a feature now — would you consider shooting that in black and white?
We actually shot over half of *Headcheese* in colour. I had purchased a Bolex H-16 on

eBay, which is a wind-up 16mm camera from the '50s. It was very hard to operate because it was non-reflexive, which basically means I couldn't see what I was actually filming while I was filming, so I had to guess on the framing, which worked only sometimes. We wanted desperately to do the entire short on 16mm, but it was just too expensive. Colour 16mm film stock cost twice as much as black and white. So we decided to do the other half in Super 8mm, solely to cut costs. Strangely, the price of colour Super 8mm film is about the same as black and white Super 8mm. So we figured, why not shoot it in colour just in case we wanted to have some colour sequences. In the end, we stripped it entirely of colour for creative reasons. I think the tone of the film, with its grain and grit, was much better served in black and white. I would love to do another film in black and white, but only if it accented the story we were telling. I wouldn't say black and white is our first choice, it's just one of them.

Is there any dialogue/monologue/voiceover on Headcheese, *or just the soundtrack music?*
We wanted to have more dialogue in the short, but since we were shooting it silently in 16mm/Super 8, we knew it would be very arduous synching it in the editing room. So there is only one sequence of actual dialogue, and the rest is voice-over narration by the main character Legion. The rest of the sound design is foley work we did to create the 'aural environment' from scratch.

Are you local to the places from Chain Saw *you filmed in?*
All of the locations featured in the original *Chain Saw* are within a thirty-mile radius of Austin, so we were able to visit all of the remaining sites and incorporate them into our script. Most of the locations are still around, thirty years later. The BBQ Shack/gas station in Bastrop looks eerily the same, the cemetery is in Leander (which used to be a town of its own, but is nearly fused with Austin after thirty years), and the lot where Leatherface's house used to stand is in Round Rock, which is basically Austin nowadays. The lot is on a hill, which has been called Quick Hill for many years by the townsfolk. The actual house was moved to Kingsland several years back and has been transformed into a family restaurant. At the time we shot *Headcheese*, the lot on Quick Hill had the old barn and remnants of past inhabitants still standing, but as of a year ago, all of it has been cleared out completely. Nothing remains on the lot except neatly trimmed grass and a highway about fifty feet away. In fact, the only reminder that Quick Hill is indeed the original location, is a faint outline of the narrow road that ran in front of the house in the 1970s — the very road that Sally escaped down in the back of the pickup truck at the end of the film.

Above:

Legion at play.

Have you shown Headcheese *to many* Chain Saw *fans? Any of the conventions or anything? What's the reaction to the film been like from the people who've seen it so far?*

Headcheese screened as part of the Brooklyn Film Festival and the Dallas Video Festival. Shortly after we completed it, a distribution company in New Jersey contacted us about distributing it on DVD. It took some time, but in January 2003, it was released in stores all over the US. The reaction so far has been great; many *Chain Saw* fans have contacted us to share their feedback. Several reviews have started to come in, even from the UK. Several fans have commented that we were able to capture the feeling of *Chain Saw* successfully, which is a great compliment. We had a different story to tell, but we wanted to have an underlying homage present — if only for the hardcore fans out there. Like the ones reading your book!

It's co-produced by Kim Henkel — has having him aboard helped at all?

Kim was one of the first people we showed the completed film to. After the credits rolled he said, 'You can put my name anywhere on that film.' We were thrilled! He loved it. Having Kim attached was something we wanted from the very start. It was the perfect way to complete the homage. Kim really liked the short, so he warned us that having his name attached could actually 'hurt' the film's chances at distribution — he thought maybe some people would perceive it as a 'rip-off' or a 'lame remake' of *Chain Saw*. We didn't feel this would be the case, so of course we let him hop on board as producer. I think it has helped the film get attention, but we honestly believe that it stands on its own without the *Chain Saw* ties. At least we like to think so. What do you think?

ALL AMERICAN MASSACRE

All American Massacre was conceived by Tobe Hooper's son William (aka Tony) as a sort of tribute/prequel to his father's two *Chainsaw* films. Shot on high-resolution digital video, it started out as a fifteen-minute short to show off Hooper's computer skills, and ended up as a sixty-minute featurette.

The story has an imprisoned Chop-Top (originally re-christened Bloody Bobby, played by *Chainsaw 2*'s Bill Moseley) being interviewed by a reporter, telling the story of how 'The Family' came into being. Flashback carnage ensues... Or would have, if the film had ever seen the light of day. Other actors involved included Todd Bates, who'd done make-up and props for *Fight Club* and *Hollow Man*. The music was by Moseley's guitarist pal Buckethead, a long-time *Chain Saw* devotee.

In 2000 the film's publicist 'Stu Carney' announced that *All American Massacre* would be available for downloading and viewing exclusively on-line that Halloween. Trailers were posted, but the scheduled download spot never materialised and the *All American Massacre* website subsequently closed. All that currently remains of the project are a few poor quality still images lurking on the internet. The film, and Tony Hooper, seem to have vanished.

Eric Lasher: Tony Hooper and I did *All American Massacre*, I worked for three years on that. I was 'Stu Carney' — that's beef stew when you think about it, carne is meat... I was the executive producer and I play Leatherface, I also doubled everyone in the film who's not female. Tony and I wrote the script — the two of us basically did everything.

It was supposed to be a one-shot thirty second thing, it turned into a one hour movie. And it kept getting bigger and bigger — it looks like a million dollar film, but it cost me $14,000 or $15,000 to make. It's all shot in my garage and in Tobe's back yard. Tony lived eight doors away with Tobe in a rented house and we shot the exteriors there. They moved to a really nice place with a garage at the back that Tony took over as a studio, he set up the editing there. Tobe raised Tony — his mother left when he was about one year old — so he's been growing up in this chainsaw world where everything's fake and weird and trippy... Tony sort of resented it but couldn't get out, so this was our idea to get Tony's work shown to everybody.

It's all about Bill Moseley, his character. It starts in a prison — actually it starts with his DNA coming out of a dripping puddle of blood — and you find him in a cell. He's the same, only he's now twenty-five years older, so half his head is exposed, there's more of the plate. The guard comes and opens the door — they lead him off and you think he's going to an execution, but he's going to an interview about serial killers for television, and he flashes back, so most of it takes place one month prior to the first film.

We were at a Halloween party one year and there was this guy Todd Bates dressed as Chop-Top, so we said, 'What are you doing for the next two weeks?' And he was trapped forever... Todd plays the young Chop-Top and also plays the Hitchhiker, so we have both characters in the film together.

We had problems right away. There's a car that pulls into a gas station with a guy driving and three girls. We shot all night — all the interior sequences in the car, all their discussions — then one of the girls dropped out, so she's doubled every-where. In fact, we had to change the original script because they're all supposed to go inside, but we couldn't have this character walking around, so he (Chop-Top/Bloody Bobby) comes out and kills her in the car. The other girl jumps out the passenger side and runs up against a van that's been sitting there the whole time, the door opens and it's Leatherface — he jumps out and he runs the chainsaw through her back and it comes out between her tits, she falls backwards and he drags her in and slams the door of the van, just like in the first film. He's only in it for about a minute, just jumps out and does this little scene very close to the end of the film. But the audience would have been knocked out.

My intent was a total assault on all your senses all the time. Our set was like the set in *Chainsaw 2* but on a much smaller scale — very, very colourful but dark, it's all in a flashback, so it's in his mind what was right, you're getting Chop-Top remembering. When you come in, you don't see the details, then slowly during the course of the movie you're seeing there's bodies right in front of you, you just didn't notice — like there's a pot sitting on the stove, and when the Hitchhiker comes in out of the rain, he goes over to the pot and pulls a dead baby out of it, pops the eye-balls out and eats them. I battled with Tony for about a month not to shoot that scene, I just thought it was too over the top, then I decided, 'What the fuck, why not? We're hardly going to get a rating for this anyway' because it was designed for the internet, a free internet movie.

It's still enthralling — and it's all of a sudden over, so much happening in a very short period, there's always something to look at. Buckethead did the music, he's playing for Guns 'n' Roses now — he's a big *Chainsaw* fan. He was originally cast as Leatherface, but he's this really tall, really skinny guy, it took us all night to get him ready, we filmed him running around for a day as Leatherface, but I ended up doing it.

We were only missing a couple of shots. I really don't know what's going on... Tony just didn't finish the project. There was so much work — everything was so much better than I expected it to be when I watched it back. I loved it when I was doing it — it bothers me more than anything else that nobody's going to see it. ∎

"A HUMAN HORROR STORY OF GHASTLY PROPORTIONS"

16 November 1957, Plainfield, Wisconsin. The disappearance of middle-aged shop-keeper Bernice Worden led Sheriff Art Schley and Captain Lloyd Schoephoerster to discover her headless, disembowelled corpse hanging upside down in a woodshed attached to the home of Edward 'Ed' Gein. Schoephoerster called for backup. Once it arrived, he and a deputy searched Gein's neglected, rubbish-filled house, revealing, amongst years' worth of accumulated detritus, body parts of at least fifteen women. The inventory, coupled with Gein's ghoulish inventiveness, led to one of the 20th century's more sensational cases of murder, grave-robbing, possible cannibalism and necrophilia (which Gein denied: corpses smelled bad), and sundry depravity.

Gein's trophies included: four human noses, nine 'death masks' made from preserved faces, ten heads with the tops sawn off above the eyebrows, chairs with seats made from strips of human skin, a wastepaper basket made from human skin, a shoe box containing nine preserved vulvas (one was a silverish colour — apparently painted in an attempt to preserve it when it began to rot — with a red ribbon attached), a hanging human head, a lampshade covered with human skin, shrunken heads, two skulls mounted on bedposts, a pair of human lips hanging from a string... Bernice Worden's heart was found in a pan on the stove, but there was no evidence of body parts stored for consumption — Worden's other organs had been thrown in a cardboard box.

Gein liked to make things: a drum fashioned from skin stretched over a large can; a bowl made from a cranium; a shirt, leggings, bracelets, a knife sheath and a purse made from human skin. His ultimate creation was a full female body suit constructed of human skin, complete with face. Gein also liked to dress up.

Some of the rooms had been sealed off and remained unused, including his mother's bedroom, nailed shut and left intact since her death. All the rooms used by

Gein were a mess, with various forms of rubbish occupying every inch of space — from a four-foot high pile of worn-out overalls to a large can full of chewed gum...

Edward Theodore Gein was born on 27 August 1906, the second son of Augusta and George Gein. His brother Henry was seven years his senior. Augusta was a religious fanatic, convinced the world was full of sin, obsessed with loose women luring her sons into immorality and a subsequent long roast in hell. She viewed George as a snivelling, booze-swilling ne'er-do-well, unfit to raise her boys, and took their upbringing upon herself. Using the money from her grocery business, she bought a large farm in Plainfield and moved the family there.

George died in 1940, Henry and Ed taking on odd jobs to maintain the farm. Augusta continued to abuse them, having decided they were destined to follow their father on the hot rails to hell. Ed accepted the belittling and imprecations, while Henry on occasion took issue with her attitude.

AMERICA'S MOST BIZARRE MURDERER

EDWARD GEIN

by Judge Robert H. Gollmar

With eight pages of blood-curdling police photographs

Above:

The book written by the judge of Gein's 1968 trial.

Henry died in May 1944, supposedly fighting a brush fire close to their home. After reporting him missing, Ed then led police straight to his body, which was in an unburned area. His cause of death was given as asphyxiation, though Henry's head was bruised. (Judge Robert Gollmar, who presided over Gein's 1968 trial and subsequently wrote *Edward Gein: America's Most Bizarre Murderer*, states there was no autopsy.)

Gein was left with his beloved mother to himself, though not for long. She died in December 1945, following a series of strokes.

Bereft of his mother, incapable of shaking off her thirty-nine year domination, Gein's psychosis blossomed and bloomed. Seen by the community as an essentially harmless fruitcake (one of his jobs was babysitting!) and always having been a loner, Gein was left to retreat into fantasy worlds fuelled by anatomy textbooks, pulp magazines (adventure stories about head-hunters seem to have been a favourite), stories of Nazi experiments and piles of local newspapers (his attention strangely drawn to the obituaries...). Gein began his nocturnal graveyard wanderings, returning with female body parts and sections of skin. Genitalia in particular interested him.

Though only convicted of two murders (Worden and Mary Hogan, missing since 1954), Gein was suspected of other local disappearances, specifically two teenage girls and two middle-aged men. Gein's premises and areas around his home were systematically searched, including extensive aerial surveys, and no traces of any corresponding remains were found. Given Gein's oedipal fixation and the nature of the remains found around his home, it seems unlikely he would choose such victims (the girls were too young, the men were, well, men), though Judge Golmar seems sure he murdered the girls, as genitals belonging to two young, unidentified females were amongst Gein's collection.

In early 1958, Gein was declared insane and sentenced to indefinite incarceration in the Central State Hospital in Waupun. On 27 March, three days before it was due to be auctioned, Gein's house burned to the ground. Three days later all his possessions not destroyed in the fire were sold, bringing in around $5,000. The most famous item was his car, which became a fixture at county fairs ('See the car that hauled the dead from their graves!').

It took ten years before Gein was declared 'fit' to stand trial. The trial took place between January and November 1968, with Gein ultimately judged insane due to chronic schizophrenia at the time of the murders. He was returned to the Central State Hospital. In 1978 he was transferred to Mendota Mental Health Institute, where he was always described as a model inmate: gentle and polite. Gein died on 26 July 1984, at the age of seventy-seven, and was buried next to his mother in Plainfield Cemetery. His headstone was stolen in June 2000, presumably by one of the miserable specimens who 'worship' him. It has yet to make an appearance on the world's largest internet auction site…

In 1959, a copy of Robert Bloch's just-published short novel *Psycho* came into the hands of Alfred Hitchcock. Norman Bates, the book's 'protagonist', was loosely based on Ed Gein (Bloch had lived less than fifty miles from Plainfield). Hitchcock suggested Anthony Perkins for the role of Bates — written by Bloch as a slobby, middle-aged, beer-swilling peeper — and the film's 1960 release changed modern cinema. Perhaps the most overrated film of the past fifty years, *Psycho* produced three legitimate sequels: *Psycho II* (1983), *Psycho III* (1986) and the TV movie *Psycho IV: The Beginning* (1990; featuring a script by Joseph Stefano, writer of the original), not to mention Gus Van Sant's pointless, virtually shot-for-shot remake in 1998, and *Bates Motel* (1987), a poorly-received pilot for a thankfully unmade television series. *Psycho's* influence also inspired countless imitators whose relevance to the Gein case is usually marginal at best, the majority being no-budget studies in shrieking, oedipal, cross-dressing murderers.

The Snivelling Oedipal Killer Jerk movie, a horror sub-genre as worthless as the Teen-Hacker in Ludicrous Outfit, with which it sometimes interbreeds, is a direct descendent of *Psycho*. The Snivelling Jerk has usually suffered a childhood trauma (cheapest and most popular is seeing his mother/sister/father having sex) which causes him to spy on young women, kill young women, build a shrine with bodies (or parts thereof), mutter and mumble to himself while creeping around, and finally kidnap a young woman who reminds him of his mother/sister/father. He dresses in his mother's clothes, shows his latest victim the shrine, a fight ensues and he dies. That's it. Sometimes there are hints at cannibalism and/or necrophilia: *Maniac, Wicked Wicked, 3 on a Meathook, Don't Go in the House, It!, I Dismember Mama, Skinner* — knock yourself out, watch them all. (It should be noted that *Ed and His Dead Mother*, a bizarre black comedy starring Steve Buscemi, has nothing to do with Ed Gein or *Psycho*.)

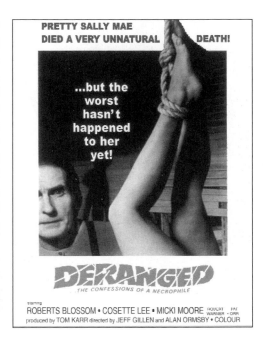

PRETTY SALLY MAE DIED A VERY UNNATURAL DEATH!

...but the worst hasn't happened to her yet!

DERANGED

THE CONFESSIONS OF A NECROPHILE

starring
ROBERTS BLOSSOM • COSETTE LEE • MICKI MOORE   HORUH   PAI   WARNER • ORR
produced by TOM KARR directed by JEFF GILLEN and ALAN ORMSBY • COLOUR

Gein was also the basis of the Buffalo Bill character (who 'covets' female skin) in Thomas Harris's *Silence of the Lambs*; Jonathan Demme's Oscar-winning film adaptation was produced by one-time *Texas Chain Saw Massacre* production manager Ron Bozman.

The two films based most closely on Gein's life and atrocities are *Deranged* (1974) and Chuck Parello's *Ed Gein* (2000). Directed by Alan Ormsby and Jeff Gillen, scripted by Ormsby and produced by Tom Karr, *Deranged* is now a rather obvious '70s exploitation period piece, but it possesses an authentic squalor and grubbiness lacking in Parello's film. It's also far more entertaining. The opening crawl states: 'The motion picture you are about to see is absolutely <u>true</u>. Only the names and the locations have been changed.' Up pops Tom Sims (Leslie Carlson), a cloddish on-screen narrator, to introduce us to the story of Ezra Cobb and inform us, 'It is a human horror story of ghastly proportions and [*pause*] profound reverberations.' Naturally.

Tom Karr: It was beautifully written by Alan Ormsby... I hired him to take the newspaper articles that I had gotten from the *Chicago Daily Tribune* from their library — they had all the stories about Ed Gein and what he had done and what the police had found... I got together with Ormsby and he put together a concept that was basically what I wanted... So how does the movie *Deranged* deviate from Ed Gein? Well, there's only one area where this happens. In the movie you see Ezra Cobb bringing his mother home from the cemetery... I went back to Alan Ormsby and said, 'Let's have Ezra bring his mother home and keep her in the bed where he

Above:
Ezra Cobb talks
turkey with his
companions.

can feed her and talk to her, and they can play cards together or they can gossip with the other girls that he collected and they could have a complete family.' [*The Making of Deranged* documentary]

Jeff Gillen: One of the things that I was fascinated by — the parts that Alfred Hitchcock totally chose to ignore or overlook or only used a very minimal part of — was the amount of dress-up or disguise, Ed Gein's actual putting on bits and pieces of skin and making musical instruments and useful tools. He was extremely fascinated by the bits and pieces of bone and flesh he put together. [*The Making of Deranged* documentary]

While *Deranged* does stray from many of the proven facts (though less so than *Ed Gein*) its assets still far outweigh its 'deviations', especially Ezra's realistically dingy farmhouse with its unlit corridors, musty rooms and filthy, cluttered kitchen — a marked contrast to the bright, spacious, neat and tidy household of *Ed Gein*. Particularly fine is Roberts Blossom's creepy performance as Ezra.

Jeff Gillen: I thought Roberts Blossom was perfectly cast. He involved himself deeply in the role. The scooping of the brains and the playing with the eyeballs and the dealing with the skull — at the time we were filming we were in hysterics… It hit the screen and I guess it was just too graphic an image. But Roberts Blossom did such a wonderful job that you would think he was doing something like playing with jello! He was so detached from the emotional aspects of it that it became an extremely frightening scene, although we had loads of laughs doing it. [*The Making of Deranged* documentary]

Deranged does handle its vein of sick humour remarkably well, frequently managing to strike a balance between grotesque and amusing: Ezra, oblivious to Momma's deathbed ranting ('The wages of sin is gonorrhoea, syphilis and death!') attempts to feed her soup, with explosive results, while his skull sawing, eyeball and brains scooping is so over the top as to become cringe-inducingly comical.

Jeff Gillen: There's a very fine line between what is funny and what is horrible, and I think we were able to cross that line back and forth a few different times in the film. When you were at the height of your laughter, suddenly we would hit you with a horrible image — that was what we were hoping to do. [*The Making of Deranged* documentary]

Below:

More of

Ezra's friends.

David Gregory's short documentary, tagged on the end of *Deranged*'s limited UK video release, uses clips from the much lengthier *The Deranged Chronicles*. Directed by Michael D. Moore and originally produced in 1993, it features some excellent behind-the-scenes footage, informative interviews and some entertaining stream-of-consciousness voiceover from special effects man Tom Savini. *The Deranged Chronicles* was reissued with added footage in 1999 for the film's twenty-fifth anniversary.

Filmed as *In the Light of the Moon*, *Ed Gein* won prizes for Best Film and Best Actor (Steve Railsback, who also served as executive producer) at the thirty-third Sitges film festival. While Railsback is a match for Roberts Blossom in the pop-eyed creepy smirking stakes, it's hard to see how the film received such an accolade. Besides the frequently levelled criticism of liberties taken with the story, it's a curiously flat and lifeless affair, with a drab, made-for-TV look, and — Railsback notwithstanding — performances ranging from somnolent to somnambulant. Amongst its numerous story quirks are: Ed's explicit murder of Henry; major changes (both psychological and in physical appearance) to Augusta and Bernice Worden (here called Mrs

Below:
Steve Railsback
as Ed Gein:
with mask...

Bottom:
... and without.

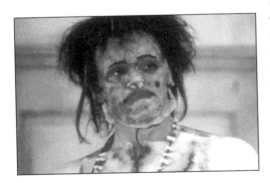

Marshall); the compressing of twelve years' worth of perversion into what appears to be a few weeks; Gein's (immaculately clean) house pointlessly redesigned; the circumstances of Gein's apprehension changed considerably; a heavily implied incestuous relationship with his mother... Some of these criticisms could obviously be levelled at *Deranged*, and one hardly expects complete adherence to the facts in a movie like this, but the changes wrought to *Ed Gein*'s story add further irritation to an already unappealing product. When even 'The Christian Spotlight', a remarkable internet film review database, takes issue with *Ed Gein*'s divergence from the known facts, there *must* be something wrong... Despite (or perhaps because of) its obvious good intentions, it's a laborious eighty-minute trudge, enlivened only by Steve Railsback — an actor who can now lay claim to portraying two of America's most notorious maniacs, having delivered a suitably manic Charles Manson in the 1976 TV movie *Helter Skelter*, with Marilyn Burns as Linda Kasabian.

Railsback also starred as angst-ridden blockhead astronaut Tom Carlson in Tobe Hooper's *Lifeforce*, a bizarre performance veering from comatose to apoplectic in the same scene.

Above left:

Sitges promo

booklet for

Ed Gein.

Perhaps because his case is one of the world's most perverse outside the pages of Krafft-Ebing's *Psychopathia Sexualis*, Gein's legacy endures: books, magazine articles, lunch boxes and internet shrines to him abound, musical 'tributes' to his 'work' are innumerable (the most recent being *Plainfield Cemetery*, an album by Swedish death metal band Deranged). Gein's activities also provided the lyrical basis for numerous 'pop' songs, a random handful of which includes: 'Ballad of Ed Gein' (Swamp Zombies), 'Dead Skin Mask' (Slayer), 'Old Mean Ed Gein' (The Fibonnacis), 'Ed Gein' (Macabre), 'Skinned' (Blind Melon) and 'Nothing to Gein' (Mudvayne). Amongst the legion of bands taking their names from him are much-loved New York punkers Ed Gein's Car, The Ed Gein Fan Club, Ed Gein, and Gein & the Grave Robbers.

Above:

Ed Gein figure by

Spectre Studios.

For further illumination, simply tap 'Ed Gein' into Google, and prepare to feel the weight of the world descend upon your shoulders. ■

A HORROR FILM TO SCARE
THE SHIT OUT OF YOU

'In a sense it's really amazing, what happens and how it happens, in terms of the manufacture of movies. The real miracle is there are *any* get made that are worth seeing. That there are many, many bad ones is no surprise — the shock is those rare ones that somehow endure the process and come out worth seeing.'

So said Kim Henkel when I was musing on the snake-bit nature of the *Chainsaw* series. And he's absolutely right, summing up the whole thirty-year saga of attempts (including by himself) to duplicate the success of *The Texas Chain Saw Massacre*. No matter how we deconstruct it (and I think we've atomised it here) the original *Chain Saw* still is, always will be, far more than the sum of its parts. Whatever Sallye Richardson felt entered it that night in 1974 refuses to depart. It remains one of the greatest horror films of all time, not just for those who saw it at the cinema in the '70s, but for those experiencing it for the first time on video or DVD.

I first read about it in the *New Musical Express* in '74 or '75 and had to grind my teeth in frustration until finally seeing it in 1978 (when I was informed I was 'really sick', in a not particularly ironic or amused manner, by the couple I'd dragged along — perhaps we shouldn't have got so stoned first). In 1976 the Sex Pistols were amongst its first English devotees, the Tyla Gang and Ramones had songs about it — but even though it became a punk icon, it's both an artefact of an earlier era and something entirely out of time. Trying to analyse its appeal is almost as pointless as theorising why people still like Elvis or the Beatles (or even the Sex Pistols) — it's more than just being in the right place at the right time, there must be something which continues to attract people, something which makes it exhilarating for each new generation.

Sure, almost every example of '60s and '70s kitsch/trash idiocy has its advocates, but the films usually have little currency beyond fanatics. *The Texas Chain Saw*

Massacre transcends its $125,000 budget, 16mm origins and, like it or not, is part of cinema history. And while Bryanston's exploitation campaign was impressive (what could whip up critical frenzy better than dumping a copy of a horror film on the Museum of Modern Art, then sending out a press release to inform the media?), we've seen enough over-hyped product to know that hype alone does not deliver in anything but the short term — who would now care to admit believing *The Blair Witch Project* was ever anything more than contemptible?

Above:

Leatherface:

he doesn't like

you, he wants

to kill you.

The Texas Chain Saw Massacre materialised at a time when North American cinema was at the height of its creativity. Besides the obvious *Easy Riders, Raging Bulls* coterie, the late '60s/early '70s also produced George Romero, David Cronenberg, Wes Craven and John Carpenter, whose early films not only operated outside the mainstream but also were aesthetically at odds with average exploitation fare. Tobe Hooper and *Chain Saw* slotted neatly into that group, and one of the reasons for the film's endurance is not only does it terrify you, but it possesses an aesthetic which lends itself to as many pseudo-intellectual hypotheses as the mutant academicians of cult culture can postulate. Post-hippie, Watergate-era, Vietnam/culture-shock, revolt-of-the-underclass musings mean nothing if the film doesn't work as a *horror film* to *scare the shit out of you*. That's what it is, that's what it does. We can do an A. J. Weberman and rummage through the contents of Hooper's and Henkel's garbage cans, trying to figure exactly what the hell caused this phenomenon, but Weberman didn't succeed with Bob Dylan, and we probably won't with *Chain Saw*. Maybe it really is a film about meat. Maybe it really is a film about the Vietnam era. But we don't ponder that as we're watching, we try to stop cowering in our seats.

The same can be said for *Shivers* or *Rabid*, *Last House on the Left*, *Halloween*, Romero's *Living Dead* films — you can circle jerk yourself to death discussing the socio-economic ramifications, but not while you're watching. All great horror films have sub-texts, but they share one primary objective: to borrow a phrase from Anne Billson, *they remind you you're going to die*. They want to scare the shit out of us by relentlessly reminding us of the inevitability of our death, and we emerge feeling traumatised, slightly desperate, having made it through the on-screen victims' experiences while confronting the realisation that we ourselves are going to die. To produce that feeling successfully a film must become more than the sum of its parts: the film-makers must convince us *we* are the victims, we're *in* the movie. (Any thoughts of 'It's only a movie' have been long forgotten.) And that's what *The Texas Chain Saw Massacre* does, that's why it works, why it stands alone in the series, and that's the true nature of the horror film: we survive with Sally, but we die with Kirk, Pam, Jerry and Franklin.

Well, it's another theory to dismiss, if nothing else. Perhaps it goes some way towards accounting for why *The Texas Chain Saw Massacre* possesses qualities lacking elsewhere in the series — not to say they're bad films, they just don't engage us on the same terms. Returning to Kim Henkel's opening observation, they didn't endure the process of manufacture, failed to entirely survive the damage inflicted by producers, studios and ratings boards. *The Texas Chain Saw Massacre* is timeless, almost peerless, maybe even a work of art; it has assumed a life of its own beyond anything the makers could have envisaged. Thirty years later they want to re-imagine it: in Hollywood anything is possible. Except perhaps trying to fully understand the phenomenon that is *The Texas Chain Saw Massacre*... ■

Cast of Characters

ERIC BALFOUR (actor: *The Texas Chainsaw Massacre* 2003)

WAYNE BELL (boom operator/post-production sound/co-music: *The Texas Chain Saw Massacre*, sound: *The Texas Chainsaw Massacre 2*, music: *The Return of the Texas Chainsaw Massacre*) lives in Austin. He continues to work in sound recording/design, and also makes documentaries. He worked with Eagle Pennell on *The Whole Shootin' Match* and *Last Night at the Alamo*, co-wrote the music for *Eaten Alive*, and recorded sound for *Mongrel* and *Future Kill*. (He'd also like to point out that horror movies make up only a tiny proportion of his work over the past thirty years.)

'My ideal would be to take a film from the beginning, all the way to the final product, to shepherd every aspect of the soundtrack — because sound is half the movie experience, sound is where your story gets told, sound trumps picture: you can show a picture and have two different tracks and the meaning of the pictures is completely different for each track… The power of the soundtrack — not just the music, but all the parts together — is incredible, a lot of film-makers don't quite get it. It's what first attracted me, and that's still what I do.'

JESSICA BIEL (actress: *The Texas Chainsaw Massacre* 2003)

RON BOZMAN (production manager: *The Texas Chain Saw Massacre*) is a Hollywood producer and assistant director, frequently working with Jonathan Demme. He shared a 'Best Picture' Oscar, a BAFTA Best Film award, a Director's Guild of America award for Outstanding Directorial Achievement in Motion Pictures and a Producer's Guild of America Golden Laurel Motion Picture Producer of the Year Award for *Silence of the Lambs*.

JOE BOB BRIGGS aka John Bloom (actor: *The Texas Chainsaw Masscre 2*). Gonzo Movie-Goer, originator of 'We Are the Weird'. His latest book *Profoundly Disturbing: Shocking Movies That Changed History* contains a lengthy chapter on *The Texas Chain Saw Massacre*, besides *Deep Throat*, *Triumph of the Will* and a bunch of other goodies. Here's a quickie email interview that arrived too late to be fitted into the *Chainsaw 2* section:

How did you get involved in Chainsaw 2?
Tobe Hooper knew I was a big fan of *Chain Saw*, so when I went to the set to do an

article on Dennis Hopper for *Rolling Stone*, the screenwriter Kit Carson suggested they put me in the movie. Tobe loved the idea, so I essentially wrote the two scenes for myself. Tobe also wanted to use the two babes in the scene, so I worked them in. It was all kind of done as a lark.

What happened in your scene? How long did it last?
I walk out of a movie theatre with the two bimbos, and I'm explaining with great authority how fake the effects were in the movie, how that's not how people really die in real life. After I've gone on for a while, trying to instruct these two women in the finer points of real gore, Leatherface appears and I look up at him, not fearful so much as in awe, like someone seeking an autograph. My last words are, 'Well, nail my dick to a tree!' — before he plunges the chainsaw into my stomach, I scream, and various articles of bloody clothing fly past my head. Whole thing takes about thirty seconds, I would imagine.

Was it shot by Tobe or that weird Newt guy?
It was shot by Tobe. He was grinning the whole time.

Did they ever tell you why they cut it? Was it one of the deleted scenes included on the laser disc release?
Cannon Films was trying to shorten the film by several minutes right before its release, and they found this scene expendable. They were right, it really didn't advance the plot at all. Tobe called to apologize, said it wasn't his decision. And yes, it was restored on the DVD, but it's a grainy scratchy work print.

Were you around the set for long? Any observations?
I was there for about a week. I spent some time with Kit Carson and with Dennis Hopper. Hopper's agents had told him not to make the movie, that it would ruin his career. But he wanted to spend the summer in Austin, where he could play golf. He was just starting his second career after coming off drugs and liquor.

ANDREW BRYNIARSKI (actor: *The Texas Chainsaw Massacre* 2003)

MARILYN BURNS (actress: *The Texas Chain Saw Massacre* and *The Return of the Texas Chainsaw Massacre*) lives in Houston. After *Chain Saw* she got tied to a bed and generally abused in *Eaten Alive*, played Linda Kasabian in *Helter Skelter*, and co-starred in the snake-bit *Future Kill* with Edwin Neal. Here, Marilyn looks back fondly on the experience of making *Future Kill*:

'This is torture... [*agonised silence for a long period...*] I think they put all their vision into the Giger artwork [for the poster]. We needed more focus on... the movie. Ed... they... had... a vision... I would never... I don't want to say anything that would hurt anybody's feelings... You know, if you had sent me an email saying you wanted to talk about *Eaten Alive* and *Future Kill*, I think I'd have just deleted it.'

ROBERT A. BURNS (art director: *The Texas Chain Saw Massacre*) has worked on a multitude of films including *The Hills Have Eyes*, *The Howling*, *Re-Animator* and *Microwave Massacre*. He direct-ed the notorious *Mongrel* ('a dog of a movie') and starred in *Confessions of a Serial Killer*, more closely based on the Henry Lee Lucas case than the better-known *Henry, Portrait of a Serial Killer*. He's also an expert on acromegalic actor Rondo Hatton (check his website).

Above:
Marilyn Burns
in Future Kill.

'I have four different screenplays that are being championed by people in LA trying to find the funding, some for me to direct. The most promising is *Unbroken*, a true story of suspense that Stuart Gordon has optioned. He is trying to put together the financing for me to direct it in LA later this year. He feels he is right on the verge of completing the deal. (Yeah, "The check's in the mail," and "I won't cum in your mouth.")'

JEFF BURR (director: *Leatherface: Texas Chainsaw Massacre III*) has directed numerous fantasy and horror films including entries in the *Puppet Master* series, *Pumpkinhead II* and *Johnny Mysto: Boy Wizard*.

L. M. KIT CARSON (script: *The Texas Chainsaw Massacre 2*) is a native of Dallas, Texas, and a writer, producer and actor (sometimes all three together). Came to prominence as an actor in the '67 cult hit *David Holzman's Diary*, directed by Jim McBride, who later direct-ed the Carson-scripted *Breathless* remake. Co-director of *The American Dreamer*, a 1971 portrait of Dennis Hopper at work on *The Last Movie*, recently co-executive produced and acted in the award-winning *Hurricane* (aka *Hurricane Streets*), and co-wrote, co-produced and acted in *Bullfighter*.

LARRY CARROLL (co-editor: *The Texas Chain Saw Massacre*) became a successful editor, producer and director in Hollywood.

JAMES L. CARTER (director of photography: *Leatherface: Texas Chainsaw Massacre III*) has worked on over forty films, from *Don't Answer the Phone* and *Satan's Mistress* to *My Dog Skip* and *Tuck Everlasting*...

MARY CHURCH (script girl/stunts: *The Texas Chain Saw Massacre*) has become a production manager and producer in Hollywood, working extensively in TV.

ALLEN DANZIGER (actor: *Eggshells* and *The Texas Chain Saw Massacre*) runs a party favours business in Austin called Three Ring Service.

'We started doing singing telegrams and moved on to clowns, jugglers, Las Vegas nights, corporate picnics — anything to do with entertainment. The catfish rodeo had a short life: we started off with the idea of hooking them, but changed it to lassoing them, so you could catch them and they go right back, but people got upset with us for hurting the fish, so I said, "Enough of that" — we did it, we proved that we could do it, but we got too many complaints, so we scrapped it — a couple of years and that was it for catfish. A few weeks ago we did the Spam-O-Rama — everything you can do or make with spam — it was a big deal! That started here in Austin.'

MIKE DELUCA (associate producer: *Leatherface: Texas Chainsaw Massacre III*) is now President of Production at DreamWorks Pictures.

JOHN DUGAN (actor: *The Texas Chain Saw Massacre, The Return of the Texas Chainsaw Massacre*)

TOBY EMMERICH (President of Production, New Line Cinema)

ROBERT ENGELMAN (producer: *Leatherface: Texas Chainsaw Massacre III*) produced numerous films (including *Frankenstein: The College Years, Mr Nanny* and *Blade*), and worked as an assistant director throughout the '80s (*The Border, Footloose, Pee-Wee's Big Adventure* and many more).

R. LEE ERMEY (actor: *The Texas Chainsaw Massacre* 2003). Gun-toting neo-fascist military supremacist character actor in dozens of movies — outstanding in Kubrick's *Full Metal Jacket*.

JOHN HENRY FAULK, the storyteller in *Chain Saw*'s graveyard scene, was a famous Texan blacklisted during the '50s. Born in Austin in 1913, Faulk was a humorist, raconteur, civil rights activist and WWII veteran, who began a series of radio shows in 1946. In 1956, towards the end of Senator Joe McCarthy's anti-communist witch-hunts, Faulk's union activity led to a brush with AWARE, a New York-based organisation who, for a fee, would investigate individuals for 'subversive' affiliations. Branded a communist by AWARE and subsequently unable to broadcast, Faulk sued, running up against Roy Cohn, McCarthy's psychopathic right-hand man. After a six year legal case Faulk was awarded $3.5 million, only to have it reduced to $500,000 by an Appeals Court. Victorious but broke (his award was swallowed by legal fees, and CBS would not re-hire him), Faulk returned to Austin. In 1963 he wrote *Fear on Trial*, an account of his legal battle, and until his death was involved in Austin politics, wrote plays, had a regular spot on the 'Hee-Haw' downhome TV series, and travelled the US lecturing students about civil rights.

In 1975 Faulk was played by William Devane in *Fear on Trial*, a TV movie based on his book. Faulk had appeared in *Lovin' Molly* with Paul Partain and Marilyn Burns; Partain later acted in *Blue Thunder* with William Devane... And Faulk (together with Lou Perryman) also appeared in *Trespasses*, starring Robert Kuhn, with sound/music by Wayne Bell.

He died in April 1990 — a library and theatre in Austin are named after him, and numerous awards given in his name.

Allen Danziger: For me one of the neatest things was meeting John Henry Faulk: he was a raconteur, I remember listening to him on the radio as a kid in New York, talking about civil rights. He was just a phenomenal guy and it was a real treat for me to meet him, to listen to him talk as we were on our way to the set.

Levie Isaacks: I knew John Henry Faulk pretty well, I had used him in some political commercials. We tried to do a radio show, but the problem was that he had no discipline — he'd tell a story one time and it'd be ten minutes, next it'd be eight minutes... You couldn't control him, he just had to go his way — but they were wonderful stories.

Kim Henkel: I knew John Henry — I can't remember how I met him, probably from Austin politics, he was round and about — and I'd read his book. I wouldn't call him a 'character', more of a political activist — not as a candidate but he was actively involved in local politics.

DAVID L. FORD was the producer of *Eggshells* and *The Windsplitter*, and later of *Hotwire* (in which Jim Siedow appeared) and *Uphill all the Way*, both directed by Texas 'legend' Frank Q. Dobbs.

JEFF GILLEN (co-director: *Deranged*) died in June 1995 of a heart attack. He also collaborated with Alan Ormsby on the 1972 low-budget horror *Deathdream*, for which Tom Savini provided special effects.

DUANE GRAVES (director: *Headcheese*): 'Our distributor, EI Independent Cinema in New Jersey is currently looking for a horror project for us (Justin Meeks and myself) to direct. In the meantime, we've finished a new feature length horror script to shop around and also another black and white horror short titled *Voltagen* shot on 16mm, which may find its way out on DVD in the near future.'

ED GUINN (actor: *The Texas Chain Saw Massacre*) was a member of legendary '60s Texas psych band The Conqueroo, closely associated with the even more legendary Thirteenth Floor Elevators. He has a recording studio in Austin. Here's a short email interview with Ed:

How did you become involved with Chain Saw?
Bob Burns hired me because my brother in law and I had a diesel truck.

Had you seen Eggshells, *Tobe Hooper's previous film?*
No.

Was the running over of the Hitchhiker scene rehearsed much? Did it seem weird to run some-one over, even if it was a dummy?
I don't remember if it took lots of takes. I do remember having to run up and down the road over and over and that just about killed me. Never been much of a jock!

Is having acted in this film something that keeps coming back to haunt you? Has it been a help or a hindrance to your career in any way? (People like me harassing you...)
It is a little odd to think, given the stuff I have done and been involved in in my life, that this movie generates interest over the years like nothing else. Gag!

Did you like the film? Was its success a surprise to you?
Not particularly on either count. The success was of no consequence to me — I got paid when I did it and that was all I ever expected.

You've got a recording studio now... I think Gunnar Hansen told me you wrote music for com-
mercials — is that right?
I got out of the composition business some time ago and have been writing software
with some partners for about fifteen years. It pays better :)

You did music for Bob Burns' film Mongrel *in the early '80s — had the two of you kept in*
touch since Chain Saw?
Sure, I talk to Bob every now and then.

Have you worked on any other film projects?
An AFI student film and lots of docs and industrials etc.

JERRY HALL (Governor Preston Smith's press secretary, instrumental in setting up the
Texas Film Commission)

GUNNAR HANSEN (actor: *The Texas Chain Saw Massacre*) now lives in Maine. He has
published four books, including *Bear Dancing on the Hill* (a volume of poetry) and
Islands at the Edge of Time, about the barrier islands on the US coast from Texas to
North Carolina. He also writes screenplays and makes documentary films.

Film appearances include *The Demon Lover*, *Hollywood Chainsaw Hookers*,
Campfire Tales, *Mosquito* (with his friend, legendary Stooges guitarist Ron Asheton),
Hellblock, *Freakshow*, *Rachel's Attic* and *Hatred of a Minute*.

KIM HENKEL (actor/script ideas: *Eggshells*, co-script/associate producer: *The Texas Chain
Saw Massacre*, director/script/co-producer: *The Return of the Texas Chainsaw Massacre*)
teaches English and screenwriting 'down on the border — you can spit into Mexico.'
After his adventures in Hollywood and the screen trade he returned to Austin and
worked with Eagle Pennell on *Last Night at the Alamo*. Wayne Bell, Lou Perryman and
Brian Huberman were also involved in this classic Texas indie film. 'I wrote the screenplay and we were short of hands so I got drafted to be an actor. I hate being in front of
the camera so I completely rewrote the role so you had to drag words out of the character's mouth. It was a testimony to my loathing to being in front of a camera.' Hopefully
his *Exurbia* screenplay ('Sort of a horror piece but not in the traditional sense – like the
underbelly of the American Dream... I had some interest from New Line, but we ended
up at loggerheads. It's an interesting little script...') will one day be produced.

DOUG HOLLOWAY has nothing really to do with this book. Part of Eagle Pennell's crew on
Whole Shootin' Match, went on to direct *Fast Money*, in which Lou Perryman appeared.

Levie Isaacks: Basically what Doug did: he was so impressed by *Whole Shootin' Match* that he took the cast and Eagle, he had this script and a little bit of money — not very much, I think most of us worked for free on that one... It was shot on 16mm, and in those days 16mm was still in amateur category, and *Fast Money* didn't have anybody known in it. Eagle started out as DP, but it was the same story: he just drank too much, he drank while he was working, so finally Doug fired him — originally I was doing the lighting, but I ended up finishing it for him.

SCOTT HOLTON (publicity: *The Texas Chainsaw Massacre 2*), now deceased, also worked on Tobe Hooper's remake of *Invaders From Mars* (he was a life-long fan of the original) and *InnerSpace*.

TOBE HOOPER (director/photography/co-editor/some music: *Eggshells*, director/co-script/co-music/additional photography: *The Texas Chain Saw Massacre*, director/co-producer/co-music: *The Texas Chainsaw Massacre 2* — see separate chapter starting on page 112 for other credits)

WILLIAM 'TONY' HOOPER, son of Tobe. Director's Runner on *Lifeforce,* model maker on *Chainsaw 2* (working on the dinner table and the bone furniture), produced various special effects on *Spontaneous Combustion* and designed the Mangler Machine (a job taking three months) for *The Mangler*. Directed the still-unseen *All American Massacre.*

BRIAN HUBERMAN (director: *The Return of the Texas Chainsaw Massacre: The Documentary*): 'I was a graduate of the National Film School in Beaconsfield (England), part of the first intake that crawled out into the world in '74. I got offered the job to go to Rice University fairly quickly and that's where I've remained, as a teacher and a film-maker.' In addition to *The Return of the Texas Chainsaw Massacre: The Documentary*, his work includes *John Wayne's The Alamo,* a documentary included on the DVD, video journalist for The Learning Channel's *Trauma* and *Paramedics* documentary series, PBS documentaries on blues men, transsexuals and housing in Houston (not all in the same film, sadly), various anthropological concerns, and much on Davy Crockett, including a film about the controversial *De la Pena Diary.*

LEVIE ISAACKS (director of photography: *The Return of the Texas Chainsaw Massacre*): 'When I was going to UT, I worked at a local television station, I was a newsman, and in that kind of market you did everything: I shot the stories, edited them, wrote them, recorded them. That's how I met Kim — a friend was working at South-West

Development Laboratories, and that was Kim's day job when he was writing *Chain Saw*. So I sort of met Tobe through Kim.

'When I first came to LA one of the first people I called was Tobe. I'd done a picture for Roger Corman, showed him the work I'd done and ended up doing a number of projects as cinematographer with Tobe: *Spontaneous Combustion*, *I'm Dangerous Tonight*, *Real Ghosts* for CBS, then a *Tales From the Crypt*. The producer from *Real Ghosts* became the producer for *Tales From the Crypt*, and he carried me over, so I have to give Tobe credit for helping me get started out here in Los Angeles.'

After photographing over a dozen episodes of *Tales*, Isaacks shot numerous cinema and TV movies before becoming cinematographer on *Dawson's Creek* and *Malcolm in the Middle* (of which he's also directed several episodes).

ROBERT JACKS (actor: *The Return of the Texas Chainsaw Massacre*)

BILL JOHNSON (actor: *The Texas Chainsaw Massacre 2*) lives in Austin. Besides film and theatre acting, he's a highly respected voice coach, does voiceovers for various software games series, and if he has time, operates a cat sitting service. Film appearances include the inescapable *Future Kill*, *The Texas Comedy Massacre* and Oliver Stone's *Talk Radio*. He also appeared as 'Vice Cop' in Doug Holloway's *Fast Money*.

TOM KARR (producer: *Deranged*) acted in and was associate producer (with Michael D. Moore, who directed the *Deranged* documentary) on the 1995 psycho-gore movie *Creep*.

RICHARD KIDD (owner of Motion Picture Productions): 'I spent my entire career doing what I suppose is classed as 'corporate business', where you're doing things that are never seen in the theatrical world, but they sure pay a lot of bills! After *Chain Saw*, we'd all gone our separate ways, the original five was totally split, so I started a company where I could always remember who I worked for — 'Richard Kidd Productions' [*laughs*]. I did that for a couple of years in Austin then moved to Dallas, stuck with it till I sold the whole operation to some big boys out of New York in '95. I waited for

Above:
'They need
someone who
looks like Baby
Huey' – the real
Bill Johnson.

the cheque to clear and I retired! Never regretted it for one minute! My wife and I bought a boat and spent the last four years cruising round the world.'

RICHARD KOORIS (director of photography: *The Texas Chainsaw Massacre 2*): 'I moved to Austin in 1966 and got a master's degree in film production — the first master's degree from UT. I started teaching there while I was getting my degree. I was shooting just about anything I could get my hands on just to get experience as a DP: commercials, the film for the 1968 World's Fair, a lot of documentaries. We did a dramatic film called *Stasis* in 1966, it won the *Esquire* film competition, which was a pretty high-profile contest at that time. It was a black and white fifty-five minute mini-feature, based on a short story by Jean-Paul Sartre, 'The Wall' ('Le Mur'). I was DP/camera operator. The fellow who directed it was Rod Whitaker, better known by the name Trevanian, who wrote *The Eiger Sanction* — he was my professor and kind of mentor from the time I got to Texas to the early '70s. I studied very closely with him and he had a great influence on me.'

Below:

'The plate could use a little more pus' – the real Bill Moseley.

He now owns Gear, and 501 Studios, a large complex in Austin supplying most film-making requisites, from equipment rental to sound stages. He also works as a director/cameraman for Synthetic Pictures, with clients including Wal-Mart, Miracle-Gro, American Heart Association and Budweiser. He also shot Bob Burns' *Mongrel*…

ROBERT KUHN (financier/legal stuff: *The Texas Chain Saw Massacre*, executive producer/ co-producer: *The Return of the Texas Chainsaw Massacre*) is a partner in a law firm in Austin. He acted in and executive produced *Trespasses*, and thinks he'll probably spend the rest of his life in litigation attached to *The Return of the Texas Chainsaw Massacre*.

ERIC LASHER was stills photographer on Tobe Hooper's *Invaders From Mars*, *The Texas Chainsaw Massacre 2*, *Spontaneous Combustion*, *I'm Dangerous Tonight*, *The Mangler*, *Crocodile*, *Nowhere Man* ('I took the photo 'Hidden Agenda' — the picture the show was based around'), *Tales From the Crypt* and *Freddy's*

Nightmares. Currently 'doing a pre-edit on a Travel Log/Documentary that I directed and shot at the end of 2002 in Eastern Europe, called *Vagabonds: Around the Bloc in 80 Days.* We did sixteen countries, twenty-three cities in eighty days, almost all in what was 'The Soviet Union'.'

TERI McMINN (actress: *The Texas Chain Saw Massacre*) got hung on a meathook then retired from cinema after *Chain Saw*. She supposedly charges $40 for an autograph. Start saving.

R. A. MIHAILOFF (actor: *Leatherface: Texas Chainsaw Massacre III*)

FRED MILLER (producer: *Peter, Paul and Mary*)

JIM MORAN (director: *Leatherface Speaks*)

BILL MOSELEY (actor: *The Texas Chainsaw Massacre 2*) lives in Los Angeles, and most recently starred in Rob Zombie's *House of 1000 Corpses.* Other film appearances include *Pink Cadillac, Army of Darkness,* Tom Savini's *Night of the Living Dead,* and *Honey, I Blew up the Kid.*

Above:
Ed Neal in
Future Kill.

EDWIN NEAL (actor: *The Texas Chain Saw Massacre*) lives in Austin. He acted in and co-produced Ronald Moore's notorious *Future Kill,* acted in *My Boyfriend's Back* (with Renee Zellweger and Matthew McConaughey) and did voice work for *Sonic the Hedgehog: The Movie.*

LISA NEWMEYER (actress: *The Return of the Texas Chainsaw Massacre*)

TED NICOLAOU (location sound: *The Texas Chain Saw Massacre*) has directed over twenty features, many for producer Charles Band, including five films in the *Subspecies* series, three *Dragonworld* films and a couple of *Leapin' Leprechauns…*

MARCUS NISPEL (director: *The Texas Chainsaw Massacre* 2003)

MARK ORDESKY (President, Fine Line Features)

BILL PARSLEY, *The Texas Chain Saw Massacre's* main financier, remained in Austin working in the state legislature and speculating on the side in anything that took his fancy, from oil to banking to movies. With Warren Skaaren, tried to produce a *Chainsaw* sequel at some point in the '70s. Luckily, he was unsuccessful.

PAUL A. PARTAIN (actor: *The Texas Chain Saw Massacre*, *The Return of the Texas Chainsaw Massacre*) has worked mainly in the electronics industry, though he did appear in *Race with the Devil*, *Outlaw Blues* and *Blue Thunder*.

'I will let you know that in the last couple of years I have gotten back my dream of being an actor. I have auditioned for three features: *The Rookie*, *The Life of David Gale*, and *The Alamo*. Got a small part in *David Gale* and some of it actually made it to the screen (in the AA scene, third drunk on the right). Got to audition for the director in *The Rookie*, but I just did not shift gears fast enough once I realized that my characterization of a coach was 180 degrees out from what John Lee Hancock had in mind… blew that one big time. On *The Alamo*, so far they don't seem to need grey-haired fat guys. Now if you are a young half-starved Mexican, they can use you today.'

DANIEL PEARL (director of photography: *The Texas Chain Saw Massacre*, director of photography: *The Texas Chainsaw Massacre* 2003) has shot around 250 commercials and over 500 music and concert videos (including Billy Idol's 'Dancing With Myself', directed by Tobe Hooper), winning MTV's Best Cinematography Award twice. Working in this area he met, and subsequently worked on several occasions with, Marcus Nispel, director of the latest *Chainsaw* 're-imagining', and Michael Bay. In feature films he's worked extensively with director Larry Cohen.

Robert A. Burns: I was talking to a friend in LA, it must have been almost ten years ago, and I said something about Daniel being the King of music videos, and he said, 'King, hell — he's the *Emperor!*'

DOROTHY (DOTTIE) PEARL (make-up: *The Texas Chain Saw Massacre*) is now a Hollywood make-up artist, working with Jessica Lange for many years. Films include *1941*, *Tootsie*, *The Postman Always Rings Twice*, *Groundhog Day*, *Race with the Devil*, *Poltergeist*, and *She Came to the Valley* (an Albert Band western on which Robert Burns and Daniel Pearl also worked).

EAGLE PENNELL died in 2002, aged forty-nine, of alcoholism. Director of *Hell of a*

Note (a short), *The Whole Shootin' Match* (supposedly Robert Redford's inspiration to start the Sundance Festival), *Last Night at the Alamo*, *Ice House*, a sequence of *City Life* (shot by Levie Isaacks) and *Doc's Full Service* (on which some of his direction was phoned in while drinking). His presence loomed over this book — almost everyone involved in any aspect of the Austin film-making scene during the '70s and '80s had an Eagle story to tell, and many of them collaborated with him at some point. *The Austin Chronicle* features an excellent obituary, with pieces by Wayne Bell, Brian Huberman and Lou Perryman.

Above:
Caroline Williams
and the great
Lou Perryman
in Chainsaw 2.

TONIE PERENSKI (actress: *The Return of the Texas Chainsaw Massacre*)

LOU PERRYMAN (assistant director: *Eggshells*, assistant camera: *The Texas Chain Saw Massacre*, actor: *The Texas Chainsaw Massacre 2*) is a living legend: raconteur, Renaissance man, long time friend, collaborator and sparring partner with Eagle Pennell, appearing in *Hell of a Note*, *The Whole Shootin' Match* and *Last Night at the Alamo*. Kim Henkel is currently preparing a documentary on him: 'You turn on the TV — the other day it was *Blues Brothers* — all of a sudden Lou pops up, or *Boys Don't Cry* — all of a sudden Lou pops up, or *Poltergeist* or God knows what — and there's Lou.

But right now he's driving a cab in Austin. He's gone through a lot of different careers... He's a colourful character.'

RON PERRYMAN: Lou's 'mad genius' older brother. Worked with Tobe Hooper throughout the '60s, co-director of *Peter, Paul and Mary*, collaborator on *Eggshells*, inventor and photographer *par excellence*... Fell out of orbit in the early stages of filming *Chain Saw*, though he reappeared briefly during post-production to shoot Warren Skaaren's corpse sculpture.

Sallye Richardson: Ron didn't want to do a horror film, he didn't think it was appropriate. So Ron and Tobe were going in different directions — Ron was more talk and less action, more and more the old hippie: let's go out and watch the grass grow. He enjoyed doing that kind of thing and Tobe just didn't have time for it. Ron had this film about hoboes he wanted to do — he always wanted to make that film, but as far as I know he never did.

Wayne Bell: My memory is that at a certain point as this thing [*Chain Saw*] was coming together and it became apparent what it was, Ron somewhat distanced himself. He has a bit part in *Chainsaw 2* that Tobe wanted him to do, it was one of the first things we shot — there's a chilli cook-off and Ron is playing one of the judges, a big tall guy...

Lou Perryman: The chilli cook-off was part of that 'mystery meat' motif — it could be *anything* in that chilli... But Ron ended up feeling humiliated and regretful that he had done it — he felt there was an ulterior motive on Tobe's part.

SPENCER PERSKIN (music: *Eggshells*) was a founder member of the legendary '60s psych outfit Shiva's Head Band, and is still making music today.

GARY PICKLE was once partner in MPP with Richard Kidd, Tobe Hooper, Ron Perryman and Mike Bosler. Now a producer, he also runs MPA studios in Austin.

SALLYE RICHARDSON (assistant director: *Eggshells*, co-editor/assistant director: *The Texas Chain Saw Massacre*) graduated from UT, majoring in film, and lived in Austin, Colorado and Los Angeles before moving to Dallas in the early '80s. She has continued to work in film — editing, corporate/commercial/advertising and documentaries — and ended up working for Richard Kidd again as a director, producer and VP of his company. She collaborated on a screenplay about inventor/electrical engineer/scientist Nikola Tesla, and is working on the rights to a Terry Goodkind novel for another project.

TOM SAVINI (special make-up effects: *The Texas Chainsaw Massacre 2*) is probably the world's most famous horror film special effects make-up artist, working extensively with George Romero (including acting). Directed the excellent *Night of the Living Dead* remake in 1990. One of his earliest jobs was working on *Deranged*.

DAVID J. SCHOW (script: *Leatherface: Texas Chainsaw Massacre III*) is the foremost short story writer of the '80s 'splatter punk' movement, author of *The Kill Riff* (the definitive rock 'n' roll/horror novel), *The Shaft*, many short story collections, numerous screenplays (including a couple of *Critters* and *The Crow*) and non-fiction work (*The Outer Limits Companion*).

BRAD SHELLADY (director: *The Texas Chain Saw Massacre: A Family Portrait*) was the chief case investigator for Henry Lee Lucas from 1988 to 2001, which he wrote about in Russ Kick's *Everything You Know Is Wrong*. 'I am no longer in the film field (if one could say I ever truly was) and prefer the audience view of films as opposed to behind the camera. I now spend my time in forensic investigation and as a sometime author. But *Family Portrait* will always be a work I am proud of and would do it again in a second. Maybe I can get Michael Bay to bankroll a remake, ya think?'

JIM SIEDOW (actor: *The Texas Chain Saw Massacre* and *The Texas Chainsaw Massacre 2*): '*Texas Chain Saw Massacre* was the first horror movie I ever did — I'm really a lover!' Jim still lives in Houston. Born in 1920 and a veteran of over eighty stage plays, he finally decided to retire, but is happy to attend conventions or cast reunions when his health allows. Also appeared in *Hotwire*, produced by David L. Ford, and Tobe Hooper's *Amazing Stories* episode.

WARREN SKAAREN died in December 1990. Around the time of leaving the Texas Film Commission and securing *Chain Saw*'s disastrous deal with Bryanston, he became chair-man of FPS Inc in Dallas, a film and TV production studio involved in supplying equip-ment to the TV series *Dallas*, amongst many. Thanks to some nifty work by the William Morris Agency, by the mid-'80s he had become one of the highest paid and most suc-cessful script doctors in Hollywood, working on *Top Gun*, *Beverly Hills Cop II*, *Batman* and *Beetlejuice*, also writing several unproduced scripts. He was also involved with numerous charitable organisations, foundations and societies.

MICK STRAWN (production design: *Leatherface: Texas Chainsaw Massacre III*) has worked extensively in TV, including the *Freddy's Nightmares* series, the *Hercules* movies and the fabulously titled *Frankenstein: The College Years*.

MIKE SULLIVAN (prop master: *The Texas Chainsaw Massacre 2*, credited as Michael O'Sullivan) currently teaches on-line for the University of Phoenix, and recently worked on Robert Rodriguez's *Spy Kids* movies. An actor, art director, designer and founder of the Actor's Clearing House agency in Austin, he also worked on Dennis Hopper's *The Hot Spot*, *Gettysburg*, *Lonesome Dove*...

'Michael O'Sullivan is my name for SAG because there was already a Mike Sullivan. I'm down there on the imdb in a couple of different ways — I tried to consolidate that stuff but I finally just gave up on it...

'It has been my approach to be as detailed as possible, to put as much effort and quality into every set and every prop. Part of this is because I am compulsive, but I also come at film from an actor's point of view. I try to provide the actors with the details of their fictional lives. I have always taken pride that the camera can go anywhere on a set and the detail will be appropriate for both the setting and the characters.

'I have, at times, taken this to extremes. During *The Hot Spot* I had t-shirts and caps made for a little league baseball team sponsored by Harshaw Motors and took pictures of the teams, so that the pictures on the walls behind the characters would be 'real'. Of course, the producers had a fit that I spent the extra money. They were probably right — the pictures were never ID'ed, but they could have done a close-up on them. Or on the logos for Harshaw Motors on the gimme-caps and ballpoint pens on the desk — or on the invoices in the file cabinets that they never opened. Come to think of it, I guess I am compulsive.'

WILLIAM VAIL (actor: *The Texas Chain Saw Massacre*) also appeared in the ludicrous Bobbie Bresee vehicle *Mausoleum* (as the monster) and *Poltergeist* before becoming a set designer, working mostly in TV.

CAROLINE WILLIAMS (actress: *The Texas Chainsaw Massacre 2* and [uncredited cameo] *Leatherface: Texas Chainsaw Massacre III*) has appeared in numerous TV series and feature films including *Stepfather II*, *Days of Thunder* and *How the Grinch Stole Christmas*.

BILL WITLIFF (aka Whitliff, Wittliff) wrote the screenplay for and produced *Lonesome Dove*, and wrote screenplays for *The Perfect Storm*, *Barbarosa*, *Raggedy Man* (amongst many). Also a publisher (the Encino Press, whose publications include *In a Narrow Grave*, Larry McMurtry's book of essays), a photographer, collector of photographs (he set up the Wittliff Gallery of Southwestern and Mexican Photography) and about a thousand other things. He also invested $5,000 in *The Texas Chain Saw Massacre*... ∎

Credits, Select Bibliography and Weblinks

CREDITS

EGGSHELLS
(USA 1971)

Director: Tobe Hooper
Producers: David L. Ford & Raymond O'Leary
Executive Producer: David L. Ford
Music: Spencer Perskin/Shiva's Head Band, Jim
Schulman/Timberline Rose, Hooper/Perryman
Photography: Tobe Hooper
Editors: Tobe Hooper, Robert Elkins
Assistant directors: Louis Perryman, Sallye Richardson
Collaborator: Ron Perryman
Tales of Ben Skabarsak by Kim Henkel

Cast
Mahlon Forman — Mahlon
Boris Schnurr (Kim Henkel) — Toz
Ron Barnhart — Ben Skabarsak
Amy Lester — Amy
David Noll — David
Pamela Craig — Girl in park
Allen Danziger, Sharon Danziger — couple with baby

THE TEXAS CHAIN SAW MASSACRE
(Vortex/Henkel/Hooper, USA 1974)

Procucer/Director: Tobe Hooper
Story & Screenplay: Tobe Hooper, Kim Henkel
Executive Producer: Jay Parsley
Production Manager: Ronald Bozman
Cinematographer: Daniel Pearl

Editors: Sallye Richardson, Larry Carroll
Music Score: Tobe Hooper, Wayne Bell
Assistant Director: Sallye Richardson
Lighting: Lynn Lochwood
Assistant Cameraman: Lou Perryman
Location Sound Recording: Ted Nicolaou
Post Production Sound/Boom Man: Wayne Bell
Art Director: Robert A. Burns
Grandfather's Make-up: W. E. Barnes
Make-up: Dorothy Pearl
Camera Assistant: J. Michael McClary
Script Girl: Mary Church
Additional Photography: Tobe Hooper
Stunt Driver: Perry Lorenz
Stunts: Mary Church
Associate Producers: Kim Henkel, Richard Saenz
Songs: Roger Bartlett & Friends, Timberline Rose,
        Arkey Blue, Los Cyclones

Cast
Marilyn Burns — Sally
Allen Danziger — Jerry
Paul A. Partain — Franklin
William Vail — Kirk
Teri McMinn — Pam
Edwin Neal — Hitchiker
Jim Siedow — Old Man
Gunnar Hansen — Leatherface
John Dugan — Grandfather
Robert Courtin — Window Washer
William Creamer — Bearded Man
John Henry Faulk — Storyteller
Jerry Green — Cowboy

Ed Guinn — Cattle Truck Driver
Joe Bill Hogan — Drunk
Perry Lorenz — Pick Up Driver
John Larroquette — Narrator

THE TEXAS CHAINSAW MASSACRE 2
(Cannon, USA 1986)

Director: Tobe Hooper
Producers: Menahem Golan, Yoram Globus
Script: L. M. Kit Carson
Executive Producers: Henry Holmes, James Jorgensen
Co-Producer: Tobe Hooper
Associate Producer: L. M. Kit Carson
Editor: Alain Jakubowicz
Director of Photography: Richard Kooris
Production Designer: Cary White
First Assistant Director: Richard Espinoza
Second Assistant Director: Mark Lyon
Unit Production Manager: Henry Kline
Music: Tobe Hooper & Jerry Lambert
Costume Designer: Carin Hooper
Special Make-up Effects: Tom Savini
Stunt Coordinator: John Moio
Sound Mixer: Wayne Bell
Model Maker: Tony Hooper
Script Supervisor: Laura Debolt Kooris
Special Effects Coordinator: Eddie Surkin
Second Unit Directors: Newt Arnold, John Moio
Music Supervisor: Paula Erickson
Music Editor: Michael Linn
Songs: Timbuk 3, Torch Song, The Cramps, Oingo
    Boingo, Concrete Blonde, Roky Erickson,
    Lords of the New Church, Stewart Copeland

Cast
Dennis Hopper — Lieutenant "Lefty" Enright
Caroline Williams — Vanita "Stretch" Block

Jim Siedow — Cook
Bill Moseley — Chop-Top
Bill Johnson — Leatherface
Ken Evert — Grandpa
Harlan Jordan — Patrolman
Kirk Sisco — Detective
James N. Harrell — Cut-Rite Manager
Lou Perry — L. G. McPeters
Barry Kinyon — Mercedes driver
Chris Douridas — Gunner
Judy Kelly — Gourmet Yuppette
John Martin Ivey — Yuppie
Kinky Friedman — sports anchorman
Wirt Cain — Anchorman
Dan Jenkins — TV commentator
Joe Bob Briggs — Gonzo moviegoer

**LEATHERFACE: TEXAS CHAINSAW
MASSACRE III**
(New Line, USA 1989)

Director: Jeff Burr
Producer: Robert Engelman
Script: David J. Schow
Based on Characters Created by Kim Henkel and
    Tobe Hooper
Associate Producer: Michael DeLuca
Executive in Charge of Production: Deborah Moore
Director of Photography: James L. Carter
Production Design: Mick Strawn
Editor: Brent Schoenfeld
Costume Design: Joan Hunter
Special Make-up Effects: Kurtzman, Nicotero & Berger
    EFX Group
Mechanical Effects: Bellissimo/Belardinelli Effects
Music: Jim Manzie with Patrick Regan
Stunt Coordinator: Kane Hodder
1st Assistant Director: Benita Allen

2nd Assistant Director: Skot Bright
Script Supervisor: Jesse Long
Production Mixer: Robert Janiger
Special Effects Coordinator: Thomas L Bellissimo
Mechanical Effects Designer: Dean Miller
Leatherface Makeup Applied By: Suzanne Sanders
Art Director: Ella Blakey
Music Supervised: Kevin Benson
Songs: Laaz Rockit, Hurricane, SGM, Blackmale,
    Death Angel, Wrath

Cast (in alphabetical order)
Jennifer Banko — Little Girl
Ron Brooks — TV newsman
William Butler — Ryan
Miriam Byrd-Nethery — Mama
David Cloud — Scott
Beth DePatie — Gina
Tom Everett — Alfredo
Ken Foree — Benny
Kate Hodge — Michelle
Toni Hudson — Sara
R. A. Mihailoff — Leatherface
Viggo Mortensen — Tex
Joe Unger — Tinker
Dwayne Whitaker — Kim
Michael Shamus Wiles — Checkpoint Officer
Caroline Williams [uncredited]

THE RETURN OF THE TEXAS CHAINSAW MASSACRE aka TEXAS CHAINSAW MASSACRE: THE NEXT GENERATION

(Ultra Muchos Inc & River City Films Inc, USA, 1994)

Director & Script: Kim Henkel
Producers: Robert J Kuhn, Kim Henkel
Executive Producer: Robert J Kuhn
Editor: Sandra Adair

Director of Photography: Levie Isaacks
Score: Wayne Bell
Costume Desinger: Kari Perkins
Production Designer: Deborah Pastor
Casting: Isabelle Emmanuelle Coulet
Supervising Sound Editor: Tom Hammond
Associate Producer: Charles Kuhn
Production Sound Mixer: Scott Szabo
Special Make-up Effects: J. M. Logan
Art Director: Ann Yzuel
Stunt coordinator: David 'Stutter' Sanders
Script Supervisor: Samara Paysee

Songs by: Pariah, Tail Gators, Erik & Erik, Skatenigs,
    Blind Willie's Johnson, Loose Diamonds, Daniel
    Johnston, Pushmonkey, Beau Jocques and the
    Zydeco Hi-Rolelrs, Santiago Jiminez Jr, Cecilia
    Saint, Naughty Ones, Kelly Willis/Rich
    Brotherton/John Ludwick/Don Harvey, Deborah
    Harry/Robert Jacks/Kaye Klier/Sterling
    Price-McKinney, Roky Erickson, Russ C Smith,
    Coffee Sergeants

Cast
Renee Zellweger — Jenny
Matthew McConaughey — Vilmer
Robert Jacks — Leatherface
Tonie Perenski — Darla
Joe Stevens — W. E.
Lisa Newmyer — Heather
John Harrison — Sean
Tyler Cone — Barry
James Gale — Rothman
Chris Kilgore — Rothman's Chauffeur
Vince Brock — I'm Not Hurt
Susan Loughran — Jenny's Mother
David Laurence — Jenny's Stepfather
Grayson Victor Schirmacher — Grandfather

Jeanette Wiggins — Woman Eating Chocolates

Carmen Nogales — Girl in Red Dress

Lisa Caraveo — Brenda

Les Martin, Adam White, Bill Wise — Hecklers

Loren Guerra — Bud's Pizza Attendant

Derek Keele, Debra McMichael
    — Cops at Bud's Pizza

Geri Wolcott, Axel L. Schiller — Couple in RV

Andy Cockrum — Stuffed DPS officer

Roger Roe, Angee Hughes, Rebecca Rosenberg —
    stuffed family

John Dugan — Cop at Hospital

Paul Partain — Hospital Orderly

Anonymous [Marilyn Burns] — Patient on Gurney

Fred Ellis — Voice of Narrator

Wayne Bell, Bob Simmons — Voices of Radio News

THE TEXAS CHAINSAW MASSACRE

(New Line Cinema/Next Entertainment/Platinum
Dunes/Radar Pictures Inc, USA 2003)
(Due for release in Oct 2003)

Director: Marcus Nispel

Script: Eric Bernt, Scott Kosar

Based on characters by Kim Henkel & Tobe Hooper

Producers: Michael Bay, Mike Fleiss, Andrew Form,
    Bradley Fuller

Executive Producers: Ted Field, Jeff Allard

Line Producer/Unit Production Manager: Joe Dishner

Original Music: Marilyn Manson

Director of Photography: Daniel Pearl

Editor: Glen Scantlebury

Casting: Lisa Fields

Production Design: Greg Blair

Art Director: Scott Gallagher

Set Decoration: Randy Smith Huke

Costume Design: Bobbie Mannix

Sound: Stacy Brownrigg

Special Effects: Rocky Gehr

Stunt Coordinator: Tony Cecere

Cast

Jessica Biel — Erin Hardesty

Jonathan Tucker — Morgan

Eric Balfour — Kemper Hardesty

Erica Leerhsen — Pepper

Mike Vogel — Andy

R. Lee Ermey — Sheriff Hoyt

David Dorfman — Jedidiah Sawyer

Lauren German — Teenage Girl

Heather Kafka — Henrietta Sawyer

Terrence Evans — Old Monty

John Larroquette — Narrator

SELECT BIBLIOGRAPHY

Books

Robert H. Gollmar — Edward Gein, America's Most
    Bizarre Murderer, Hallberg & Co 1982

Phil Hardy (ed) — The Aurum Film Encyclopedia:
    Horror, Revised Edition, Aurum 1993

J. Hoberman & Jonathan Rosenbaum — Midnight
    Movies, Harper & Row 1983/Da Capo Press 1991

David J. Hogan — Dark Romance: Sexuality in the Horror
    Film, McFarland 1986

Stephen Jones — Creepshows, The Illustrated Stephen
    King Movie Guide, Titan Books 2001

Stephen King, Stephen King's Danse Macabre,
    Macdonald & co (UK), 1981

Richard Meyers — For One Week Only, The World of
    Exploitation Films, New Century Publishers, 1983

Kim Newman — Nightmare Movies, Proteus
    1984/Bloomsbury 1988

Danny Peary — Cult Movies, Vermilion 1982

Robert H. Rimmer — The X-Rated Videotape Guide,
    Harmony Books 1984/Prometheus Books 1993

Donald C. Willis — *Horror and Science Fiction Films II*, Scarecrow Press 1982

Magazines

Castle of Frankenstein, No 25, June 1975

Cinefantastique, Vol 16 No 4/5, October 1986

Fangoria — numerous issues cited through the text, invaluable for Tobe Hooper interviews & *Chain Saw* articles

Film Comment, August 1986

Shock Xpress, Vol 2 No 2, Winter 1987

Video Watchdog — generally

WEBLINKS/CONTACT INFORMATION

There are dozens of websites connected to all aspects of *The Texas Chain Saw Massacre* and its associated cult/culture. Most can be found relatively easily, others require a bit more digging around. (Be aware that many sites contain information that's incorrect.) Many of those below have links to other useful sites.

Cast & crew sites:

www.robert-a-burns.com
Excellent site with tons of information, highly recommended

www.paulpartain.com
Paul Partain's site

www.gunnarhansen.com
Gunnar Hansen's site — buy an original foundation stone from the *Chain Saw* family house!

www.geocities.com/jsiedow.geo/JimHomepage.html
Jim Siedow's page

www.leatherface2.com
leatherfacetwo@hotmail.com
Bill Johnson's site/email address

www.choptopsbbq.com
Bill Moseley's site

www.threeringservice.com
Allen Danziger's company, book your entertainment here!

www.davidjschow.com
Excellent David J. Schow site

duke@rice.edu
Direct contact for Brian Huberman, to buy copies of *Return of the Texas Chainsaw Massacre: The Documentary*

www.headcheesemovie.com
Info/contact for Duane Graves/*Headcheese*

www.the-arthouse.org.uk/jimmoran.htm
rjs.moran@ntlworld.com
Jim Moran's site, and email contact for buying copies of *Leatherface Speaks*

www.joebobbriggs.com
Joe Bob Briggs's site: huntin', shootin', fishin', politics and babes (plus some gore)

www.outlawforpeace.com/spencer/toc.html
Spencer Perskin's (Shiva's Headband) site

Other sites:

www.austinchronicle.com
Inevitably the first stop for research into anything Texan — movies, music, culture — absolutely essential. Look for pieces written by Marc Savlov

www.weeklywire.com
More Texas stuff. No longer publishing but has an essential archive

www.texaschainsawmassacre.net
Tim Harden's encyclopedic *Chain Saw* site

www.houseofhorrors.com/texas.htm
Pretty good *Chain Saw* site

www.geocities.com/leatherfacette
Excellent *Texas Chainsaw Massacre 2* site

www.angelfire.com/ca/TCM4
The only *Return of the Texas Chainsaw Massacre* site!

www.mtivideo.com
Where to buy *Texas Chain Saw Massacre: A Family Portrait*

www.boxofficemojo.com
Best site for box office figures

www.dmentd.com/fx-savini-main.html
Excellent piece on Savini's Grandpa make-up from *Chainsaw 2*

www.fangoria.com/
Back issues, features, news etc

www.theavclub.com/avclub3636/avfeature_3636.html
Good Tobe Hooper interview

www.living-dead.com
Excellent horror site with Paul Partain & Bill Moseley interviews (amongst much other stuff)

www.texasmonthly.com
Excellent site for all things Texas

www.tsha.utexas.edu/handbook/online/index.html
The Handbook of Texas Online, another extremely useful site

http://laws.lp.findlaw.com/5th/9851016cv0.html
Legal site with details of the *The Return of...* case against CAA

www.tranquileye.com/historyofporn/mafia.html
Detailed article with plenty of information about the Perainos, backed up by quotes from government documents and newspaper articles

http://courttvweb1.courttv.com/archive/onair/shows/mugshots/indepth/hollywood/
Detailed pieces on links between pornography and organised crime

www.crimelibrary.com/gein/geinmain.htm
About the best Ed Gein piece on the net, well written and researched

These sites have been down for some time but may one day wake up again...

www.tobehooper.com
www.allamericanmassacre.com

THE BOOK OF ALIEN

By Paul Scanlon & Michael Gross

In 1979, a movie was released that was to capture the imagination of the world, and become a science fiction classic... *Alien*.

The Book of Alien is the definitive companion to the movie, which celebrates its 25th anniversary in 2004. Taking you right behind the scenes of the production, there are interviews with the key people involved, including legendary designer H. R. Giger and director Ridley Scott. Lavishly illustrated with scores of stunning design paintings, production art and film stills unpublished elsewhere, the book covers every creative stage, and graphically demonstrates just why the movie won an Oscar for its visual effects. Simply a must-have for any *Alien* fan.

'A highly realistic sci-fi future, made all the more believable by the expert technical craftsmanship'
Variety